I

MUTUAL SAVINGS BANKS

MUTUAL SAVINGS BANKS

The Evolution of a Financial Intermediary

WELDON WELFLING

THE PRESS OF CASE WESTERN RESERVE UNIVERSITY

CLEVELAND • 1968

Preface

Conclusion.

Mᴜᴛᴜᴀʟ savings banking in the United States dates from 1816;
1966 marked the completion of 150 years of the institution's history. Two savings banks vie for the honor of being the first in this
country: The Philadelphia Saving Fund Society, which was the
first to open for business, and the Provident Institution For Savings
In The Town of Boston, which was the first to obtain a charter.
Both are leading mutual savings banks at the present time.

The impetus for establishing this type of financial institution
was the philanthropic interest of leading citizens in the seaboard
cities in reducing the level of poverty among the emerging wage-
earning classes. Coupled with altruism was a degree of enlightened
self-interest; any device that reduced the degree of poverty would
also diminish the burden of taxes for poor relief that had appeared
in England and was beginning to emerge in America. The model for
the establishment of these banks was the savings bank developed by The Reverend Henry Duncan in Scotland, and others
shortly thereafter established in Scotland and England. In fact,
similar mutual savings banks were established in several European
countries at approximately the same time—about the beginning of
the nineteenth century—although their existence does not seem to
have been widely known in this country.

After 150 years of existence in the United States, the mutual
savings banks are institutions far different from their prototypes.
Anyone walking by the imposing buildings that house the contemporary savings banks in New York City, for example, might be
surprised that the first savings bank to be organized in that city in
1819 was granted a charter because, in the words of the legislature,

> the society for the prevention of pauperism in the City of New
> York, have petitioned the Legislature for an act of incorporation,
> for the laudable purpose of encouraging in the community habits of

industry and economy, by receiving and investing . . . such small
sums of money as may be saved from the earnings of tradesmen,
mechanics, laborers, minors, servants and others . . . and the Legislature [consider] it their duty to cherish all laudable attempts to
ameliorate the condition of the poor and laboring class of the
community. . . .

While the basic function of accepting deposits on the one hand
and investing the funds in a restricted variety of highly safe assets
on the other has continued to characterize savings banking, the
nature of the banks has evolved with the changing economic environment. In 150 years, the United States has changed from a new
and economically underdeveloped country, where all but a small
fraction of the population lived in rural areas and were self-
sufficient to a high degree, to an industrial nation with a population of approximately 200 million, highly concentrated in
metropolitan areas. While there are still the "poor and indigent,"
the nature of poverty has changed. In 1816, the poor were, by and
large, the "laboring class," whose wages were not far above the
level required to keep body and soul together and raise a family—
the subsistence level to which wages were naturally supposed to
gravitate in the view of the economists of the day. Today the poor
are by and large those who are unable to enter the "laboring
class"—the unemployed or unemployable. In contrast, the great
bulk of the population has an income level far above subsistence,
and "discretionary income" has become a common term.

After perhaps a third of the history of savings banks had
elapsed—that is, by the end of the Civil War and shortly thereafter—it was plain that the role of savings banks in the economy
was not principally that of a philanthropic organization designed
to ameliorate the condition of the destitute; its primary function
was to provide a safe place of deposit for the growing numbers of
wage earners and small businessmen, who had neither the resources nor knowledge with which to make direct investments. As
time passed, other institutions were developed and changed their
character. Commercial banks, originally designed to finance commerce, and often consisting of groups of merchants themselves,
eventually became the "department stores of finance" of today.

Building and loan associations arose to meet a need for mortgage credit and evolved into the system of modern savings and loan associations. Insurance companies, originally specializing in insurance protection, branched into annuities and then into the savings field. Trust companies, industrial banks, finance companies, and others sprang up in response to market demands on either the borrowing or saving side.

Partly as a result of their original philanthropic purpose, the savings banks left the field wide open to other institutions in the country outside of New England and the Middle Atlantic states. Although they became important, even dominant, financial institutions in those restricted areas, in the rest of the country the broad function of the financial intermediary was performed by other institutions. Out of total savings held by individuals in the forms of savings deposits and shares, savings bonds, and reserves of life insurance companies, amounting to about $480 billion at the end of 1965, mutual savings bank deposits were $52 billion, or about 11 per cent. In the 18 states where mutual savings banks exist, however, they held about 33 per cent of the "deposit-type" savings of individuals, and approximately 52 per cent in New York State and 65 per cent in Massachusetts and Connecticut.

The existence of an institution with assets in excess of $61 billion at the end of 1966—about half the aggregate of the savings and loan associations and nearly the same proportion of commercial bank savings deposits—raises many interesting questions concerning the institution's current functions and future. At the core of the situation are the pertinence of the mutual nature of the banks and the system of trusteeship under which the banks developed. In the evolution of different kinds of intermediaries and in the present active competition for saved funds there also arise many questions of appropriate investment and loan powers for the respective contenders. Whether savings banks and savings and loan associations should be permitted to make, for example, personal loans, and the extent of participation by commercial banks in the residential mortgage market, are examples. Related to these powers are others, such as the power to branch and the maximum limit, if any, that should be imposed on the size of deposits.

paper presented

Overlying all the other questions is that of federal chartering of savings banks. If there were to be a federal chartering law, all the other questions would have to be answered in it.

The study that follows is an effort to supply historical and contemporary information that will throw light on these current questions. The history of the savings banks is a fascinating one. As noted above, they began as philanthropic organizations and have changed with the economy, until they are significant factors in money and capital markets, especially in the northeastern section of the country. The plan of the study is to trace this history in sufficient detail to provide a current history of savings banks in the United States and to use this history as a background for an examination of the current importance and problems of the industry.

I have been fortunate in having available several earlier studies that have greatly shortened the task of surveying the historical development of savings banks in this country. Prominent among these is Emerson Keyes' extremely useful *History of Savings Banks,* the two volumes of which were published in 1876 and 1878. I have also drawn on John Lintner's *Mutual Savings Banks in the Savings and Mortgage Markets* and my earlier study, *Savings Banking in New York State,* as well as the monograph prepared by the Research Department of the national association for the Commission on Money and Credit, *Mutual Savings Banking.* Several other useful studies are referred to at appropriate points in the text. The statistical compilations at hand at the National Association of Mutual Savings Banks and the excellent *Annual Reports* and *National Fact Books* made unnecessary much spade work that would otherwise have been required.

I am grateful to numerous people for valuable suggestions and information. Among these, I especially want to express thanks to the European savings bankers who were so generous with their time and information during my study of their operations, the staff of the International Savings Bank Institute in Amsterdam, and the staff of the National Association of Mutual Savings Banks. I also profited from discussions of many points with Professor David A. Bowers of Case Western Reserve University. In addition, I gratefully acknowledge grants from the American Philosophical Society

(Penrose Contingent Fund) and the Mutual Savings Foundation of America, without which I could not have undertaken this study at this time. The usual responsibility of the author for statements of fact, opinion, or judgment, however, remains with me.

Weldon Welfling

and also the general development, operations, services, functions and legislations, related to Mutual Savings Banks

Contents

Tables

Charts

I | Historical Background

CHAPTER 1

Philanthropic Origins
and Early Development

IN 1816, the United States was a new nation that had but recently won its independence by war and had then within a few years fought a second war against the mother country. In both wars, trade was disrupted, new attempts at manufacturing were started, and price inflation was drastic. Although the overwhelming preponderance of the population lived in rural areas—Benjamin Franklin remarking that there were about a hundred farmers for every artisan or merchant at the end of the Revolution—price fluctuations, worthless currencies of first the Continental Congress and later many state banks, and shortages of such essentials as pots, pans, and nails complicated the lives of nearly everyone. In the cities, the return of imports to market after 1815 sometimes bankrupted new small manufacturers and threw people out of work.

The Early American Economy

When the new federal government was established in 1789, the population of the country was about 4 million virtually all located along the Atlantic. By 1820, the number had risen to about 9.5 million and the expansion of the country to the west had begun. Jefferson, surprised by the availability of the Louisiana Purchase from France, thought that it might be a thousand years before that area was settled by any significant number of people. The westward movement proceeded rapidly, however, with a virtually constant stream of immigrants spilling over from the seaboard and adding to the flow of population past the Appalachians.

The Census of 1790 revealed six cities—so-called—of more than 8,000 population, in which resided 1 out of every 33 people. The number grew by 1820 to 13, holding 1 out of every 20 people. New York City was jostling Philadelphia out of its position as the largest and leading city, and was considerably aided by the opening of the Erie Canal in 1825, which connected the seaboard with the "West."

The factory system began to spread in the first decades of the nineteenth century. Spinning and weaving were moving from the household to the factory, and were slowly joined by the manufacture of nails, lumber, clothing, shoes, and—where charcoal and ore were available along the coast—iron. Discovery of how to use anthracite increased the possible sites for producing iron, and output rose from around 50,000 tons in 1810 to a million tons by the time of the Civil War 50 years later. Steam was used to drive iron-working machinery as early as 1801, but principal reliance was on water power, which dictated the location of scores of textile mills in southern New England. Wood was the principal fuel until about 1850. Many products were the result of combined factory and household production. Spinning was taken over by mills, but lack of looms left weaving in the home much longer. A great deal of the work on clothing and weaving was "put out" by manufacturers to be done at home under the domestic system.

Wages and the Poor

It was not until about 1830 that some of the more skilled artisans gained a ten-hour day. Normal hours were "sunrise to sunset." In most factories, 12 to 14 hours were the normal workday until after 1850, when the hours dropped to 11 or 12. Children and young women made up most of the work force in many textile mills. Around 1820, women could earn 50 cents a day in most factories, or 25 cents as seamstresses. Typical wages for men were $.75 to $1.25; farm labor expected $.50 and skilled artisans in cities $1.25 to $1.50. The Census of 1820 enumerated those over ten years of age and engaged in gainful occupations. The distribution of the work force in 1820 and in 1860 is shown in Table 1–1. There was still evidence in 1820 of the colonial system of progression through apprentice and journeyman to craftsman, the latter often owning his own business and in turn employing apprentices and craftsmen, but the division between capitalist and laborer was becoming clearer.

TABLE 1-1[1]

PERCENTAGE OF GAINFULLY EMPLOYED
IN CHIEF OCCUPATIONS, 1820 AND 1860

Occupations	*1820*	*1860*
Agriculture	71.9	59.7
Manufacturing and mechanic arts	12.2	18.4
Trade and transport	2.5	7.4
Domestic and personal service	10.0	9.5
Professions	2.8	2.9
Mining	.3	1.6
Lumbering	.8	.2
Fishing	.2	.3

As had occurred in England after the Industrial Revolution, the creation of cities with a class of wage earners brought with it the social problem of poverty and poor relief. Sixty years after the formation of the first American savings banks, Emerson W. Keyes, the historian of the savings banks of that time, wrote in 1876:

> We think, then, that it must be conceded, that in any natural state of society the wages of the laboring classes in seasons of prosperity will ever be such as to enable them, *if they will,* to reserve a portion for future need. The neglect to do this, or the want of opportunity to do this, must ever be a fruitful source of poverty, indigence, pauperism, *crime.* . . . [The savings bank] preserves

1. P. K. Whelpton, "Occupational Groups in the United States, 1820-1920," *Journal of the American Statistical Association,* xxi, 340; quoted in Chester Whitney Wright, *Economic History of the United States* (New York: McGraw-Hill Book Co., 1949), p. 331.

from *falling into destitution* that large class of the poor who are ever hovering upon the brink of pauperism.[2]

Poor Relief Laws in England to reduce the problem led several groups in the United States practically simultaneously to try another experiment imported from Great Britain. Thus the savings banks were born as devices to prevent the spread of poverty.

Precedents for Savings Banks

Since everything has a precedent, the origin of savings banks could undoubtedly be traced back to antiquity. The usual forerunners of the modern savings bank, however, are generally taken to be the suggestion of Hugues Delestre in 1610 that "the wage worker . . . might deposit his savings and withdraw them again, in part or in whole as he might require, with interest according to the time they had been on deposit"; Daniel Defoe's suggestion, in *Essays on Projects,* in 1698, that workmen pay into a pension office a percentage of their wages, which with interest would provide protection against pauperism; the reorganization of a philanthropic organization in Hamburg into a savings bank or source of annuities in 1778; and similar philanthropies by Duke Peter Frederick Gunther in Oldenburg in 1786 and by Queen Catherine in Würtemberg in 1819.[3] Jeremy Bentham published a proposal for "Frugality Banks" in 1797. Other prototypes have been suggested as arising in Berne, Geneva, Kiel, London, and Italy. The Rev. Joseph Smith made a suggestion similar to that of Delestre in 1799 in Wendover, England. Smith's idea was to "receive any sums in deposit during the summer, and to return the amount at Christmas with the addition of one third to the whole, as a bounty upon the depositor's economy." His "Sunday Penny Bank" and others operated around 1800, with "interest" obtained from charitable sources.[4]

---

2. Emerson W. Keyes, *A History of Savings Banks in the United States* (New York: Bradford Rhodes, 1876), I, 11. Original italics.

3. James Henry Hamilton, *Savings and Savings Institutions* (New York: Macmillan Co., 1902), pp. 155-56.

4. See H. Oliver Horne, *A History of Savings Banks* (Oxford: Oxford University Press, 1947) for the history of savings banking in England.

The early experiments in England were related to the formation of what were known as Friendly Societies. In his *Science of Wealth,* in 1872, Prof. Amasa Walker remarked,

In England, these 'friendly societies', as they are called, are numerous, and often exert a very happy influence. They are formed for a great variety of specified objects. Some of these are merely charitable,—for assisting members when searching for employment,—for relieving them in case of disability from sickness, and for similar purposes. Others are for the diffusion of intelligence, like lyceums, mechanics' institutes, etc., or for moral and social elevation and improvement, as associations to discourage the use of intoxicating drinks, and other pernicious and degrading habits.[5]

While they were usually organizations of workingmen, one "Friendly Society for the benefit of women and children" was established by a Mrs. Priscilla Wakefield at Tottenham High Cross in 1798, primarily to provide annuities, weekly sums in cases of illness, and burial costs, but it later added a fund for loans and a "bank for savings." In the *Essay on Population,* Malthus saw some slight hope against his fears of constant poverty for labor in "county banks," where young laborers might accumulate some capital and in the process postpone marriage.

The bulk of the credit for the early establishment of savings banks, however, goes to the Rev. Henry Duncan of Ruthwell, Dumfrieshire, where he established a bank in 1810. Duncan worked assiduously to publicize his bank in other parts of the country in order to encourage imitators. He published numerous articles and pamphlets and encouraged the establishment of a similar bank in 1814, by the Edinburgh Society for the Suppression of Mendicity.[6] A local London magistrate, Patrick Colquhoun, claimed to have originated the idea of savings banks in a treatise on indigence in 1806, and was in fact instrumental in advising the founders of the Bank for Savings in New York in 1819.

5. Amasa Walker, *The Science of Wealth* (Philadelphia: J. B. Lippincott, 1872) p. 192.

6. See Sally Hall, *Dr. Duncan of Ruthwell* (Edinburgh: Oliphant, Anderson and Ferrier, 1910); E. W. Brabrook, *Provident Societies and Industrial Welfare* (London: Blackie & Sons, 1898); and William Lewins, *A History of Banks for Savings (in Great Britian and Ireland)* (London: Sampson Low, Son & Marston, 1866).

Philanthropic Origins: Philadelphia

In the United States, the first savings banks were the Philadelphia Saving Fund Society, which opened in 1816 in Philadelphia, although chartered later, and the Provident Institution for Savings in Boston, which was chartered in 1816.

The philanthropic aspect of the formation of the early banks is illustrated by the list of founders of the Philadelphia Saving Fund Society which included the names of Condy Raguet, Clement C. Biddle and John Strawbridge. Condy Raguet was apparently the moving spirit in the project. He was also interested in the Pennsylvania Company for Insurances on Lives and Granting Annuities and in other financial and business enterprises in Philadelphia, and was a state senator. In addition, he was a prolific writer on monetary and other financial matters, publishing articles, pamphlets, and essays on banking reform.

Following the English example, these gentlemen formed a voluntary association, each contributing $10 to a fund of $250 to get the bank started. In addition, the Managers, as the corporators were called, volunteered their services in turn to perform the clerical work of the bank. To limit their personal liability, the managers applied to the state for a charter. The charter limited the number of managers to 25 and imposed no restrictions on their investment powers.

From time to time, the charter was amended. One of the early amendments provided for an unusual manner of filling vacancies among the managers. The managers were to nominate a list of five to a Board of Appointment, which was to select one of the five; the board consisted of the Chief Justice of the State, the President and Judges of the District Court and the Court of Common Pleas, and later, after a change in the state constitution, of the five judges of the Court of Common Pleas. As Keyes remarked, "The admission of unworthy persons to membership in the Board would seem to be in this way very carefully guarded against."

After thirteen months of operation, the deposits of the Society were only $8,945, and when the corporation took over the funds in 1819 they totaled $45,114. By 1821, deposits reached

$200,000, and, in the financial panic year of 1837, the Society paid out $712,445 to depositors, while taking in $422,699.

At first, the charter set an annual flat rate of interest of 4.8 per cent (presumably so it could be calculated as .4 per cent per month), and provided that any surplus would be divided among the depositors every three years. Deposits were limited to $500 per year—a figure that appears rather high for the times, but was perhaps designed to allow for the initial deposit of hoards—and to an over-all limit of $300,000. Of course, the over-all limit on deposits had to be raised by amendment to the charter from time to time, while the limit on individual deposits was also changed; the latter was $200 from 1828 to 1869 to prevent "abuse of the bank by the rich" seeking temporary attractive investment.[7]

The bank in Philadelphia followed in broad outline the history of such banks in England. In Scotland, home of Dr. Duncan's bank, the trustees deposited all the funds in the joint stock banks, which paid special interest rates on them. In England, however, there were few branches of joint stock banks available, and the private banks did not pay interest on deposits. Hence, the banks purchased "public securities" and mortgages. In Edinburgh, depositors were required to withdraw their funds and start their deposits anew when they reached £10, on the grounds that with such funds they could patronize the joint stock banks. The Philadelphia Society also invested first in public stocks (meaning bonds) and in 1818 made its first mortgage loan. It often found that the demand for mortgage loans on the part of private lenders was such that it was easier for the bank to hold securities. Mortgage loans, however, were callable and were found actually to be more liquid in the early days than were the public stocks.

Other Early Banks

The Provident Institution for Savings in Boston received the first legislative sanction in America or Great Britain for such an institution in 1816; the British act of Parliament recognizing savings

---

7. James W. Willcox, *A History of the Philadelphia Saving Fund Society, 1816-1916* (Philadelphia: J. P. Lippincott, 1916).

banks came a year later. As in Philadelphia, knowledge of the experiments at Ruthwell and Edinburgh had led philanthropists, especially James Savage, to initiate the project. A religious monthly publication, the *Christian Disciple,* carried an announcement in December, 1816:

Savings Banks

Under this novel title, it is proposed to form an institution in Boston, for the security and improvement of the savings of persons in humble life, until required by their wants and desires. A meeting of gentlemen has been called, and a large and respectable committee appointed to apply to the legislature (now in session) for an act of incorporation, and to digest suitable rules and bylaws, to be proposed to an adjourned meeting. Similar institutions exist in England and Scotland. . . . In Philadelphia it is proposed to establish one of these societies. We agree in the following sentiment, and wish every success to the laudable schemes contemplated: "It is not by the alms of the wealthy, that the good of the lower class can be generally promoted. By such donations, encouragement is far oftener given to idleness and hypocrisy, than aid to suffering worth. He is the most effective benefactor to the poor, who encourages them in habits of industry, sobriety and frugality."[8]

Within the month the charter was enacted. It provided for 48 incorporators, who might add to their number. It did not limit the society's investment powers, but provided that deposits could be accepted and the funds invested "at best advantage." After necessary expenses, the proceeds were to be distributed to the depositors. When it opened in the spring of 1817, the Provident Institution for Savings promised interest at one per cent quarterly, but after the first dividend in July paid 1.25 per cent. By 1822, deposits had already reached $600,000, at which time the rate was restored to one per cent quarterly, with a provision that the surplus would be distributed every five years, the amount being apportioned to the length of time deposits then on the books had been in the bank. This practice was followed in 1827 and 1832, and there seems to have been a division in 1834; then during the

8. Keyes, *op.cit.,* I, 38.

ensuing five-year period, covering the panic of 1837, losses absorbed the excess earnings.[9]

In 1818, a group of leading citizens of Baltimore obtained a charter for the Savings Bank of Baltimore. The charter was virtually a duplicate of that of the Philadelphia Saving Fund Society; the first section listed the names of the 134 incorporators, "and it includes the names of almost every prominent merchant in Baltimore as well as the social and political leaders of the community."[10] The nature of the bank is shown by the weekly limits on deposits, which fluctuated between $10 and $50 in the early years of the bank. From time to time, the bank examined its list of depositors and returned the funds of those not considered to be "entitled to make deposits according to the original object of the Institution."

In 1819, came the charters for the Philadelphia Saving Fund Society, the Bank for Savings in the City of New York, the Society for Savings in Hartford, Conn., and the Savings Bank of Newport, Rhode Island. The charter for the Bank for Savings introduced express prohibitions against trustees or managers receiving directly or indirectly any compensation for their services and against their or officers' borrowings from the bank. Such provisions became standard in later charters and legislation.

Antipathy to Banks of Issue

The avoidance of the word "bank" in many early titles reflects the fact that, at this time in American history, banks were a subject of heated debate. Great animosity to banks had been built up by the effects of paper money, whether issued by the colonies, states, Continental Congress, or banks. Hammond points out that toward the end of the eighteenth century, the word "bank" had three meanings: (1) a corporate institution, such as the Bank of Eng-

9. Keyes, *op. cit.* See also *The Provident Institution for Savings in The Town of Boston, 1816-1966* (Boston: The Provident Institution for Savings, 1966).

10. P. L. Payne and L. E. Davis, *The Savings Bank of Baltimore, 1818-1866* (Baltimore: Johns Hopkins University Studies in Historical and Political Science, 1954), p. 27.

land; (2) an issue of bills of credit by a colonial government; and (3) an association of private persons which issued its own bills of credit.[11] The colonial bills of credit were issued originally to cover emergency expenses but later, especially by Rhode Island, to lend, in order to create a supply of money. The private associations took the form of land banks, which exchanged spendable notes for pledges of land. In 1780, "some ninety merchants and other men of substance established a bank in Philadelphia for the sole purpose of obtaining and transporting . . . three millions of rations and 300 hogsheads of rum" for the army.[12] This "bank" led to the formation of the Bank of North America in 1781, largely through the efforts of Robert Morris, who was Superintendent of Finance for the Continental Congress. Although chartered by the Congress, this bank sought assurance of legality by obtaining charters from several states; its charter from Pennsylvania, a duplicate of the Congressional one, was the one under which it operated. In 1785, the agrarian sections of Pennsylvania succeeded in having the charter revoked because "the accumulation of enormous wealth in the hands of a society who claim perpetual duration will necessarily produce a degree of influence and power which can not be entrusted in the hands of any set of men whatsoever without endangering the public safety."[13] The political climate changed and the charter was restored before the bank went out of business, but the episode illustrates the fear and animosity of much of the populace toward banks. The bank existed until 1929, when it was absorbed by the Pennsylvania Company for Insurance on Lives and Granting Annuities, now the First Pennsylvania Banking and Trust Company.

Several other commercial banks pre-dated the earliest savings banks. Some of the other new banks established at this time were the Bank of New York, which opened in 1784 and received a charter in 1791 largely through the efforts of Alexander Hamilton; the Massachusetts Bank, also dating from 1784; and the Bank of Maryland, established in 1790. The Bank of Maryland failed in

---

11. Bray Hammond, *Banks and Politics in America* (Princeton, N.J.: Princeton University Press, 1957), pp. 9-10.

12. *Ibid.*, p. 42.

13. *Ibid.*, p. 54.

1834, while the Bank of New York is still in operation. The Massachusetts Bank converted to a national charter in 1865 and eventually merged with the First National Bank of Boston.

At this stage, incorporation implied monopoly, since, in the English tradition, the various trading companies and banks had received corporate charters as monopolies. In the early days of this country, banking was largely in the hands of Federalists. As a result, banking was all the more a political issue. This situation was also reflected in the origins of the Bank of the Manhattan Company. New York City suffered from a severe epidemic of Yellow Fever in 1798, the cause apparently being impure water. The city failed to obtain authority from Albany to construct a water system, whereupon some private citizens, led by Aaron Burr with the help of Alexander Hamilton, proposed a private company. The city government seconded the application for a charter for a water company, and such a company—the Manhattan Company—was set up with capital of $2 million, of which the city owned $200,000. The directors, like Burr, were mostly Republicans (it will be remembered that at this time Republicans were Jeffersonians and anti-Federalist; they later took the name Democrats). The charter permitted the company "to employ all such surplus capital as may belong or accrue to the said company in the purchase of public or other stock or in any other monied transactions or operations not inconsistent with the constitution and laws of this state or of the United States, for the sole benefit of the said company." Burr made no secret of the fact that the Manhattan Company "might have a bank, an East India Company, or anything else that they deemed profitable,"[14] although later the claim was made that the legislature had been hoodwinked into chartering a bank.

Alexander Hamilton apparently was somewhat taken in by the maneuver to obtain a bank charter in Republican hands. It was not unusual, however, to couple a bank with other undertakings, and later the practice was common for turnpike, canal, and railroad companies to raise funds in this manner. Hamilton set about to obtain another charter for a bank to be run by Federalists, which eventually resulted in the formation of the Merchants Bank.

---

14. *Ibid.*, p. 152.

There was, however, much publicity about bribery, and other pressures in the legislature over its charter augmented the general antipathy to banks and banking. After the demise of the First Bank of the United States in 1811, there was a rash of bank chartering in several states—this was the period of growth of state banks, which contributed to inflation during the War of 1812— and even more publicity over bribery in obtaining charters. In some cases, the state governments purchased some of the stock, as they did with other companies later. Pennsylvania obtained sufficient income from its investment in the Bank of Pennsylvania, founded by Gallatin in 1793, and in other ventures to avoid any direct taxes for 40 years.

This early history of banking illustrates the popular fear and antipathy the public exhibited toward banks. It was based largely on the fear of size and monopoly and on the experience of inflation. Thomas Jefferson said:

> He who lent his money to the public or to an individual before the institution of the United States Bank of twenty years ago, when wheat was well sold at a dollar the bushel and receives now his nominal sum when it sells at two dollars, is cheated of half his fortune; and by whom? By the banks, which, since that, have thrown into circulation ten dollars of their nominal money where was one at that time.[15]

John Adams agreed that, "Every dollar of a bank bill that is issued beyond the quantity of gold and silver in the vaults represents nothing and is therefore a cheat upon somebody."[16] Condy Raguet, a founder of the Philadelphia Saving Fund Society, wrote in 1829 that bank loans lead to rising prices and "purchases are made for no other reason, than that the buyers suppose they can sell the next day at a profit. . . . Every new sale of commodities and property on credit creates new promissory notes, and these create a new demand for discounts."[17] W. M. Gouge, another essayist of the period, agreed:

---

15. Quoted in Harry E. Miller, *Banking Theories in the United States Before 1860* (Cambridge, Mass.: Harvard University Press, 1927), p. 20.

16. *Loc. cit.*

17. Condy Raguet, "Principles of Banking," *Free Trade Advocate* II (1829), 7.

Banks do not increase the loanable capital of a country, but only take it out of the hands of its proprietors, and place it under the control of irresponsible Bank Directors. Great facilities are thereby afforded to many men for borrowing, to whom no man ought to lend. They are led by bank loans to engage in business for which they are not fitted by either nature or education.[18]

Gouge also agreed with Raguet's early business cycle theory just quoted.

The first savings banks in Philadelphia and Boston consequently were proposed as a "Society" and an "Institution," rather than as banks. It is rather likely that the founders did not think of their proposed institutions as "banks," but they perhaps also avoided the term because of the opposition its use was likely to stir up. These gentlemen, being merchants and men of affairs, undoubtedly thought of banks as institutions that financed commerce by issuing banknotes on the security of shipping documents and other claims. In addition, the English prototypes were associated with the Friendly Societies, which were older and more important institutions than the savings banks they sponsored. In Massachusetts, by 1834, 24 savings banks had been chartered and all but two were organized; all but one were called Institutions rather than banks. The exception was the Savings Bank for Seamen (Boston, 1833), later renamed the Suffolk Savings Bank.

Beginnings in New York

The first effort to establish a savings bank in New York did utilize the word "bank" and ran into the difficulties that might have been expected. The original steps were taken in 1816, when Thomas Eddy corresponded with Patrick Colquhoun in London, and brought together some of the leading citizens to consider a proposal for a savings bank. Eddy wrote Colquhoun in 1817:

Among the many philanthropic institutions with which your country abounds, there is none that appears to me more likely to be useful than Savings Banks. They are certainly most admirably calculated to be beneficial to the poor, by promoting among them a

18. W. M. Gouge, *Short History of Paper Money, and Banking in the United States* (1833), p. 45.

spirit of independence, economy and industry. Immediately on receiving from thee an account of the Provident Institution in your metropolis, I proposed to a number of my friends to establish a similar one in this city. A plan was formed, and a number of our most respectable citizens agreed to undertake the management of it; but we found that we could not go into operation without an act of incorporation. . . .[19]

The response of the legislative committee to whom the bill was assigned was as follows:

That however desirable it may be to encourage the poorer class of community to save their hard earnings, and to produce habits of industry and economy by holding out motives of interest to them so to do, still the committee are not convinced that, under the present state of society in this country, an institution like this, which may be beneficial under other circumstances, and in older countries, can be put into operation with advantage. The expense necessarily attendant in such an establishment will lessen, if not defeat, the benevolent views of the petitioners. And the committee have yet to learn, whether the object might not be accomplished, with a greater prospect of success, and at the same time avoid a new incorporation, by making an arrangement with one of the banks in New York, to allow one of their clerks to transact the business for a small extra allowance.[20]

The committee was willing to introduce the bill for debate, but it did not pass in that session. It is interesting that during negotiations the name of the proposed bank was changed to a "saving corporation" and then back to bank.[21] Subsequently, a ". . . number of philanthropic gentlemen of this city, whose minds had been earnestly engaged in considering the condition of our poor,

---

19. Keyes, *op. cit.*, I, 309.

20. *Ibid.*, p. 311.

21. Because of the formation of the association and the application for a charter prior to the successes in Philadelphia and Boston, Keyes claimed that, "Though not successful in this first effort to secure a charter, Savings Banks had here their inception in this State." *Ibid.*, p. 316. Because of the use of the word "here", it is not clear whether he means merely that this was the first savings bank in New York State, or whether he means that the savings bank movement began in New York. This history of the formation of the Bank for Savings is based primarily on Keyes' account.

and seeking out plans for the welfare of the industrious and laboring classes" met in 1817 and established the Society for the Prevention of Pauperism. A committee was formed to draw up a statement of the principal causes of pauperism and how they might be attacked. Such a statement was drawn up and distributed widely in 1818. Among the causes of pauperism was "want of economy." "Prodigality is comparative among the poor, it prevails to a great extent in inattention to those small but frequent savings when labor is plentiful, which may go to meet privation in unfavorable seasons." The obvious remedies are savings banks, insurance, and benefit societies. Another fruit of the Society for the Prevention of Pauperism was the Society for the care of Juvenile Delinquents, or House of Refuge.

The Society brought the next petition for a charter for a savings bank. Among the organizers in 1816 had been De Witt Clinton, who was elected Governor in 1817. In 1818 his message to the legislature included the following remarks:

Our statutes relating to the poor are borrowed from the English system, and the experience of that country, as well as our own, shows that pauperism increases with the augmentation of the funds applied to its relief. This evil has proceeded to such an alarming extent in the city of New York, that the burdens of heavy taxation which it has imposed, menace a diminution of the population of that city, and a depreciation of its real property. . . . Under the present system, the fruits of industry are appropriated to the wants of idleness; a laborious poor man is taxed for the support of an idle beggar; and the vice of mendicity, no longer considered degrading, infects a considerable portion of our population in large towns. I am persuaded that the sooner a radical reform takes place, the better. . . . Charity is an exalted virtue, but it ought to be founded on reason and regulated by wisdom. While we must consider as worthy of all praise and patronage religious and moral societies, Sunday, free and charity schools, houses of industry, orphan asylums and savings banks, and all other establishments, which prevent or alleviate the evils of pauperism, by inspiring industry, dispensing employment, and inculcating economy; by improving the mind, cultivating the heart, and elevating the character, we are equally bound to discourage those institutions which furnish the aliment of mendicity, by removing the incentives to labor, and administering to the blandishments of sensuality.[22]

While the legislature was considering the petition from the Society, another group petitioned for a charter for an "interest and savings bank," which they thought would soon attract deposits "equal to its capital" and which would be the only bank offering to pay interest on deposits. This bill failed, however, probably in part because of the general antipathy to banks, but also because of opposition from other banks. The legislature also failed to act on the petition for a savings bank, but took up the matter again in 1819, when it had a memorial from the Society "praying certain legal provisions in regard to tavern licenses, and also the incorporation of a savings bank." Although there was considerable disagreement between the House and the Senate over some provisions of the charter, there was eventual agreement on the various provisions, and the charter of the Bank for Savings was granted in 1819.

Besides its provisions relating to trustees and officers, the charter permitted investment in "stock created and issued under and by virtue of any law of the United States, or of this State, and in no other way." The first board of managers consisted of a president, three vice presidents, and 24 trustees. The board could fill vacancies by its own election and was required to report to the legislature and to the "common council" of the city annually.

Nature of Early Banks

The Bank's first report in 1820 stated that it had opened, on July 3, 1819, in a room granted rent-free by the Academy of Arts in the New York Institution and that on that day the trustees had taken in deposits of $2,807. By the end of the year—in six months—deposits amounted to $153,378, made by 1,527 depositors, and $6,606 had been withdrawn, leaving $148,372 invested in public funds. The Bank requested an amendment to its charter to allow mortgage loans. Depositors consisted of mechanics, laborers, tradesmen, domestics, minors, widows, orphans, apprentices, and unclassified. Three trustees each month took turns as

22. *Ibid.*, pp. 323-25.

the committee for the month "to attend at the bank." They received deposits, saw that entries were duly made, made inquiries
. . . as to the situation of the depositors, and ask[ed] such further questions as might promote the welfare either of the individual or of the institution. By this means the whole of the board of trustees have become familiar with the depositors, and while their confidence in those to whom they have committed the safeguard and improvement of their little funds has been confirmed, it has afforded an opportunity, readily embraced by the trustees, of giving such advice to many of the depositors as they believed would tend to promote careful habits and moral feeling.

Several other comments in the first report reflect the philanthropic base of the institution and the economy of the times.

The man who attends to the regular discharge of his duties, and is enabled to lay up a weekly sum from his hard-earned income, is too often the dupe of the idle, the profligate, the designing, or the unfortunate. Incaution, and sometimes an excusable vanity, prompts the possessor of an increasing fund to reveal it to his less prosperous neighbor. The desire of accumulation, and the hope of bettering his condition, will induce the listener to try the means with which his friends can furnish him on some object of speculation. He tries, and both are ruined. . . . Many cases have come before the trustees wherein the above was justified by ample details. The causes, as after stated by the sufferers themselves, arose alike from their want of some secure place of deposit, and their ignorance how to improve what they had laid up. The sums are generally too small to be received at any of the banks; and where this is not the case, it was found equally as difficult to retain it as if it had been actually in the owner's hands; the temptation to loan was the same. Though many depositors understood how to invest their money in public stocks, yet anticipating an early use for it, or fearing a loss from the fluctuation of the funds, they preferred letting it lie useless. In numerous instances sums from $100 to $300 had lain unimproved for many years, while others had loaned and lost the whole. . . .

The trustees are glad to report, that the habit of saving among the depositors becomes very soon not only delightful, but permanent. Those who have brought their one dollar, are anxious to increase it to five, and so on. The number of re-deposits sufficiently confirms this fact; and such has been the effect on emigrants from Great Britain, that the very guineas which they have received from the banks for Savings at home, they have deposited in the one in this city immediately after landing.[23]

The trustees were also gratified that a few sailors had been directed to the bank and "the trustees will do all in their power to increase the number." They were also pleased that clergymen, although unable to save very much as "their means in general are small and their families large," were making deposits, for the trustees were impressed by "the number of destitute widows of once respectable and useful clergymen." The number of deposits for minors was also "not one of the least blessings which shall flow from this institution." "The trustees take this public opportunity of thanking the gentlemen connected as tellers, clerks and porters in the different banks, for the cheerful manner in which they have rendered their services on the evenings of deposit."

Reference to the evenings of deposit suggests that the early savings banks were part-time operations. Many opened at first one or two evenings a week, others for short periods on selected days of the week. For example, when the Bowery Savings Bank was opened in rent-free quarters in the Butchers and Drovers Bank in 1834, some of the trustees were present on Monday and Saturday evenings between five o'clock and eight o'clock to receive deposits. A few months later, the cashier of the Butchers and Drovers volunteered his services. All the deposits received the first year were deposited at this commercial bank at 5 per cent interest; at the end of the year, the Bowery paid 5 per cent on deposits up to $500 and 4 per cent on larger deposits; it had met expenses of $459.93 for "procuring a set of books and other expenses," and had $243.42 left over.[24] It was also common for the early savings banks to provide different hours or separate facilities for lady depositors. The president of the Bowery Sav-

---

23. It was not until the Coinage Act of 1853 that the United States succeeded in supplanting entirely foreign coins in general circulation with United States coinage.

24. William Dana Orcutt, *The Miracle of Mutual Savings* (New York: The Bowery Savings Bank, 1934), pp. 27-29.

ings Bank, Thomas Jeremiah, sent the following comments, which are quoted in *A History of Savings Banks in the United States* (II, 195), to Emerson W. Keyes when the latter was preparing his history of savings banking:

> The measure of establishing a savings bank in the Bowery, to be called the Bowery Savings Bank, originated with the directors of the Butchers' and Drovers' Bank, and while the great object for which such institutions was intended may have received a proper degree of attention, yet the prevailing idea was undoubtedly the prospect of some collateral advantages. The relation of these two institutions will be apparent from the fact that nine out of the thirteen directors of the Butchers' and Drovers' Bank were among the original incorporators of the Bowery Savings Bank.
>
> The success of this last institution sufficiently illustrates that no necessary embarrassment or hazard should be charged upon the business relations which legitimately exist between banks for discount and Banks for Savings. . . .

The Secretary of the Provident Institution for Savings in Boston wrote to the Society for Prevention of Pauperism, while the latter was seeking a charter, that all of the business of the Provident was conducted by the Treasurer, whose books were examined weekly by a committee of the trustees, who took turns monthly for this task. He stated:

> The greatest good is, in affording the humble journeymen, coachmen, chamber-maids, and all kinds of domestic servants, and inferior artisans, who constitute two-thirds of our population, a secure disposal of their little earnings, which would otherwise be squandered, or unwisely lent to petty fraudulent dealers, on a promise of usurious interest, which is three times out of four, wholly disregarded. More than a hundred instances have occurred in our experience, of such losses, by lending to neighbors or cousins; and these operate as the most powerful argument, with that class of people, to come to the Savings Bank.
>
> Some examples of adjuring spiritous liquors, and laying up what was worse than wasted, have encouraged us.[25]

The Provident also reported that half of the deposits were in

---

25. Society for Prevention of Pauperism, *Documents Relative to Savings Banks, Intemperance and Lotteries* (New York: 1819), p. 4.

sums of less than $30. The nature of the clientele was indicated by the list of depositors:

1 widow of a clergyman, 89 widows, 2 nurses, 309 single women, 62 married women, 9 mantua-makers, 8 tayloresses, 1 orphan, 402 minors, 19 charitable societies, 1 church, 1 trustee for a minor, 21 merchants, 41 traders, 15 printers, 37 lawyers, 5 gentlemen, 5 physicians, 6 druggists, 1 comedian, 3 clergymen, 6 school-masters, 90 mechanics, 6 bakers, 4 taylors, 5 barbers, 8 shoemakers, 1 butcher, 18 farmers, 25 clerks, 25 sailors, 2 soldiers, 33 laborers, and 158 domestics.[26]

The Savings Bank of Baltimore informed the Society that:

We do not take over 500 dollars at any time, for any one person. We have an Irishman, a hard-working stone mason, who has deposited 500 dollars, at 3 different times. Several free blacks, have, from time to time, deposited 100 dollars, and more. We have several instances of women, who, during the whole summer, deposited a dollar per week. This is the most desirable kind of depositors, for all this is saved from luxury and dress. Several journeymen mechanics deposit their 3 to 5 dollars per week. Just at present, our weekly deposits are small—as the expenses of a family, in the winter, are heavy, and less can be saved than in summer.[27]

The Institution for Savings in the Town of Salem and its Vicinity informed the Society that in six months it had received $26,250, from 184 depositors. The secretary noted that three fourths of the depositors were "females, sailors not being disposed to deposit their earnings, which if husbanded at all, can be turned to greater advantage, when taken with themselves as adventures on their voyages."[28] Rather apologetically, he noted that the expenses of the institution for the first six months— $104.35—were expected to be lower in the future as it had been necessary to furnish the treasurer "with the necessary books and other articles."[29] The Philadelphia Saving Fund Society remarked that depositors who had found it necessary to withdraw funds had said "how thankful they were that they had this

26. *Ibid.*, p. 6.
27. *Ibid.*, pp. 7-8.
28. *Ibid.*, pp. 10-11.
29. *Loc. cit.*

resource to apply to, *in time of need*," and the secretary concluded, "I have no hesitation in recommending to you, to establish a similar institution in your city, *fully believing it the most
efficient means of decreasing the evils of pauperism.*"[30]

Clearly, as illustrated by the efforts of the trustees in starting
the banks and by the tone of these letters, the first savings banks
were entirely philanthropic institutions aimed at ameliorating
or preventing pauperism. Probably the founders of the early
banks had no conception of the size and importance these institutions would attain. They seem to have thought of them as
places where, from time to time during the week, small deposits
(and a few sizeable ones like that of the Irish stonemason) could
be made by people with very limited funds and limited opportunities to invest them, and that it would be a simple matter to
invest these funds in federal and state securities. Little thought
apparently was given at first to other investments or loans, to
the question of cash and other liquid reserves, or to building up
a surplus as a form of protection or as a means of increasing
earnings.

Rapid Early Growth

In the 40 years from 1820 to the Civil War, growth of the banks
was rapid. Savings banks were established in industrial cities of
New England and New York, usually by the same sort of public-
spirited individuals as had started the first ones, but sometimes
as "feeders" for commercial banks, for prestige, and for other
related reasons. By the time of the Civil War the banks were
firmly established in the northeastern section of the country as
important financial institutions. Elsewhere, growth was virtually
nonexistent, although some banks were established in western
Pennsylvania, Ohio, Chicago, and elsewhere.[31] However, as the

---

30. *Ibid.*, p. 14 (original italics). These statements are quoted in Weldon
Welfling, *Savings Banking in New York State* (Durham, N.C.: Duke University Press, 1939), pp. 8-9.
31. It is reasonably certain, however, that the savings banks noted in
early references and statistical sources in Chicago and most other areas
west of Ohio were not mutual savings banks, but stock corporations.

West was being settled there was no pre-existing class of "gentle-men" with the sense of civic responsibilities that was held by the wealthier merchants of Philadelphia, Boston, Baltimore, and New York. The influence of gentlemen Quakers and Puritans was not predominant in the pioneer settlements, nor, indeed, was there a "lower class" dependent upon the wealthier for employment or for assistance when employment was lacking.[32]

The demise of the Second Bank of the United States in 1836 provided the opportunity for a rapid growth of state-chartered commercial banks, for which there was an insistent demand as a source of funds for agricultural and commercial ventures. These banks were often not above accepting small deposits, as the more aristocratic merchant banks of the East had been. The growth of the commercial banks prior to the Civil War was rapid, as shown in Table 1–2. After some reduction in the numbers and dollar volume involved in the early 1840's, growth was persistent.

TABLE 1-2[33]

STATE BANKS, SELECTED YEARS, 1835–60

Year	Number[a]	Banknotes	Deposits[b]
		(in millions of dollars)	
1835	704	104	83
1840	901	107	76
1845	707	90	88
1850	824	131	110
1855	1,307	187	190
1860	1,562	207	254

[a]Excludes unincorporated (private) and mutual savings banks.
[b]Probably includes small amounts of unincorporated and mutual savings bank deposits.

While the West was being settled and new cities being created, the older cities where savings banking started were growing to unprecedented size. New York and Philadelphia were

32. Quakers played leading roles in establishing the early banks in Philadelphia, New York, Baltimore, and Wilmington, Delaware.
33. Board of Governors, *Banking Studies*, 1941, pp. 417-18.

both about 37,000 in population in 1790; New York had reached more than 800,000 by 1860 and Philadelphia exceeded 500,000. In this 70-year period, Boston grew from 25,000 to 175,000 and Baltimore from 15,000 to 205,000. Pittsburgh was still only a settlement in 1810 but had a population of 50,000 by 1860, and Chicago, reporting a hundred settlers in the early 1830's, had over 100,000 by the Civil War. Second and third savings banks were soon established in imitation of the first in each seaboard city, and later the numbers grew rapidly. The 1850's were a period of especially rapid growth (see Tables 1–3 and 1–4).

TABLE 1-3[34]

DEPOSITS IN MUTUAL SAVINGS BANKS, 1820–60

	New York	Massachusetts	Other New England	Other	Total[a]
1820	$ 432,576	$ 400,000	$ 106,000	$200,000	$ 1,138,576
1830	2,623,304	2,500,000	1,075,000	775,000	6,973,304
1840	5,431,966	5,819,554	2,800,000	- - -	14,051,520
1850	20,832,972	13,660,024	8,938,134	- - -	43,431,130
1860	67,440,397	45,054,236	36,782,871	- - -	149,277,504

[a]Totals are for the preceding columns. No data available for "other" states for 1840, 1850, 1860.

---

34. Based on data in Keyes, *op. cit.*, II, 532. As Hammond remarks, "One must not expect too much from nineteenth century bank statistics." These data are the best Keyes could find after exhaustive efforts, including correspondence with each savings bank, not all of which was answered. Keyes remarked, "With due allowance for error, which it will be a pleasure to have corrected by anything more reliable or authentic, the statement is presented as the nearest approximation to accuracy which the present knowledge of the subject will admit of. We believe, however, that the aggregates will never be materially changed. They have cost an immense amount of labor, and we are not likely to be furnished with data for their correction any more authentic or complete than those already employed by us." The Comptroller of the currency, in his *Annual Report* in 1916 used the same figures.

TABLE 1-4[85]

NUMBER OF SAVINGS BANKS AND ACCOUNTS, AND
AVERAGE DEPOSIT, 1820–60,
NEW YORK AND MASSACHUSETTS

	New York			Massachusetts		
	Number of banks	Open accounts	Average deposit	Number of banks	Open accounts	Average deposit
1820	2	3,153	$137	3	2,962	$135
1830	5	18,085	145	20	15,000	166
1840	12	38,231	142	31	37,470	157
1850	22	111,112	187	45	78,823	173
1860	72	300,693	224	89	230,068	196

Thus, by 1860, commercial bank obligations in the form of notes and deposits outstripped savings bank deposits by a clear margin. The predominance of savings banks in New England and New York, however, kept a closer parity; commercial bank-notes and deposits in 1860 in New York were $139 million and in Massachusetts $51.4 million. By and large the distinction between commercial banks and other financial institutions was maintained. While the former issued their own circulating notes in exchange for commercial debts, they were also developing a system of transferring deposits by check and of crediting proceeds of loans to these deposit accounts. At the same time, however, they began to accept small deposits not subject to check. Statistics do not separate time from demand deposits, but there are many references to the payment of interest on deposits; often, of course, interest was paid on demand deposits also.

The general public

. . . was beginning to require the services of financial intermediaries, both as a place for safekeeping and as an extender of credit. More equitable enfranchisement and representation, culminating in the wave of Jacksonian Democracy that swept away all remaining property qualifications for voting, inevitably resulted in the more equitable distribution of wealth. . . . Per capita national wealth grew from $170 in 1790 to $590 in 1860. Moreover, an ever

35. *Loc. cit.*

greater proportion of acquired wealth was held in the form of specie or currency rather than land, and was therefore much more vulnerable to theft or loss. . . .[36]

Deposits in the savings banks reached about $150 million and were held by some 700,000 depositors by 1860.

The management of these funds required a change in the original nature of the savings banks. They could no longer be entirely part-time operations carried on as philanthropic sidelines by public-spirited citizens. While new banks were being established much along the lines of the early ones, older banks were moving to new quarters, staying open each day, and hiring full-time officers and clerks. Problems of investing funds became more complex, management of liquidity for deposits amounting to large sums presented a challenge, and in general the savings banks became sophisticated financial institutions. The financial panics of 1837 and 1857 had repercussions, including heavy withdrawals and depressed assets, on these depositories as they did on commercial banks and the commercial community. Questions such as that of an appropriate surplus, appropriate rates to be paid to savers, relationships with depository commercial banks, and others required attention from both savings bankers and regulatory officials. As incorporation of banks in general was divorced from the old system of incorporation by legislative acts, general laws were passed in order to apply uniform investment and other powers to all of the savings banks in a given jurisdiction.

Charter Provisions

Investment powers were originally granted in the charters. As already noted, some of the early charters left the determination of these powers to the incorporators themselves. Others made no provision for holding cash; some required the periodic distribution of surplus while others ignored the question. Some permitted investment only in "public funds," while others specified other assets.

---

36. Savings Division, The American Bankers Association, *Response to Change* (New York, 1965), p. 9.

Of the five charters granted to savings banks in Baltimore between 1818 and 1868, four placed no restrictions on the investments that could be made by the trustees. The charter of the Dime Savings Bank (1854) limited holdings of real estate, permitted investment in "securities and stocks of this State or the United States, or . . . the stocks and bonds of the city of Baltimore, authorized to be issued by the Legislature of this State, or loaning . . . on the securities of said stocks or bonds, or on improved real estate" provided the real estate was worth at least twice the amount of the loan.[37] The restrictions, however, apparently were neither observed nor enforced; at least by 1872, the investments included Missouri, Vermont, Maine, and railroad bonds. Thon has calculated the percentages of earning assets at the beginning of certain years for the Savings Bank of Baltimore as follows:

TABLE 1-5[38]

INVESTMENTS AS PERCENTAGE OF EARNING ASSETS,
SAVINGS BANK OF BALTIMORE, VARIOUS DATES

	1821	1839	1849	1859
Railroad bonds	- -	4.9	1.7	1.7
State, county, municipal	45.8	22.7	26.8	24.2
U.S. Government	30.2	- -	10.6	19.4
Public utility securities	- -	- -	2.2	1.2
Bank stocks	15.5	5.7	4.4	2.4
Loans	- -	66.9	54.3	51.1

In New York State a variety of charter provisions came into existence and proliferated as original charters were amended to grant additional powers. In 1820, the Bank for Savings received authority to make loans to New York City; in 1827, it received authority to invest in the stocks of the State of Ohio, the first authorization to go outside New York State. The charter of the

37. Robert W. Thon, Jr., *Mutual Savings Banks in Baltimore* (The Johns Hopkins Press, 1935), p. 29.
38. Thon, *op. cit.,* pp. 43, 45. For 1821, the tabulation is incomplete as there were also bank deposits of about 9 per cent of assets.

Albany Savings Bank in 1827 authorized investment in the stocks of banks in that city or in Troy. In 1829 the Brooklyn Savings Bank was authorized to invest in New York City securities and in "Brooklyn Village stock." In that year the Seamen's Bank for Savings was granted power to invest in Pennsylvania and Ohio stocks. In 1830, the Bank for Savings won approval for investment in the stocks of any state and for loans to the "Public School Society of New York on satisfactory real security." The charter of the Poughkeepsie Savings Bank in 1831 authorized mortgage loans where the security was twice the loan, thereafter a common provision.

General Laws

By the end of the Civil War period, however, general laws typically superseded charters as sources of bank powers and regulation, although this development came rather late in New York State. By 1834, although total deposits amounted to only about $3.5 million in the savings banks of Massachusetts, there were already 22 banks and additional requests for charters. The legislature responded with "An Act to Regulate Institutions for Savings," of which the following were the chief provisions:[39]

1. Officers were to be a president and a treasurer, plus such others as were found necessary, and "such number of trustees or managers as the corporation shall agree upon."

2. The officers were to be selected by the corporation, except that the treasurer was selected by the trustees.

3. Any citizen of the Commonwealth was eligible to be a member of the corporation.

4. Individuals' deposits were limited to $1,000, but not deposits of religious or charitable organizations.

5. Deposits could be invested as follows:
   a. in bank stock, up to 50 per cent of the commercial bank's capital stock, or in bank deposits at interest, or in loans secured by bank stock to 90 per cent of value;
   b. in real estate mortgages, up to 75 per cent of deposits, but without restriction as to value of property;

---

39. The act is quoted in Keyes, *op. cit.* I, 47-50.

   c. in the public funds of the United States, or the Commonwealth or any county, city or town in Massachusetts;

   d. "if the moneys held on deposit . . . cannot be conveniently invested" in the manner listed above, in loans on bonds or other personal security, with at least one principal and two surety promisors, up to 25 per cent of deposits.

   6. Officers could not borrow from the bank, but the ban did not extend to trustees.

   7. Income was to be divided among the depositors "in just proportion;" no provision was made for a surplus.

   8. An annual report was required.

Subsequent charters were simple references to this act.

In 1838, the legislature provided for three bank commissioners, who were to examine each bank and savings bank annually. Their first report showed bank stock to be the largest investment, mortgages second, loans on personal security third, and bank deposits fourth. In 1841, the banks were empowered to lend on the security of railroad stocks, but only under strict limitations: The stock must command at least par in the market, the road or franchise could not be subject to a mortgage, and the loan could not exceed 85 per cent of value.

The question of whether the Act of 1834 superseded provisions of charters granted earlier was answered by the courts in the affirmative in litigation involving the Provident Institution for Savings.

Other Developments to 1860

From the passage of the Act of 1834 to the Civil War, growth of the savings bank system in Massachusetts was rapid. By 1860, there were 89 banks with 230,000 depositors and deposits of over $45 million.[40] The average deposit approximated $200; virtually one person in five was a depositor, and deposits averaged $36.59 per capita. Growth responded to cyclical influences; deposits rose rapidly in 1852 and 1858–59, but scarcely at all in 1842, as

---

40. *Report of the Bank Commissioners,* 1861, *passim.*

had also been true of the panic year of 1837. Growth led to
expansion of the list of authorized investments to include the
securities of all New England states, and, apparently to limit the
influence of affiliated commercial banks, the amount of cash was
restricted to 7 per cent of deposits. *Next para ⟶*

Growth brought attendant problems. Liquidity management
became more of a problem. Investments in bank stocks proved
to have problems of liquidity, or as it was then called, converti-
bility. Stocks of country banks had limited markets, while bank
stocks generally could be depressed as they were by the outbreak
of the Civil War. The loans on personal security tended to
become business loans, and sometimes of the sort not sought by
the commercial banks. To the extent that such loans were attractive to the commercial banks, antagonism was created between the two types of banks. Mortgages were beginning to
demonstrate illiquidity and occasionally lack of safety in
depreciating neighborhoods, but some of the savings banks were
employing the principle of amortization and requiring annual
reductions of principal. The general opinion was that income
property provided the best security.

As the banks approached $150 million in deposits, their rela-
tionships with commercial banks brought critical attention. On
the one hand, they were sometimes competitors; on the other
hand, they were sometimes dominated. In 1860, according to the
Commissioners, 27 savings banks operated in the same rooms
with commercial banks. As Keyes explained, the practice

. . . had its origin, naturally enough, in the fact, that in small neighborhoods, where it was thought a Savings Bank might be of service to
the manufacturing classes, it would be found that the patronage
secured would hardly be sufficient to warrant the expense of an
independent establishment. Economy would therefore be promoted,
by transacting the business of the Savings Bank in the office, and
through the officers of an ordinary bank. A small addition to the
salary of such officers would compensate them for the service rendered, and the bank would be at no additional expense, and the
slight inconvenience suffered by the accomodation thus afforded
would be compensated by the balance of Savings Bank funds left
with it for deposit and use. But the tendency of such connection

was to make the affairs of the Savings Bank subordinate to those of the bank of discount. Whenever the affairs of the Savings Bank became prosperous, and its business profitable, these would be made to inure to the benefit of the stock corporation.[41]

And the Commissioners complained in 1861 that "In our examinations we have often found the books of a Savings Bank sadly in arrear, because the treasurer had been too much occupied with his duties as cashier to keep them written up."

A general savings bank act was passed in Virginia in 1838. It appears that unincorporated savings banks began operations in Richmond around 1830, as an act was passed in 1832 to permit them to continue to operate but not to issue banknotes; philanthropy does not seem to have been the motive for their establishment. Later incorporations differed from the New England type in that depositors were members of the corporations and thus voted for the directors; the Harper's Ferry Savings Institution was incorporated in 1833, and several others followed in 1838. The general act prohibited purchase of securities below "face and interest," and a supplementary act repeated the prohibition against issuing notes. Savings banks, as such, did not attain importance and after the war banking was left to commercial banks.[42]

The first savings bank in Connecticut was the Society for Savings, in Hartford, which opened about the same time as did the Bank for Savings in New York, in 1819. By 1848, there were 12 savings banks in the state. Investment powers tended to be broader as new charters were granted, until in 1843 charter provisions were supposedly supplanted by a general law. Both earlier and later charters, however, contained provisions contrary to the general law. The general law, for example, appeared to prohibit investment in bank stock, but individual charters permitted it. Connecticut also differed from other states in requiring minimum percentages of deposits to be invested in mortgage loans, rather than imposing maximum limits. The Act

41. Keyes, *op. cit.,* I, 64-65.

42. *All-Bank Statistics* recognizes no mutual savings bank history in Virginia, nor does the National Association of Mutual Savings Banks. These banks apparently were not mutual savings banks.

of 1843 authorized investment only in mortgage loans, but charters authorized investments in the usual variety of securities.

Individual charters neither required nor authorized banks to build up a surplus, but an act passed in 1847 permitted the banks to do so on a sliding scale of $5,000 for the first $250,000 of deposits and 1 per cent of additional deposits, to a maximum of $15,000. This amount was raised in 1854 to 2.5 per cent of total deposits, and after the Civil War to 5 per cent.

"Saving and building associations" were also formed in Connecticut, but reached only $2.4 million in shares in 1858. According to Keyes, "the result of this experiment does not appear to have been satisfactory, for in 1858 their formation thereafter was prohibited, and provision was made for closing those already formed."[43]

The year 1819 also saw the first savings banks in Rhode Island. Three were chartered but only two, the Savings Bank of Newport and the Providence Institution for Savings, were organized at that time. The Pawtucket Institution for Savings followed in 1828. Early charters provided for a large body of corporators who in turn selected a much smaller board of trustees. Investment powers were similar to those in Massachusetts, but a common provision was authority to invest in "private securities at the discretion of a standing committee of the board." A general law appeared in Connecticut in 1858; it authorized investment in the bonds of the federal government or any state, stocks of any bank, and securities of any municipality, "as they may deem safe and secure," as well as loans secured by these obligations or mortgages. Dividends were not covered by the act, but left to charter provisions, as were limitations on individual and total deposits. The question of requiring or permitting a surplus was generally ignored.

General laws did not come until 1869 in Maine and New Hampshire and 1875 in New York State. There were certain acts applying to all savings banks, such as those requiring examinations or reports, but not such as to be called general acts regulating investment, loan, and other powers.

The year 1819 figures in New Hampshire history also, as in

43. Keyes, *op. cit.*, I, 140.

that year the legislature considered but did not approve a charter for the Portsmouth Provident Society; however, a charter was granted in 1823 to the Portsmouth Savings Bank. This bank originated from much the same circumstances as did the other early savings banks. "The bank organized here soon after the Sunday school was established, and for the same purpose, and to a considerable extent, by the same persons."[44]

Maine also embraced savings banking in 1819—before it became a state—by chartering the Institution for Savings of the Town of Portland. This bank provided one of the few instances of failure, as it did not weather the difficulties of 1837 and failed in 1838.

Growth was slow prior to the Civil War; there were 11 banks by 1855, and deposits reached $1.5 million in 1860. Apparently, three of these 11 were in actuality commercial banks that were discontinued in the 1860's and succeeded by mutual savings banks.

The Saco and Biddeford Savings Institution was chartered in 1827. It had a large body of corporators, which could determine its own number; the corporators were authorized to invest the deposits "to best advantage."

Along with the rest of the American economy, the savings bank system was to flourish in the period of history following the Civil War. By 1860 the system was already entrenched as a leading financial institution in New England and New York, in many areas outstripping in assets commercial banks as well as other types of institutions. The original philanthropic character was dominant in many of the smaller banks and remained strong even in the large city savings banks, whose management had begun to move into the hands of professionals.

44. Letter from the solicitor of the bank in 1869 to Emerson W. Keyes (I, 201). A New England vignette is provided by the Treasurer's report on the fiftieth anniversary of the bank, which points out that one of the deposits made on the first day was $240, which was reduced to $188 in 1838; in fifty years dividends amounted to $1,191.71, "of which there has been withdrawn $871.49, leaving the present deposit $560.22."

CHAPTER 2

From Agricultural to Industrial Society, 1860–1914

BETWEEN the Civil War and World War I the United States emerged as a leading industrial nation. This change was reflected in countless ways. Human and animal power provided nearly three fourths of total productive energy around 1860, but only a third by 1910. Manufacturing establishments clearly indicated the triumph of the factory system: They numbered 141,000 in 1860 and 268,000 in 1914. Between these two dates the value of manufactured products rose from about $3 billion to more than $24 billion. Census data showed a population growing by a fifth or a quarter every decade; the figures were:

Year	Population in Millions	Per Cent Increase
1860	31.4	- -
1870	39.8	26.7
1880	50.2	26.0
1890	62.9	25.3
1900	76.0	20.8
1910	92.0	21.1

A city of a million population was reported for the first time by the census of 1880.

The Developing Economy

Although agriculture declined from more than a quarter of total output in the 1870's to about a fifth in 1900, in absolute terms it grew. Like industry, it also required more capital. The value of farm implements and machinery in use increased from about $150 million shortly before the Civil War to $750 million in 1900, while the tonnage of fertilizer consumed rose from 53,000 to 2.7 million.

The Westward Movement after 1860 naturally shifted the centers of growth from the areas principally served by savings banks. Population west of the Mississippi was about 4.5 million at the start of the Civil War, 20 million by 1900, and 30 million by 1915. Population in the older sections did not, of course, decline in an absolute sense. The Northeast—including Indiana, Illinois, Michigan and Ohio—went from 18 million in 1860 to 40 million in 1900 and 50 million in 1915. Mining, cattle raising, timber, and farming, along with numerous auxiliary opportunities, called people west. Milling and meat-packing centers rose where few people had lived shortly before, while manufacturing establishments increased in the older sections. The young eastern farmer or resident of a small town was more and more faced with the choice of moving either to the West or to the city. Until 1885, most of those who moved were northerners. This was not because their lot was harder than was that of southerners. "The reason probably lay in higher per capita savings enabling the northerner to move and start anew, his experience as farmer, 'mechanic', or small businessman that was readily adaptable to conditions in the West, his innate energy and restlessness and, particularly before 1885, his far superior means of transportation."[1]

The shifts and growth of the population were accompanied by other developments that were reflected in the nature of financial institutions. Increasing city populations implied more wage earners and other receivers of money incomes. More and more of

1. Harold F. Williamson (ed.), *The Growth of the American Economy* (New York: Prentice-Hall, 1951), p. 350.

the economy's transactions were being conducted through the use of money, including the transaction of saving. There were more dollars per person; incomes were appearing not only more as money incomes, but as incomes of more dollars. Even if real incomes had not been rising as a long-run trend, the same percentage savings would have provided more nominal dollars of savings for financial institutions to handle. At the same time, real incomes were in fact rising. Kuznets' estimates of net national product for the remainder of the nineteenth century are:[2]

Decade	Annual Average in Billions
1869-78	$ 9.3
1879-88	17.9
1889-98	24.2

These data are expressed in 1929 dollars and thus reflect real output. Consequently, while population was less than doubling, output was nearly tripling.

In spite of the rapid growth of population and output, the country was far from fully developed during this half century. It was not until 1887 that legislation was passed to subdivide Indian reservations among individual Indians and to make citizens of those who accepted. Bison still roamed the plains in herds of literally millions after the Civil War, and probably 10 million were slaughtered between 1870 and 1883, when the herds were finally nearly depleted, for the twin objectives of obtaining hides and removing the buffalo as a support for Indian tribes.

Railroad mileage was about 53,000 at the end of the Civil War, 74,000 by 1875, and 128,000 by 1885; it reached a peak of 253,000 in 1917. Railroad building probably provided a quarter of net capital formation during the 1880's. In 1865, there was a fairly complete network in the corner of the country bounded by the Ohio River and the City of Washington on the south and

2. Simon Kuznets, *National Income, A Summary of Findings* (New York: National Bureau of Economic Research, 1946), p. 32.

the Mississippi on the west. New York and New England were connected with Chicago. Four fifths of the 53,000 miles were in the East. After 1860, steel rails replaced iron, and steel permitted many improvements in size and design of locomotives and cars. By 1870, the Mississippi River was bridged in several places, and the Union Pacific line reached the West Coast. While many duplicating lines were built in the East after the war, in the 1880's competing lines criss-crossed the West. About a half billion dollars of railroad securities were issued as an annual average in the early 1870's, until checked by the financial panic of 1873, and about a billion came on the market in the early 1880's.

During this period agriculture formed itself into cotton, tobacco, wheat, corn, and grazing "belts." The same period saw the rise of the petroleum industry, following Drake's well in western Pennsylvania and a boom in the 1860's when oil was used for illumination and lubricants. Pennsylvania was producing 26 million barrels in 1881, 31 million in 1891. Ohio, California, Texas, and Oklahoma fields followed, and output reached 200 million barrels in 1910. Around 1910, a market for gasoline for automobiles and other engines began to develop. Iron ore mines were developed in Wisconsin and Michigan, and were then surpassed by the Mesabi Range of open-pit mines. Copper mines were developed in Montana and Arizona in the 1870's and 1880's. By 1870, steam coal was exceeding water power as a source of industrial energy; shortly the United States became the leading producer of hard coal as well as of steel.

Developments in steel were coordinated with those in other fields. The Bessemer furnace permitted production of steel for rails, and the introduction of the open hearth made possible purer and more economical steels from a wider variety of ores. Rolling mill output rose from a half million tons in 1860 to over five million by 1890 and to 16 million by 1900. Andrew Carnegie put together his steel company, which had a capitalization of $25 million in 1891, and which became part of the first billion-dollar company, United States Steel, in 1901.

The dramatic changes in living standards to be brought about by the automobile and numerous other developments of the early twentieth century began to be hinted. Predecessors of the automobile, powered by steam, had appeared in Europe before the availability of petroleum, and illuminating gas had also been used as a fuel. In England, Parliament had found it necessary by 1865 to require that any mechanical vehicle using the public roads must have at least three drivers, not exceed four miles per hour, and be preceded by a man carrying a red flag. In the 1890's, Ford, Duryea, Olds, Haynes, and Apperson produced a few cars. In 1900, 4,200 were built, representing half of total registrations; by 1913, registrations reached 1.25 million cars and 68,000 trucks. By 1903, the Wright Brothers were getting an airplane to fly.

In 1860, most skilled labor still worked 11 hours per day; The figure was reduced to ten by 1891. The standard workweek in industry was still 60 hours in 1900. Steel workers put in seven 12-hour days a week, but the building trades had won six days of eight hours. Average annual earnings reached $490 in 1900 and $630 in 1910, most of which increase was matched by that in living costs. Before 1900, most homes were illuminated by kerosene; gas and electric companies vied for street-lighting contracts. In the cities, few houses were yet wired for electricity, but the better ones were piped for gas.

Growth in Number and Size of Banks

These widespread and fundamental changes in the economy were reflected in the further development of savings banks, which in some respects reached their highest relative position in the economy in this period. Their dominant position in the northeast section of the country became pronounced, while their relative importance in the nation as a whole was also great. Some efforts to spread the system to the other parts of the country were made, with little permanent effect. Rapid growth was experienced, however, in the traditional savings bank territory.

From a base of approximately $150 million of deposits in 1860, savings banks held over $2 billion in 1900 and nearly $4 billion in 1915. Increases were irregular but in general rapid. Deposits on decennial dates were (in millions):[3]

1860	$ 149
1870	550
1880	783
1890	1,336
1900	2,130
1910	3,306
1915	3,893

Progress in the several states is shown in Table 2–1. After the Panic of 1837, Massachusetts, with 31 savings banks, had slightly more deposits than did New York with 12 banks; since then New York has been the leading state in terms of deposits.

The outbreak of the Civil War brought panicky financial markets, depressed security prices, and a degree of hoarding. The Commissioner of Banks in Massachusetts reported for 1861:

> The present condition of industry in the country will not encourage petitions for the incorporation of new savings banks, nor, in our opinion, would it justify the legislature in granting such petitions, if presented. The facilities for depositing savings are already everywhere ample, and the number of small and languishing institutions is quite too large.

In fact, however, between 1860 and 1865, deposits in savings banks rose from $150 million to $243 million, while the number of depositors rose slightly faster, from 981,000 to 1.6 million.

The preceding growth and the prosperous conditions during and immediately after the Civil War led to an accelerated growth in the number of savings banks, until this growth was slowed down by the effects of the Panic of 1873. The all-time peak number of banks was reached in 1875, when it was 666. Four fifths of the present savings banks were organized by 1875, and half of that fraction came into existence between 1860 and

---

3. As noted in an earlier connection, banking statistics prior to 1900 are not highly accurate. Many of the same figures appear in several original and official sources, which relied partly on each other for data—such as the Comptroller of the Currency and state banking departments. Data for 1896 and later were reworked by the Federal Reserve System for *All-Bank Statistics*, published in 1959.

TABLE 2-1[4]

DEPOSITS AND NUMBER OF SAVINGS BANKS,
BY STATE, SELECTED YEARS, 1896–1915

(DEPOSITS IN MILLIONS OF DOLLARS)

	1896		1900		1905		1910		1915	
	Deposits	Number	Deposits	Number	Deposits	Number	Deposits	Number	Deposits	Number
Connecticut	149.5	89	183.8	89	232.8	89	274.2	87	316.6	82
Delaware	3.9	2	5.0	2	7.6	2	9.6	2	12.3	2
Indiana	4.0	5	6.4	5	10.1	5	11.8	5	13.0	5
Maine	57.5	52	66.1	51	78.2	51	89.9	52	97.4	48
Maryland	49.3	24	58.1	18	66.7	15	89.4	24	96.8	19
Massachusetts	453.2	187	533.8	186	662.8	189	761.4	190	917.6	196
Minnesota	7.5	11	10.6	10	13.1	9	20.2	9	26.1	8
New Hampshire	48.2	44	47.2	43	62.0	45	78.4	46	96.5	47
New Jersey	35.2	25	51.0	25	71.4	25	94.8	24	117.4	26
New York	715.0	127	922.1	128	1,252.9	130	1,526.9	142	1,774.2	140
Ohio	26.2	4	39.7	4	50.8	3	56.8	3	62.6	3
Pennsylvania	76.4	14	103.5	12	140.0	9	174.6	10	222.0	10
Rhode Island	67.5	30	73.5	29	60.0	18	72.3	18	83.4	15
Vermont	23.3	22	27.6	22	34.3	22	43.1	21	53.6	20
West Virginia	.3	1	.5	1	.9	1	1.3	1	1.5	1
Wisconsin	.2	1	.6	1	.9	2	1.4	3	2.0	5
TOTAL	1,717.2	638	2,129.5	626	2,744.5	615	3,306.1	637	3,893.0	627

4. All-Bank Statistics, tables for individual states.

1875. Of 514 banks surviving in 1960, 90 had been organized by 1850, 113 were organized between 1850 and 1859, 121 were organized during the 1860's, and 86 were established between 1870 and 1874; thus, 104 of the banks were organized after 1874.[5]

Table 2–2 shows the number of banks surviving in 1960, which existed in the three leading states on certain dates. In addition to these organizations, a relatively large number of charters seems to have been granted between 1860 and 1875 for banks that did not actually commence business.

TABLE 2-2[6]

SURVIVING BANKS (1960)
EXISTING ON SELECTED DATES: MASSACHUSETTS,
CONNECTICUT, AND NEW YORK

	Massachusetts	Connecticut	New York
1850	40	11	18
1860	79	31	48
1865	91	39	57
1870	119	45	83
1875	150	65	98
1960	185	71	127

Changing Nature of the Banks

The growth in the volume of funds handled and in the number of savings banks in operation was reflected in a modification in the nature of the banks themselves. Obviously, an institution that grows to hold nearly $30 million of deposits, as did the Bowery Savings Bank around 1875, must experience considerable change in the nature of its operations, in its motivations, and in other ways. While the benevolent and philanthropic rea-

5. National Association of Mutual Savings Banks (NAMSB), *Mutual Savings Banking* (Englewood Cliffs, N.J.: Prentice-Hall, 1962), calculated from data on p. 31. Much larger numbers of banks are cited in the *Statistical Abstracts* of the period, but it is obvious that many stock savings banks are included.

6. NAMSB, *op. cit.*

sons for the establishment of the first banks cannot be said to have disappeared, and in fact are still in evidence after 150 years, it is also true that after the first half century of operation the early founders had passed on the reins of management to their successors and that the clientele of the banks was no longer "the humble journeyman and seamstress" who were the objects of the founders' original concern. The surge in incorporations between 1860 and 1875 cannot be laid to an upsurge in the early needs for savings banks, but more to a change in the nature of those needs and increasing opportunities for meeting the needs on other than completely altruistic bases.

It is difficult to find a date when it may be said that this change took place, and it is easy to overstate the extent of the change. While some of the savings banks in metropolitan areas were clearly becoming financial institutions of very respectable size and sophistication, it must also be remembered that the larger number of savings banks held rather small total deposits, which represented modest average balances. It is clear, however, that the organizers of the newer banks shortly after the Civil War were not the Condy Raguets, James Savages, and Thomas Eddys of the first quarter of the century, but men who had before them the successful example of a working institution.

That custom and tradition have their influence is apparent in Emerson Keyes' remark, "True there are those who quite stoutly maintain that no Savings Bank ought to receive deposits in excess of $5 million, claiming that no more can be safely managed, invested and supervised."[7] Keyes was not in sympathy with this view, holding that savings banks should grow to serve properly their customers. Still, another remark of Keyes hints at the changing circumstances: He stated in connection with the effects of the financial difficulties of 1873, "Candidates for the honors and emoluments of the office of trustee of young and struggling Savings Banks are not so abundant as they were."[8]

Writing in a more recent period, William H. Kniffin noted:

Fifty years ago, when life was less strenuous than at present, and men had time to live and do things benevolent, we may find, as

7. Keyes, *op. cit.,* II, 2.
8. *Ibid.,* p. 599.

already indicated, savings banks that were established through pure philanthropy. . . . In these days of competition, to start a bank, after the old time notions, and in the old time way, would invite disaster, especially in the larger cities. The people now-a-days demand fine fixtures and well dressed men in order to convince them that this is really a bank and worthy of their regard. The difficulty attending the establishment of a modern savings bank will readily be seen when it is remembered that since 1890 there have been but 29 savings banks organized in the State of New York, and all but eight are in Greater New York. . . .

Without a proper financial motive, it is doubtful if a man capable of organizing a savings bank would give it the time necessary, which is a great deal. He must spend many hours enlisting the support of his associates. There will be incidental expenses to meet. . . . The most likely individual to assume such a task is an attorney. A bank attorneyship adds prestige to any lawyer and it is a profitable connection.[9]

Keyes was of the opinion that chartering by the legislature had led to a proliferation of savings banks in New York State by the time of the General Law of 1875, after which the restrictions of supervisory screening tended to reduce their number. Robert W. Thon concluded, however, that a general incorporation law in Maryland tended to increase chartering. In Maryland, five banks were formed between 1819 and 1868, when the general incorporation act was passed; 15 banks were formed between 1869 and 1900. Two of the 15, however, resulted from special acts.

The increased number in the latter period was probably due mainly to two causes—greater ease of incorporation and the growth of the idea of neighborhood banks. Before 1868, when charters could be secured only by special act of the legislature, a certain amount of personal prestige must have been necessary in order to secure legal sanction. This, and the natural tedium and uncertainty characteristic of legislative action, must have combined to keep down applications for charters in the early period. During this time, too, the original conception of a mutual savings bank as an agency through

---

9. William H. Kniffin, *The Savings Bank and Its Practical Work* (4th ed.; New York: The Bankers Publishing Company, 1928), p. 109.

which the rich and influential might aid the 'worthy poor' was probably strongest.

After 1868, on the other hand, when the securing of a savings bank charter involved only the fulfilling of certain prescribed formalities, the number of people desirous of incorporating naturally increased. As soon as persons of less importance could secure charters, the nature of the banks changed, and they became mostly small neighborhood affairs.[10]

Reference to the growth of neighborhood banks suggests still a different change from that suggested earlier—that banks were growing larger and presumably more impersonal. However, of 12 banks formed in Baltimore between 1872 and 1895, ten were out of business or reorganized by 1912.

Acceptance by the General Public

As the economy changed, customers of the savings banks became less "the deserving poor" and more and more a substantial segment of the population. Although the number of accounts rose rapidly, the average deposit also increased. Neither of these figures can provide an accurate measure of the "average" depositor, since an individual could have accounts at several banks, and a family could have several accounts at a single bank. The number of accounts in New England, New York, and New Jersey rose from 694,000 in 1860, to 1.6 million in 1870, and to 2.4 million in 1875. During the panic year of 1873, the number of accounts rose by more than 100,000. The panic probably served to increase average balances, as some small accounts were closed while larger accounts were opened.

The Comptroller of the Currency remarked in 1893 that "It . . . appears that while the entire deposits in mutual savings institutions are 'savings,' the reports show that over 10 per cent of the deposits in (stock savings banks) are not of that nature."[11] A different view, however, was presented in testimony in 1878. Thomas Hills argued that the savings banks were

10. Robert W. Thon, Jr., *Mutual Savings Banks in Baltimore* (Baltimore, Md.: The Johns Hopkins University Press, 1935), p. 16.
11. *Annual Report*, 1893, p. 8.

increasingly used by "capitalists" on the grounds that (1) out of
$13 million of deposits at the Boston Five Cents Savings Bank,
$4 million were in accounts of $1,000 or more; (2) in Spring-
field, 16 per cent of the deposits were in amounts of $400, $600,
or $1,000; (3) a probate filed in Suffolk County amounted to
$170,000, the personal estate being $108,759, and of this amount
$35,690 was in savings bank deposits, ranging from $500 to
$4,500; (4) the large deposits made in January in Boston must
have come from dividends on other investments; (5) "It can
hardly be claimed with a show of reason that our laboring
population, which, in 1866, were receiving high wages, could
then average but $214 to each depositor, and the same class, in
1876, after three years of great depression in all business, could
have swelled their average deposit to $329, an increase of fifty-
four per cent."[12]

A scattering of remarks by Keyes illustrates the growing use of
savings banks by more prosperous groups.

> Savings Banks are no longer confined in their range of operations
> and influences to the limited work conceived for and assigned to
> them when they were instituted. They have in late years proved
> attractive places of resort for sums far exceeding the modest sav-
> ings of humble poverty which they were ordained to succor and
> nourish. . . . It seems to be taken for granted that the bulk of the
> deposits of these institutions represents the savings of the very poor,
> and that it is desirable that this should be so. Neither the assump-
> tion nor its inference is true. . . . It is safe to say, that at least one
> per cent of the annual interest that has been paid to depositors
> since 1850, and nearly all of the surplus that has been accumulated
> for the greater security of depositors, has been derived from depos-
> its in excess of $1,000.

This student and admirer of the "savings bank interest" viewed
the development with favor, and criticized the legislative restrictions on individual deposits which have been characteristic from
the beginnings.

> In our judgment everybody should be encouraged to save. There is
> as much merit in economizing on a salary of $5,000 as on one of

---

12. "The Tax on Savings-Bank Deposits," *Remarks of Thomas Hills
before the Joint Committee on Banks and Banking* (Boston, 1878), p. 9.

$500, if indeed there is not more. And there is no more palpable and at the same time more popular fallacy than that which assumes that the ability to save $5,000 or more, carries with it the ability to shrewdly invest and care for that considerable sum.[13]

Keyes estimated that, in 1873, 81 per cent of the accounts were for less than $500, leaving 19 per cent over $500, of which 9 per cent were in excess of $1,000. He estimated that 40 per cent of total deposits were in accounts of less than $500, with 60 per cent in larger accounts and 45 per cent in accounts of more than $1,000. The average deposit at this time was $334, with accounts under $500 averaging $163, deposits over $500 averaging $1,059, and deposits over $1,000 averaging $1,749.[14]

Few Failures of Savings Banks

Prior to the Panic of 1873, there were very few failures of savings banks and these few were generally attributed to "bad investments." Typically, depositors were paid 80 per cent or more of their deposits. In a few instances, defalcations led to failure or a savings bank failed along with a closely associated commercial bank. By Keyes' count, there were 11 failures before 1872. The losses to depositors, counted in terms of gross deposits made over the period, were minute.

Perhaps 20 savings banks failed, without being able to reopen, during or as a result of the Panic of 1873. These tended to be smaller banks on which runs developed, and failures were concentrated among the younger banks. Many new charters were granted between 1850 and 1870. In New York, new charters numbered 13 in 1866, 13 in 1867, 20 in 1868, and 26 in 1869, and the situation was similar in other states. Often, the new banks were located near existing ones. The inflation and general prosperity of the 1860's, along with the ready availability of government securities, guaranteed the early success of the new banks. Interest rates were high and capital gains were created by the fact that interest on the federal securities was paid in gold, making the dollar equivalent considerably higher.

13. Keyes, *op. cit.*, II, 572.
14. *Ibid.*, p. 568.

It was not uncommon for these capital gains to be converted into new bank buildings. For example, in 1869, a trustee of the Erie County Savings Bank (founded in 1854) explained:

The large accumulation of surplus profits to the bank is a subject which requires some explanation. The theory and practice of the bank is to pay depositors a regular interest of 6 per cent, while it is receiving upon all its loans the legal interest of 7 per cent. The difference of rate is the resource of the bank to pay its current expenses. But the state of the country for the past six years has enabled the bank to realize a much greater income from its investments. The war which broke out in 1861 compelled the Government to issue large amounts of Government bonds, the interest of which was payable in gold. The bank, under the authority of the charter, proceeded to invest in these bonds, which it was compelled to do to dispose of the large amount of deposits which began to accumulate in 1862 and continued during the war. These bonds were taken at par in currency, while the annual interest was regularly paid in gold. This exceptional state of things largely increased the surplus of the bank. . . . It was from this source that the means were derived which enabled the bank to purchase the land and build and furnish its elegant banking-house. This source of special accumulation will end with the resumption of specie payments. . . .[15]

A study made by the Federal Deposit Insurance Corporation for its annual report for 1934 found that 18 savings banks suspended during 1870–74. There were 503 active banks in 1870 and 661 in 1874. During 1875–79 the number of suspended banks shot up to 123, of which virtually half (60) suspended in 1878. These suspensions brought the number of active banks down to 631. During the three subsequent five-year periods, suspensions were 13, 11, and 17, leaving (net) 649 banks in 1894. Suspensions in 1895–99 rose to 42, leaving 628 banks. In the following three five-year periods, suspensions were only eight, four, and thirteen, and there were 628 banks in 1914.

Over the whole period from 1865 to 1934, losses amounted to only $37 million, or 1.7 cents per $100 of active deposits. About

---

15. *The Erie County Savings Bank* (published by the bank, 1954), pp. 44-45.

half of these total losses occurred in 1930–33, and the losses in 1874–78 amounted to $10 million, or over a quarter of the total.

Actually, the safety record of the mutual savings banks has been better than even these statistics suggest. The data apparently include some failures of stock savings banks.[16] Further, the data are not corrected for mutual savings banks that resumed operations after suspension, without losses to depositors, nor for those whose eventual liquidation was accomplished without loss. The Commissioner of Banks in Massachusetts noted in 1941:

> A careful examination of all available records indicates that the aggregate of all depositor losses during the past century and a quarter amounted to approximately 1/40 of 1 per cent of the total deposits during that period. That record of safety has probably never been equalled by any system of financial institutions in history. This record becomes even more impressive when it is realized that the depositors received last year in interest or dividends on their accounts more than nine times as much as the aggregate of all losses sustained during the past one hundred and twenty-five years.[17]

Origins of the New York General Law

The increasing interest in obtaining charters and the failures of the mid-1870's, although few, aroused public and legislative interest in the savings banks. In New York State this interest led to the passage of the General Law of 1875, a development that had already taken place in several other states. Several laws of general applicability had been passed from time to time earlier in New York. From the beginning all charters permitted examinations by the state comptroller. In 1839, the three bank commissioners were given the power to examine savings banks, but examinations were not required, and the law was repealed in 1843. By a law of 1857, the Superintendent of Banks could

---

16. The notes of pp. 111 and 113 as to sources of data in the FDIC *Annual Report* for 1934 so suggest.

17. *Annual Report*, 1941, Part I, p. viii.

examine savings banks if he "had reason to believe" there was mismanagement or violation of law. The principal duties of the Superintendent, however, consisted of supervising the state commercial banks under the free banking system, which involved note issues secured by the pledge of securities.

The conversion of many state banks to national charters and the temporary decline in the importance of the state banking system after the tax on state banknotes was imposed released the Superintendent's office for more attention to savings banks. A bill to regulate savings banks was proposed in 1870; it was defeated at that session but passed in 1871.[18] This bill required biennial examinations of each bank, as well as semi-annual reports, which were previously required.

Earlier, following adoption of the new constitution in 1847, which frowned on incorporation by special act of the legislature, efforts had been made to obtain passage of a general law covering savings banks. Legal opinion, however, was that savings banks were not corporations within the meaning of the term in the constitution. A law requiring examinations of savings banks in New York and Brooklyn was passed in 1863. Shortly thereafter the decline in the other duties of the Superintendent and the rise in legislative chartering led the Superintendent to institute a study of the current regulations, statutes, and charters governing the savings banks. It soon became apparent that it was virtually impossible to ascertain what the rules were, as there were some 86 charters, many or all of which had been amended from time to time, as well as several laws of general applicability. Consequently, the Superintendent prepared, as di-

---

18. The pleasures of reading Keyes' history are suggested by his comments on this episode: "It was subsequently revealed that its defeat was compassed by a Savings Bank officer who had the best of reasons for desiring that the affairs of his institution should not be subjected to the rigors of any examination, the character of which he could not control. He accomplished his purpose through the co-operation of a Senator, whose position, more than his character and influence, enabled him to defeat the bill. It is some gratification to be able to record that one of these conspirators is now a fugitive from justice, and the other is doing the State more acceptable service, as an inmate of the penitentiary, than, it is to be presumed, he ever did as a legislator." Keyes, *op. cit.,* II, 37.

rected by the legislature, a general law to be submitted to the legislature in 1868. Part of this development was the preparation of a *Special Report on Savings Banks,* a voluminous work written by Emerson Keyes in 1868, which constituted the basis of his later history, frequently quoted herein. This report made the point that, ". . . [the savings banks] have out-grown their early distinctive character as charitable institutions, and take their place proudly in the front rank among the great powers of the social state." The bill considered in 1868 was primarily an effort to codify existing provisions and to take out of the hands of the legislature both amendments of individual charters and chartering new banks.

The legislature was unwilling to give up its prerogatives of chartering, and this provision was struck out in committee.[19] Without this provision, those seeking reform lost interest. Opinion among the savings banking fraternity was divided and did not provide sufficient support for the bill.

The 1875 Constitution and General Law

A compromise was reached in the next legislature with an act that required future applications for new charters to be funnelled to the legislative committees through the Superintendent, who would append his recommendations. This provision, however, appears to have been a dead letter. Then the developments of 1873 led to renewed interest and the election of a reform legislature. The new constitution of 1874 was adopted (effective January 1, 1875) and provided that "The legislature shall, by general law, conform all charters of Savings Banks or Institutions for Savings, to a uniformity of powers, rights and liabilities, and all charters hereafter granted for such corporations shall be made to conform to such general law." It was also spelled out in the constitution that ". . . nor shall the trustees

---

19. Keyes' comments are typical: "But the sentiment of the committee was not favorable to it, and the first article, which provided for incorporation outside the legislature, and thus cut off certain small patronage of small politicians who, through some inscrutable providence, have legislative honors thrust upon them, was incontinently struck out." *Ibid.,* p. 121.

thereof, or any of them, have any interest whatever, direct or indirect, in the profits of such corporation; and no director or trustee of any such Bank or Institution shall be interested in any loan or use of any money or property of such Bank or Institution for Savings." The constitution did not solve the question of where charters would originate.

In the meantime the reform legislature had had reported to it the same bill as had been written in 1868, but it was not passed. After ratification of the constitution, a bill that was similar, but permitted incorporation by the legislature, was introduced in the Assembly. The 1868 bill was introduced in the Senate, where the former Superintendent of Banks, George W. Schuyler, was Chairman of the Banking Committee. The Assembly bill was largely the product of consultation with savings bankers. After considerable study and debate in the committees, a merged bill calling for chartering outside the legislature was introduced and passed. This was the General Law of 1875. All previous acts and provisions dealing with savings banks were carefully listed and repealed.

The provisions of the General Law were basically as follows:

1. Incorporation was placed in the office of the Superintendent of the banking department.

2. Trustees were banned as borrowers or as guarantors of borrowers.

3. Individual deposits were limited to $5,000 exclusive of dividends credited.

4. Deposits of females and minors were payable to themselves (a common provision in individual charters).

5. Investments permitted were United States securities; securities of New York State and any state that had not for ten years been in default; securities of any city, county, town, or village in New York state; mortgage loans, up to 50 per cent of the value of productive and 40 per cent of the value of unproductive property, and up to 60 per cent of deposits.

6. Real estate for banking purposes was permitted.

7. An "available fund" of cash, bank deposits, or loans on eligible securities was authorized; this fund could temporarily exceed 10 per cent of deposits.

8. Loans on drafts, notes, or personal security were prohibited.

9. Annual reports to the Superintendent and examinations at least each two years were provided for.

When passed in 1875, the General Law covered 154 banks holding $319 million of deposits due to 860,000 accounts. Thus, deposits in New York State alone were twice those of the whole system in 1860 and five times the deposits in New York State alone in 1860.

Developments In Other States

Developments of this period may be summarized for other areas more briefly. In Pennsylvania the mutual form of savings banks failed to spread widely. The Philadelphia area was the starting place for building and loan association in this country, and this movement spread much more rapidly than did savings banks. The presence of a European population acquainted with these associations, the ability to purchase housing, and the absence of the early philanthropic reasons for savings banks seem to explain the growth of the building and loan associations. Many savings banks were formed, however, as capital stock banks. By 1874, there were only four mutual savings banks in the Philadelphia area, two in Pittsburgh, and one in Johnstown. The Philadelphia Saving Fund Society, the first savings bank to open in the country, represented over one half of total savings bank deposits in the state, which were $18.4 million. In Maryland, virtually all of the savings banking was done in Baltimore, where there were four banks in 1876. At that time, total deposits were about $19.7 million, of which the Savings Bank of Baltimore held $12.5 million.

Experience in the states just to the west of the traditional savings banking area was similar to that in Pennsylvania. Commercial banks, opened for a less exclusive clientele than was customary in the older eastern cities, operated in the savings field, and building and loan associations also spread westward. At the same time, savings banks with capital stock were common. In Ohio, only a few savings banks were opened prior to the Civil War. A general act covering savings banks was passed in 1867, but does not seem to have been much observed, and in 1873 an act was passed providing for the establishment of "savings and loan associations" with minimum capital stock of $50,000. The Society for Savings was founded in Cleveland in 1849, largely through the efforts of S. H. Mather. It became one of the larger savings banks, but recently was reorganized as a national bank.

In Michigan an act of 1871 endowed savings banks with all the powers of banks except note issue; here savings banks were organized as stock corporations and with rare exceptions operated in practice as commercial banks. The Ann Arbor Savings Bank kept demand and savings accounts and paid interest only on the latter.

The early version of what became the New York law of 1875 was adopted in Indiana in 1869. In 1875, there were nine savings banks in Indiana, and aggregate deposits reached a million dollars in that year.

Between these states and California there were few population centers where savings banks might be established. Minnesota provided for such institutions, but in 1875 required that they become stock organizations. In California, three mutuals were organized between 1857 and 1860, but in 1862 the legislature provided for stock associations. The earlier three differed from their eastern counterparts in that the depositors were voting members. Depositors paid an "entrance fee" of $2.00, which was devoted to the surplus. These banks had both demand deposits and those withdrawable after six months.

The older savings bank states continued to amend their laws and regulations as the system grew. In 1876, Maine adopted much of the New York law of 1875, and in 1877, codified and revised scattered previous provisions. In 1875, New Hampshire added to existing mutual savings banks a system of guaranty savings banks with capital of from $50,000 to $200,000, which consisted of nonwithdrawable deposits. These deposits earned profits rather than the regular interest paid to other depositors.

Massachusetts adopted a general law in 1876, but did not

repeal existing charter provisions; rather, the law provided that the banks could elect to operate under the new regulations. The law codified investment powers, limited dividends, and provided for division of surplus whenever it exceeded 5 per cent of deposits.

Following a study of the savings bank system in 1873–74, the legislature in Connecticut amended previous acts, but did not devise a general law. These amendments limited the relationships of savings banks with commercial banks, regulated dividends, provided for a surplus of 5 per cent to be built up, and prohibited out-of-state mortgages.

Peak of Relative Importance

The growing industrialization and geographical development of the nation brought a relatively more rapid development of other financial institutions and therefore a relative decline in the importance of savings banks. As may be seen in Table 2–3, savings banks held 61 per cent of the savings in the forms listed there, in 1880, and this percentage declined steadily throughout the period to 1915, when it reached 30 per cent. The savings banks themselves were growing rapidly, but, of course, in a limited area of the country. Consequently, they continued to dominate the savings markets in the traditional area, although their relative importance declined somewhat there as well. For example, in Massachusetts the savings banks held 88 per cent of these forms of savings in 1890 and experienced a steady decline to 73 per cent in 1915. In New York, the percentage for 1890 is estimated at 86 per cent and for 1915, 67 per cent. The percentage fell from 90 per cent in 1890 in Connecticut to 79 per cent in 1915.[20] Nationally, between 1890 and 1915 the share of commercial banks' savings deposits rose from 12 per cent of the total to 26 per cent, the savings and loan associations held 7 per cent on both dates (but fluctuated from less than 6 per cent to more than 10 per cent during the period), and life insurance reserves rose from 29 per cent to 35 per cent of the total.

20. These percentages are based on Lintner, *op. cit,* App. II-2 to II-7.

TABLE 2-3[21]

SAVINGS IN SELECTED INSTITUTIONS,
1880–1915

(MILLIONS OF DOLLARS)

	I Savings Bank Deposits	II Per Cent of Total	III Commercial Bank Time and Savings Deposits	IV Commercial Bank Time and Savings Deposits of Individuals	V Unpledged Savings and Loan Shares	VI Life Insurance Reserves
1880	783	61		105	7	385
1885	1,015	59		167	49	493
1890	1,336	53	470	297	180	729
1895	1,597	47	491	357	350	1,086
1900	2,129	44	1,087	576	460	1,659
1905	2,745	40	2,146	1,063	543	2,502
1910	3,306	34	3,720	2,082	834	3,453
1915	3,893	30	5,050	3,087	1,283	4,595

Development of Commercial Banks

During the second half-century of savings banking the commercial banking sector was influenced by the development of the national banking system. Passed during the Civil War partly to increase the market for government securities and partly to re-

21. Column I is based on Comptroller of Currency, *Annual Reports,*
before 1900; on Federal Reserve System, *All-Bank Statistics* for 1900 and
later. Column II is the percentage of column I to the total of all columns
excluding column III. Column III is based on Federal Reserve System,
Banking and Monetary Statistics (p. 34), using the 1892 figure for 1890 and
the 1895 figure, and on *All-Bank Statistics* thereafter. Column IV is
Lintner's estimates. Column V is Lintner's estimates before 1900; 1900 and
1905 are based on Goldsmith; 1910 and 1915 on American Bankers Association (see *Response to Change,* pp. 110, 116). Column VI, Lintner's
estimates before 1900, *Life Insurance Companies as Financial Institutions*
(p. 20) thereafter. The greatest change caused by use of different series is in
savings and loan shares; they appear to be underestimated before 1900. Commercial bank deposits exclude interbank and U.S. Government deposits.

form the note issue, the National Banking Act succeeded in fact in stimulating the development of the use of demand deposits as means of payment. Instead of creating a single national system of commercial banks, the act brought about the dual system of commercial banking as state-chartered banks learned to survive the later tax on their note issues by developing the check system of payments.

The number of state banks reached a high point of 901 in 1840, which was not exceeded until 1854. There were 1,562 banks in 1860.[22] National banks came into existence in 1863, largely through conversion of state charters; and state banks declined to 247 in 1868, when there were 1,640 national banks. There were more unincorporated (private) banks than national banks until 1905; the number of state banks caught up with unincorporated banks in 1893 and with national banks in 1892.

In the savings market, the National Banking Act was important for a variety of reasons. On the deposit side, the act made no distinction between demand and time deposits. Consequently, the view was generally held that national banks were not empowered to accept time and savings deposits. In any event, there was no differentiation in reserve requirements, and, at the same time, no prohibition against paying interest on demand deposits. On the loan side, national banks were not empowered to make mortgage loans. The intent of the legislation was to create a system of *commercial* banks, whose credit would take the form predominantly of banknotes secured by federal government securities.

State-chartered banks were often empowered to differentiate between demand and time deposits, and in a few states were required to do so. Reserve requirements were often lower for time deposits. Some state banks were formed as stock savings banks, and time deposits of commercial banks did show a significant rise to 1900. By and large, however, commercial banks had more pressing interests than developing the market for savings accounts and employing the funds in the manner of savings

22. Again, with due allowance for the inaccuracy of early statistics. These data are from Federal Reserve System, *Banking Studies*, p. 418.

banks. Financing the rapid growth of industry, commerce, and transportation and developing the system of correspondent banks and clearinghouses that handled the flow of checks prior to the Federal Reserve System were principal activities. By 1900, there were approximately 5,000 state banks, 5,000 private banks, and more than 3,700 national banks. Total deposits were about $3.2 billion in the state banks and $3.6 billion in the national banks (at this time savings banks held about $1.7 billion).

Between 1865 and 1900, approximately 2,000 commercial banks, about four fifths of them state banks, suspended operations. These frequent failures of commercial banks helped to maintain the position of savings banks as intermediaries. This factor operated, of course, most strongly where savings banks were already well established.

Commercial Banks in the Savings Market

The rise in the volume of monetary savings and the pressure for funds felt by the commercial banks more and more turned their attention to attracting savings deposits. Two developments in 1903 are of historical interest. In that year:

The First National Bank of Chicago wrote to the Comptroller of the Currency seeking to create a wholly owned subsidiary, with a state charter, designed to handle savings and trust functions. The Comptroller's reply was permissive, and The First thus established The First Trust and Savings Bank of Chicago, the affiliate being locked to the parent in perpetuity. This so-called Chicago Plan, widely duplicated, marked the beginning of the full-service concept of commercial banking.[23]

Also in 1903, the Comptroller of the Currency ruled that the National Banking Act neither authorized nor prohibited operation of a savings department, that all deposits were subject to withdrawal on demand, that the right to contract with a depositor for other deposits was a matter for judicial determination, and that the expediency of a national bank doing a savings

23. *Response to Change,* p. 22.

banking business was a matter for the bank's directors to decide. His letter read as follows:

August 3, 1903

Mr. H. S. Purdy
   108 W. 4th Street
      St. Paul, Minn.

Sir:

In reply to your letter of 30th ultimo, relative to the right of a national bank to operate a savings department, you are respectfully informed that there does not appear to be anything in the National Bank Act which authorises or prohibits the operation of a savings department by a national bank.

Many national banks pay interest on deposits, the receipt of each deposit being evidenced either by entries in the pass books of the depositors or by issue of certificates of deposit, as may be preferred. Deposits of this character must be shown in the reports of the bank, and loaned in the manner provided by the National Bank Act. This would prevent a national bank from accepting real estate collaterals which are deemed judicious for savings banks. All deposits, however, in a national bank are payable on demand, except when made the subject of special contract, but the right of a bank to make a contract of that nature is a matter for judicial determination.

The expediency of a national banking association, organized for the purpose of doing a business of discount and deposit, engaging in the business of a savings bank is one for consideration and determination by the board of directors.

Respectfully,
(S) Wm. B. Ridgely
Comptroller.

The inability of national banks to make mortgage loans continued at this time. Nevertheless, commercial banks of both types embarked ambitiously in the savings field. From less than $600 million in 1900, savings deposits increased sharply to about $3 billion in 1915, a five-fold increase.[24]

---

24. These are estimates based on time deposits, as individual savings deposit figures do not go back to this time. See Lintner, *op. cit.,* pp. 460-61.

Effect of Federal Reserve Act

Passage of the Federal Reserve Act in 1913, while it had more pressing objectives, encouraged commercial bank competition in the savings field. It specifically recognized the growing practice of accepting time deposits and paying interest thereon (by national banks), and opened the door to mortgage loans. State banks by 1913 were already approaching 10 per cent of total mortgage holdings. The Federal Reserve Act permitted national banks to make mortgage loans on improved farmland up to 50 per cent of value and up to 25 per cent of capital and surplus or one third of time deposits. In addition, the Federal Reserve Act differentiated between demand and time deposits and imposed a lower reserve requirement for the latter.

Building and Loan Associations

During this period the savings and loan associations, or as they were more commonly known then, building and loan associations, came into a position of some significance. Like the savings banks, the savings and loan associations trace their origin to the Friendly Societies of Great Britain. The first known association in the United States was established in the Philadelphia area in 1831, partly by English immigrants. The difference in emphasis between these associations and the savings banks was that the participants were seeking mortgage loans. Members made monthly payments on shares, and when resources permitted they bid for the available funds for the purpose of buying or building a home. When all of the members had received and repaid their loans the association dissolved. As the associations were at first voluntary and unincorporated, data on their early development are sparse and unreliable.

The next step was the introduction of serial shares whereby new members could be admitted and the association could continue in existence after accommodating all of the original members; this development became popular in the 1850's. This step was in turn followed by the introduction of permanent shares wherein shareholders' accounts were kept separate from those of borrowers. The movement was plagued between the Civil War and 1900 by the development of "national" associations, which traded on the name of the co-operatives but in fact were designed to benefit promoters. They attracted funds from wide areas and made loans over equally wide areas.

Toward the end of the nineteenth century most states had recognized the associations and were chartering, supervising, and regulating them. It is estimated that in 1888 there were over 3,000 such associations with assets of $300 million, and in 1893 there were some 5,600 associations with about $475 million of assets.[25] By 1915, unpledged share accounts were pushing toward a billion dollars.[26]

Life Insurance Companies

During the period under review, life insurance companies moved into the front rank as holders of individuals' savings. In 1915, savings banks still held as much on deposit as did commercial banks and savings and loan associations in savings accounts, but life insurance reserves for the first time began to exceed savings bank deposits. Both were approximately $4 billion in 1915; in 1880, insurance reserves had been about half of savings bank deposits (approximately $400 million versus $800 million).

Like other financial institutions, life insurance can trace its origins back to antiquity. The early trading areas devised various contracts to protect interests in both lives and properties. In the Middle Ages similar contracts were written in Italy, England, and elsewhere. The first insurance office in England is thought to have been "The Hand-in-Hand" in 1696. A Society of Assurance for Widows and Orphans was also organized in 1696 on the basis of mutual assessments. The South Sea Company was organized in 1711 to take over the national debt in exchange for a monopoly of trading in the South Seas. Much of the national debt was in the form of terminable annuities,

---

25. Leon T. Kendall, for the United States Savings and Loan League, *The Savings and Loan Business* (Englewood Cliffs, N.J., Prentice-Hall, 1963), pp. 4-6.

26. Lintner, *op. cit.,* p. 460.

which the company persuaded many holders to exchange for stock to their later loss. By 1800, several companies were operating, some as mutuals and some as stock companies.

The Friendly Societies were responsible for some of the growth of life insurance, as they were with savings banks and building and loan associations. One of the principal functions of the early Friendly Societies was provision of burial expenses and survivors' benefits. The subsequent Friendly Societies Act of 1896 described them as being ". . . for the purpose of providing by voluntary subscriptions of the members thereof . . . for the relief or maintenance of the members, their husbands, wives, children . . . during sickness or other infirmity . . . or in widowhood . . . for insuring money to be paid on the death of a member. . . ." and so on. Daniel Defoe, an early proponent of savings banks, also pamphleteered in favor of insuring against casualties and of providing pensions for old age.

In 1717, the Philadelphia Synod of the Presbyterian Church established a Fund for Pious Uses, which later became "The Corporation for the Relief of Poor and Distressed Presbyterian Ministers, and for the Poor and Distressed Widows and Children of Presbyterian Ministers," probably the first life insurance organization in this country. The insurance business as such was monopolized by English companies during the colonial period. The Insurance Company of North America was established in 1792, primarily for marine and fire risks, but it also wrote some life policies. Perhaps half a dozen companies were chartered with authority to write life policies by 1800.

There was little demand for life insurance in the economy at the turn of the century.

Businessmen, though definitely interested in marine or even fire insurance, were largely indifferent to life insurance; as for the general run of men, they were mechanics [artisans], small farmers, and tradesmen who would have considered life insurance as necessary as a fifth wheel on a wagon. Life in the preponderantly agricultural economy of the time created no great demand for life insurance; people in the rural areas and the small towns lived close to the land, families were to a large extent self-sufficing for food, clothing, and shelter, and few people were likely to starve as a result of the death of the head of the family. The land remained, children carried on, neighbors could be relied upon for help. Mutual assistance was available without the necessity of incorporating it.[27]

In addition, religious attitudes at that time were such that life insurance was considered to be a form of betting or gambling on the odds of dying.[28]

However, incorporations of insurance organizations continued in the financial centers. The Pennsylvania Company for Insurances on Lives and Granting Annuities was organized in 1809 and chartered in 1812 with $500,000 of capital. The Massachusetts Hospital Life Insurance Company was organized in 1818, and was designed to pay one third of its profits to a hospital. The spread of such companies was sufficient that in 1840 New York State passed a general law to regulate the business. In the 1840's, several mutuals that became large and successful were organized; and their success attracted a rash of incorporations in the 1850's, some of which were stock companies. Some of these companies followed unsound actuarial principles, charged insufficient rates, and paid excessive dividends, leading to failures.

Buley's comments on the formation of mutual insurance companies in the 1840's and 1850's are informative as, by implication, they are probably applicable to the formation of savings banks after the earliest days.

The feature of mutuality was not new; American insurance men were familiar with British experience with the Equitable and other mutuals and with American mutuals in fire insurance. The sudden impetus for mutuality in the life field came in part from the spirit of the times and the fact that the idea was supposed to have sales appeal, but largely from the fact that it was a means whereby resourceful men could form companies, give protection to the policyholder, and gain positions of importance for themselves without the necessity of having or acquiring a sizable sum of capital to

---

27. R. Carlyle Buley, *The American Life Convention, 1906-1952* (New York: Appleton-Century-Crofts, 1953), pp. 27-28.

28. *Documents Relative to Savings Banks, Intemperance, and Lotteries,* published by the Society for Prevention of Pauperism in 1819, quoted in Chapter 1 above, illustrate this attitude.

invest in the business. Though some of these companies during their early years did put up a guarantee fund to protect the beneficiaries, purchasers of insurance did not discriminate in favor of those companies as against those which did not. . . .

The question naturally arises as to what was the motivating force behind the activities of these men who from the very nature of the organizations which they created could not aspire to ownership of the business and the personal capital enhancement which would come from success. Talents vary; some men are traders and merchants by heritage and instinct; some are innately inventors or production-minded geniuses; other men are essentially promoters, organizers, salesmen. The inventor needs other people's money to put his ideas into material form; the production specialist needs the same to give society the advantage of his peculiar ability. The personal contributions in ability are no less capital than the savings of others. The capital of these company organizers consisted of their own energies, ideas, and abilities to win the confidence of other men. Their rewards for success were positions of responsibility and prestige, salary or commission incomes, and the satisfactions of creation.[29]

 An important feature of the operations of these new companies was their use of agents—the agency system. Although the companies advertised by newspaper and pamphlet, it was the agent who sold the policies. It may be assumed that if life insurance companies had operated like banks, staying behind counters awaiting customers, many fewer policies would have been sold.

Although the actuarial principles underlying insurance had been the object of study for hundreds of years, advances in the mid-nineteenth century came at a time that permitted the rapid growth of the industry on a sound basis. While not alone, an outstanding figure in the maturing of the industry was Elizur Wright. Wright was the son of a Calvinistic graduate of Yale who moved to the Western Reserve of Connecticut (Northeast Ohio) where he both farmed and operated an academy. The son

---

29. Buley, *op. cit.*, p. 42, pp. 46-47. It may be appropriate to note that in some instances, Quakers were prime movers in establishing life insurance companies, as they had been with savings banks.

also went to Yale, taught at Lawrence Academy in Massachusetts, and then returned home to teach mathematics at the newly established Western Reserve College founded jointly by Congregationalists and Presbyterians at Hudson, Ohio. Like most people in the area at the time, Wright became much interested in the abolition movement, and shortly he returned east to New York, at the invitation of a wealthy merchant, Arthur Tappan, to edit the *Emancipator;* in 1833 he helped organize the American Anti-Slavery Society, and in 1839 moved to Boston for similar activities. In 1844, he went to England for a variety of causes, including work for the anti-slavery movement and a study of insurance practices in England for the Massachusetts Hospital Life Insurance Company. Although he did not drop his other interests, insurance thereafter occupied more and more of his time.

In the early 1850's, he (with help from his family) compiled 203 pages of tables of net valuations, showing reserves to be held for each year of various kinds of policies; each page required up to a thousand calculations. He then campaigned for legislation to require companies to use these calculations as the basis for reserve and forfeiture practices. By 1858, Massachusetts had adopted a regulatory bill setting up two commissioners, of which Wright was one. During his ten years of tenure, Wright forced many reforms in the life insurance business in Massachusetts. He was eventually forced out of office, but served as actuary for several leading companies. He then campaigned for a model insurance company and savings bank, which would incorporate his various ideas. This, perhaps, was one of the origins of the ideas of savings bank life insurance, later to develop under the aegis of Louis Brandeis.

Although the Civil War produced the highest number, as well as rate, of casualties of any war before or since, the insurance companies prospered during the 1860's. Their policies with southerners were in general forfeited, and the war clause in other policies was not enforced but the higher risk covered by special premiums. Like the savings banks, the insurance companies found inflation bringing them increased income, while the availability of government bonds at low prices and high yields strengthened their asset position. The amount of insurance in force increased from about $200 million in 1860 to ten times that in 1870.

Another similarity lay in the rush to obtain charters in the years immediately after the Civil War. Many new companies were started, and the business was plagued by frauds and mismanagement, as described by the muckrakers, at a time when the volume of business was growing less rapidly than the number of companies. Dozens of companies failed during and after the Panic of 1873. Nevertheless, by the late 1880's, the business was about back where it had been at its postwar peak, weaker companies were being weeded out and the bulk of the business going to the larger companies, and state regulation was imposing sounder requirements. Nearly a billion dollars of new business was written in 1892. Admittedly, however, there were still abuses and improprieties, and pressure for reform was building up. In 1905, managerial difficulties at the Equitable came into the open, legislative investigations were made, and demands for mutualization of the company were insistent. Attention was called to other companies, and the result was the well known Armstrong Investigation carried out by the New York legislature in 1905. Reforms in policy contracts and in management practices resulting from this investigation brought the industry renewed respect. Insurance in force was twice as great in 1910 as it had been in 1900.

The rapid rise of insurance, and savings in the form of reserves, reflects the fact that insurance can supply a need felt by savers, namely the immediate provision of an estate.[30] The existence of reserves, of course, arises from the use of level premiums. The excess of the premiums over death claims in the early years of various policies except term insurance creates a surplus in which the policyholder has a legal interest. Thus, whole-life and related policies have an element of saving. There are other factors, also, that influence the amount of saving in this form.

---

30. For an evaluation of the reasons favoring insurance, see Lintner, *op. cit.,* Chap. IV.

Life insurance saving differs fundamentally from saving through deposit-type institutions such as mutual savings banks and savings and loan associations in at least three important respects: (1) it is long-term and contractual in nature and is therefore more stable; (2) it is motivated primarily by the desire for family financial protection in the event of untimely death; and (3) it is ordinarily expected to be left intact until the death of the insured rather than withdrawn for some consumer expenditure.[31]

Savings Bank Investments and Loans

As the different financial institutions were establishing their respective places in the economy, the investment policies and practices of the savings banks reflected the growth of the economy and their competitors. For some time after the Civil War the savings banks continued to be heavy holders of federal obligations. In New York State, for example, government securities amounted to $155 million in 1881 as compared to mortgages of $91.4 million, which latter was one fourth of total assets. At this time the entire legal list of federal, state, and municipal securities totalled only some $2 billion, while the assets of New York State banks alone amounted to about a quarter of that sum. Railroad securities were not yet on the list and, in view of the fact that some $2 billion out of the total $4.5 billion capitalization at that time paid no return, there was little pressure for adding them. Under these circumstances, mortgage lending expanded rapidly but hardly faster than the banks themselves were growing; in 1884, mortgages were still only 30 per cent of deposits or half the allowable amount.

During the 1880's, both low interest rates and the scarcity value of securities on the legal lists supported the prices of these securities and helped to create surplus accounts. In 1888, the surplus was 15 per cent of deposits in New York State and similar amounts elsewhere. Both the federal and state governments were reducing their debts; New York State redeemed the

---

31. Life Insurance Association of America, *Life Insurance Companies as Financial Institutions* (Englewood Cliffs, N.J.: Prentice-Hall, 1963), p. 2.

last of its securities held by the savings banks in 1892. Consequently, the various states expanded their legal lists, usually by including the cities of other states.

In 1893 . . . the total net indebtedness of cities in this state was $170,343,847, of which the savings banks carried $120,787,970. The logical result has been that in ordinary times municipalities of approved credit and standing have been able to borrow money to carry on public improvements at rates of interest but little exceeding the interest [on] government bonds.[32]

Under these circumstances, mortgages rose from 29 per cent of assets in 1885 to 41 per cent in 1893.

During the Panic of 1893, bond prices fell to approximately the level of their cost basis for banks in general. Especially in the larger cities, savings banks were subject to runs along with commercial banks, and resorted to requiring notice of withdrawal. Several allowed immediate withdrawal of small amounts only. The panic was followed by a long period of low interest rates, when (as later in 1930–50) it appeared that low rates had become permanent. Customary investment practice was to buy long term municipal and railroad bonds, the latter being added to the various legal lists. National banks were absorbing most of the federal debt to secure the note issue and additional amounts to secure government deposits; by 1907, the debt was down to $858.5 million, of which less than $200 million was free of these two uses. For the first time in New York State mortgages exceeded bond investments in 1906 (at 47 per cent of assets), and railroad bonds were the largest class of securities. In contrast, Massachusetts savings banks had held 48 per cent of their assets in mortgages as early as 1873.

In 1907 again, panic conditions required loss sales of bonds and the use of book values to prevent the appearance of insolvency. The vulnerability of long-term securities to price change, and the insulation of mortgage loans from quoted market prices, made the latter appear even more attractive than ever. As a

---

32. *History and Manual of the Owondago County Savings Bank*, p. 188. By a similar calculation, savings banks held $140 million out of total debt of all "municipalities" in the state of $200 million in the same year. Welfling, *op. cit.*, p. 24.

result, a trend set in wherein many banks shifted to holding shorter-term securities and increasing their holdings of mortgages. The rising percentage of mortgages to total assets continued up to the 1930's.

The outbreak of war in 1914 again brought brief panic conditions and unusually large withdrawals. For the first time in many years, total assets did not rise for the year. For some years it had been true that the dividends credited to accounts had accounted for much, sometimes all, of the annual increase.

Position on the Eve of World War I

Thus, after approximately a hundred years of existence, the savings banks found themselves dominating the financial structure of the northeastern part of the country, but with only scattered banks elsewhere. In spite of their geographical concentration, the savings banks held more mortgage loans than any other type of lender; non-farm residential mortgages held by savings banks amounted to $1.4 billion in 1915, 40 per cent more than those of the savings and loans and about twice those of either the commercial banks or insurance companies. A measure of this dominance is indicated by the fact that there were 627 savings banks in comparison with nearly 27,000 commercial banks and 7,000 savings and loan associations. Time deposits of commercial banks had surpassed deposits of savings banks by roughly $5 billion as against $4 billion, but of the $5 billion, only about $3 billion represented savings deposits of individuals.

CHAPTER 3

The Third Half-Century

THE savings banks reached the centennial mark in the United States during the period between the outbreak of World War I in Europe and American entrance as a belligerent in 1917, the centennial being duly celebrated in 1916 with an international conference and thrift campaigns. In that year total deposits of the savings banks passed the $4 billion mark; nearly $2 billion of the deposits were in New York State and over three fourths of the total in that state plus Massachusetts and Connecticut.

The third half-century was marked by clear-cut periods, corresponding respectively to World War I, the prosperous 1920's, the depressed 1930's, World War II, and the years after 1945. Each brought new influences to bear on the growth of deposits and on the uses of funds deposited.

World War I

Outbreak of war in 1914 led to panic conditions, heavy withdrawals, and imposition of 60-day notices by the savings banks. The Superintendent of Banks in New York State remarked that, "I have seen the great East Side of New York with its people raging with distrust at every form of banking in this State. In one day, in August, my department closed private banks to sixty thousand depositors. . . ."[1] Nevertheless, total savings bank de-

---

1. Franklin J. Sherman, *Modern Story of Mutual Savings Banks* (New York: J. J. Little and Ives Co., 1934), p. 108.

posits rose slightly by mid-1915 over mid-1914. Recovery was rapid, interest rates began to rise, and deposits flowed in for net gains of over $100 million in both 1916 and 1917. American entrance into the war again created much uncertainty and hoarding; until mid-1918, deposits were virtually stable, as withdrawals increased and new deposits declined. Again, the situation soon changed, as in New York State alone 190,000 new accounts were added in 1919—compared to 7,000 in 1918—and for the system as a whole deposits rose to $4.7 billion and passed $5 billion in 1920.

During the war, the Treasury issued four Liberty Loans and the Victory Loan, to an aggregate of approximately $21 billion. The savings banks increased their holdings of governments from virtually nothing in 1915 to three quarters of a billion dollars in 1920. At the same time, they were encouraging depositors to purchase governments and lending to them for the purpose. The Treasury also sold war savings certificates, partly to help avoid withdrawals from savings banks for purchase of larger securities and partly to tap new markets. The wartime increase in governments, as well as other changes in asset holdings, is shown in Table 3–1. Treasury securities amounted to 14 per cent of total assets in 1920 (Table 3–2).

The uncertainties of the war period caused increasing concern for the problem of liquidity in savings banks. It was feared that government sales of bonds could lead to declining deposits, in turn causing banks to sell bonds, thus lowering bond prices "with the result that the financial operations of the Treasury might have been greatly hampered."[2] The War Finance Corporation was established partly to lend to banks not able to borrow from the Federal Reserve banks. Although the savings banks did not resort to this agency, they did find it advisable to borrow from regular correspondents. Reported borrowings of the savings banks plus "other liabilities" exceeded $20 million in 1919. There were proposals for the savings banks to join the Federal Reserve System in order to borrow on the security of government bonds, and for making eligible paper legal for savings bank investment. In 1918, the New York legislature per-

---

2. War Finance Corporation, *First Report,* 1918, p. 3.

mitted investment in bankers' acceptances up to 20 per cent of the available fund, a reversal of the stand taken in the General Law of 1875. During the war the reserve banks did arrange for member banks to act as agents for savings banks in discounting paper.

TABLE 3-1[a]

ASSETS OF MUTUAL SAVINGS BANKS, SELECTED DATES, 1915–30

(MILLIONS OF DOLLARS)

Item	1915	1920	1925	1930
Total assets	4,257	5,586	7,831	10,164
Governments	11	783	1,076	499
State and municipal	813	650	709	920
Other securities	1,001	1,213	1,517	2,278
Cash assets	208	225	240	291
Mortgage loans	1,916	2,291	3,923	5,635
Other loans	227	336	232	312
Other assets	81	88	134	229

TABLE 3-2[a]

PERCENTAGES OF TOTAL ASSETS, MUTUAL SAVINGS BANKS, SELECTED DATES, 1915–30

	1915	1920	1925	1930
Governments	- - -	14.0	13.6	4.9
State and municipal	19.1	11.6	9.1	9.0
Other securities	24.0	21.7	19.4	22.4
Cash assets	4.9	4.0	3.1	2.8
Mortgage loans	45.0	41.0	50.1	55.4
Other loans	5.3	6.2	3.0	3.1
Other assets	1.9	1.6	1.7	2.3

[a]Based on Table 3–1.

3. *All-Bank Statistics,* pp. 46-49; June 30 or nearest available date.

Investment Shifts

Most of the increase in total assets during the 1915–20 period is accounted for by the rise in holdings of government obligations. However, other cross-currents were affecting the relative proportions of other assets. With the exception of state and municipal securities, other investments were not reduced in order to increase governments. The tax exemption, which first became important in this period, was of no value to the savings banks. From 1913 to 1917, these bonds were bid up in price from an average 4.4 per cent yield to 3.9 per cent. Yields rose in 1918 and 1919 but remained below those on other assets. Savings banks did not replace maturing issues, sold some issues, and traded others for Liberty bonds and railroad securities. The proportion of assets in municipals dropped from 19.1 per cent in 1915 to 11.6 per cent in 1920.

A modest decline also took place in holdings of other securities, which were mostly railroad obligations, but the decline was relative and not absolute. Railroad bonds were the "money bonds" of the pre-war period and high-grade bonds were considered practically riskless. A variety of troubles during the war, however, reduced their investment value. An index of railroad bond prices that was 112.7 in 1909 and 99.0 in 1915 fell to a low point of 69.2 in 1919.[4] In December, 1917, the railroads were taken over by the government. Although both legislation and the presidential proclamation promised just and reasonable compensation and maintenance of the properties aimed at stabilizing the earnings basis of 1915–17, earnings and finances deteriorated. The combined deficits of the railroads approached one billion dollars, approximately equal to the amount of securities held by the savings banks, with about one third of the total in New York State. Total holdings rose slightly during this period, but in 1919 it became apparent that the roads had lost their investment standing, and after passage of the Transportation Act of 1920 there were modest declines in holdings. From

---

4. *Savings Bank Journal*, May, 1920; "Savings Bank Investment Policies, III."

virtually a quarter of total assets in 1915, other securities declined to 21.7 per cent in 1920 and 19.4 per cent in 1925.

A higher level of interest rates than had prevailed before 1914 depressed security prices generally throughout the war period. In New York State, surplus based on market prices of assets fell below 8 per cent in 1914, rose to 9.5 per cent in 1916, and then declined to 7.7 per cent at the end of 1920, at which time surplus based on par values was 11.4 per cent. Furthermore, the "market prices" used were those supplied to the banks by the Superintendent of Banks for the purpose. Probably a third of the banks were insolvent in 1914 on the basis of actual market values, a situation similar to that prevailing earlier in 1907.[5]

Construction was retarded during the war period, and as a result mortgage loans did not increase in step with total assets but fell from 45.0 per cent to 41.0 per cent of assets between 1915 and 1920. Again, the decline was relative, as total holdings rose by about $275 million. Virtually all of the increase, however, came after 1918. At the conclusion of the war there were great needs for housing and urban business and office structures. Rent strikes and other disturbances occurred in major cities and legislatures imposed rent ceilings and considered means of forcing more mortgage lending. In New York State and elsewhere proposals were made to tax savings bank assets not held as mortgage loans. Natural forces channeled funds into this field and total loans started rising in 1919. The trend characterized the next decade, as mortgage loans reached 55.4 per cent of assets in 1930. Changes in asset proportions are shown in Chart 3–1.

Growth of Competitors

The inflation of the war years—the price level nearly tripled from its 1914 base—was the counterpart of the increase in commercial bank deposits permitted by monetary and fiscal policies. The relative size of savings banks' competitors continued to grow during this period. Trust companies were growing rapidly, while commercial banks were taking advantage of the changes

5. Welfling, *op. cit.*, p. 46.

brought by the Federal Reserve Act to become more active in
the savings field. Commercial bank demand deposits rose from
$10.3 billion in 1914 to $21.6 billion in 1920, while time deposits rose at a faster rate from $4.7 billion to $11.1 billion. The
number of commercial banks grew by 4,000 to about 30,400,
largely in rural areas, and accounts at commercial banks reached
23 million by 1920. Savings and loan associations increased during this period by about 1,800. Data on the relative growth of
commercial and savings bank deposits are shown in Table 3–3.

These data indicate the continued, if declining, importance of

Chart 3–1

**Percentage Distribution of Assets of Mutual Savings Banks
Selected Years, 1900–1966**

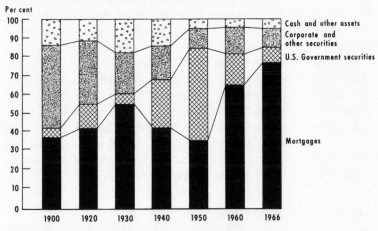

NOTE: End-of-year data except for 1900 to 1930, which are represented by mid-year data.

*Sources of data: National Association of Mutual Savings Banks and Board of Governors
of the Federal Reserve System*

TABLE 3-3[6]

DEPOSITS IN COMMERCIAL AND SAVINGS BANKS, 1915–65

(MILLIONS OF DOLLARS)

	New York State			Massachusetts			Connecticut			United States		
	Commercial		*Savings Bank*	*Commercial*		*Savings Bank*	*Commercial*		*Savings Bank*	*Commercial*		*Savings Bank*
	Demand	*Time*		*Demand*	*Time*		*Demand*	*Time*		*Demand*	*Time*	
1915	3,307	458	1,774	615	70	917	117	25	316	10,703	5,050	3,889
1920	6,049	957	2,398	1,097	267	1,189	240	91	416	21,571	11,121	5,149
1925	7,307	2,044	3,531	1,125	532	1,608	283	176	505	24,325	16,393	7,064
1930	9,027	3,120	4,566	1,130	715	2,100	325	266	653	25,648	20,192	9,088
1935	7,624	1,855	5,193	982	430	2,080	243	194	675	21,731	13,267	9,807
1940	12,490	2,037	5,670	1,383	386	2,162	405	202	741	33,646	15,608	10,605
1945	18,131	3,033	7,745	2,387	662	2,716	801	356	1,052	72,506	27,231	14,390
1950	20,932	4,001	11,574	2,844	756	3,330	1,000	415	1,341	91,882	36,729	19,922
1955	23,951	5,315	16,051	3,226	696	4,348	1,403	504	1,778	112,981	47,875	27,277
1960												
1965												

6. 1915–55, *All-Bank Statistics;* 1960 and 1965, Federal Reserve Bulletin and National Association of Mutual Savings Banks

the savings banks in their traditional areas. In 1915, savings banks held more total deposits in Massachusetts and Connecticut than did commercial banks. In Massachusetts the ratio was 133.9 per cent and in Connecticut it was 222.5 per cent. In 1915, savings banks in New York state held deposits equal to 47.1 per cent of the deposits in commercial banks, while in the country as a whole the percentage was 24.7. By 1920, these figures had declined significantly. In Connecticut, savings banks were still larger than commercial banks, but by a ratio of 125.7 per cent. In Massachusetts, the savings banks had dropped to 87.2 per cent of the commercial banks in size, in New York State to 34.2 per cent, and nationally to 15.8 per cent. Even the estimated volume of time deposits held by individuals in 1920 ($6.5 billion) exceeded the deposits in savings banks. Approximately two thirds of the increase in time and savings deposits at commercial and savings banks and in savings and loan shares and life insurance reserves were claimed by commercial banks during this period; nationally, the savings banks were no longer the largest holders of time and savings deposits.

The recognition of the power of national banks to accept savings deposits, and other provisions of the Federal Reserve Act in this field, were welcomed neither by savings bankers nor by some state banking officials. The Commissioner of Banks of Massachusetts and the Superintendent of Banks of New York State used identical wording in their reports for 1918:

> If in any state there has been created a great system of mutual savings banks, in that state the national banks, although not mutual but operated for the profit of shareholders, will be authorized to call their interest departments savings departments, and so appropriate the word which has for a generation or more been synonymous in this State with mutual institutions created under State laws. These deposits, moreover, will not be segregated, nor will the entire net income from investments be distributed among the depositors.[7]

The New York Superintendent also added:

> It is not surprising, in view of the extension of Federal control over

7. New York *Annual Report,* 1918, p. 11, and Massachusetts *Annual Report,* 1918, pp. viii-ix.

various classes of business and industry as a result of the necessities of the war, that the attention of the advocates of centralization and Federal domination should be attracted by the prosperity and success of State banking institutions. In their desire to bring under Federal control all classes of banking institutions, they seem, in the first instance, to have conceived the idea of conferring all the multifarious powers of the different classes of State institutions in all the States upon National Banks and to create a Federal system of department banks into which all banking institutions would be ultimately driven. Such a bank would rather closely resemble one of our great department stores. . . . Instead of having a uniform system of National Banks consisting of strictly commercial banking institutions and needing no other definition than the name, we would have heterogeneous varieties of hybrid institutions of as many kinds perhaps as there are States or possibly of as many types as there are classes of State banking institutions in all the States.[8]

Much of the effort of those opposing the new legislation was directed toward requiring segregation of assets acquired with commercial time and savings deposits. Criticisms took the form of claims that mixed deposits reduced commercial bank reserves for deposits, that savings were subject to commercial risks, and that payment of savings depositors could be delayed while assets were used to pay demand depositors.

Relative Growth in the 1920's

The decade of the 1920's was marked by continued growth of some of the savings banks' competitors and by a pronounced shift into mortgage lending. Between 1920 and 1930, time deposits at commercial banks increased by 81.6 per cent while savings at life insurance companies rose by 145.3 per cent. The increase in savings banks' deposits was 55.1 per cent; however, the growth of shares of savings and loan associations was slightly over 200 per cent. Of the increase in time and savings deposits at commercial and savings banks and in savings and loan shares, the commercial banks captured 51.9 per cent. Of the total increase of these plus life insurance reserves, the insurance com-

8. New York *Annual Report,* 1918, p. 11.

TABLE 3-4[9]

COMMERCIAL AND SAVINGS BANK DEPOSITS
IN CONNECTICUT, MASSACHUSETTS, AND NEW YORK,
1920 AND 1930

(MILLIONS OF DOLLARS)

	Connecticut			Massachusetts			New York State		
	Commercial		Savings Bank	Commercial		Savings Bank	Commercial		Savings Bank
	Demand	Time		Demand	Time		Demand	Time	
1920	239.9	91.4	415.6	1,096.9	266.6	1,189.0	6,049.0	957.1	2,398.3
1930	325.8	266.5	653.3	1,129.7	715.0	2,100.3	9,026.8	3,120.3	4,566.1
Increase	85.9	175.1	237.7	32.8	448.4	911.3	2,977.8	2,163.2	2,167.8
% Increase	35.8	191.6	57.2	3.0	168.1	76.8	49.2	226.0	90.4

9. Data from *All-Bank Statistics*. Note, however, that the dollar volume of growth was larger for the savings banks in all three states, increasing their absolute margin of size with respect to time deposits.

panies captured 40.6 per cent, and the savings banks 16.2 per cent.

In each of the large savings bank states, the increase in deposits was much slower for the savings banks than for the time deposit departments of commercial banks. The data in Table 3–4 show that the savings banks grew at a very respectable rate but were still outpaced in the time deposit field. It was in this decade that the growth of demand deposits slowed down and, indeed, in some years declined. Monetary policy as exercised by the Federal Reserve System put commercial bank reserves under conscious control. This change in the banking situation, especially in view of the demands for funds during the period, strengthened the commercial banks' interest in competing for time deposits. As a result, they sought both large corporate and other business time deposits and savings accounts of individuals. They found the former to be more volatile and sensitive to interest rate attractions than the latter. Much of the growth in total time deposits was accounted for by the shifting of large deposits into the time category. Demand deposits of all commercial banks increased only some $4 billion between 1920 and 1930, and declined in the two years 1921 and 1928. In some respects, and on a larger scale, the competition by commercial banks for "time money" in the decade of the 1960's was a replica of developments after 1920.

The rise of national banks as principal dealers in time deposits, the very rapid increase in the assets of insurance companies and trust companies, and the opening of many new savings and loan associations gave rise to opinions that perhaps the savings banks had served their purpose and were doomed to gradually declining relative importance. Increasing interest in direct investment in securities by the public and apparent declining ability of savings banks to attract funds buttressed this view. While in this decade the savings banks were growing by large annual amounts of dollars, these increases were at a slower rate than those being posted by competing institutions, and were to a large extent accounted for by dividends credited to accounts. This factor in most years accounted for at least half of the annual gain in deposits. Further, the banks were no longer increasing the number of accounts as rapidly as their total deposits, and annual withdrawals were rising in relation to annual new deposits.

Mortgage Lending

During the decade of the 1920's, the increase in real estate lending by the savings banks was dramatic. Real estate loans rose from $2.3 billion to $5.6 billion, or 146 per cent, while total assets increased from $5.6 billion to $10.2 billion; the real estate loans in 1930 were slightly in excess of total assets of 1920, and 73 per cent of the increase in assets was represented by real estate loans. Such loans represented 54.9 per cent of assets in late 1930. In Connecticut the percentage of assets in real estate loans rose from 37.6 per cent to 53.0 per cent, in Massachusetts from 43.6 per cent to 53.5 per cent, and in New York State from 47.4 per cent to 63.6 per cent.

The reasons for this rapid increase in mortgage loans may be listed as: (1) the inflow of funds requiring investment (total assets nearly doubled); (2) the decline in attractiveness of railroad securities and the failure of the volume of these securities on the legal lists to rise during the decade; (3) the limited volume of other private securities legal for investment; (4) the decline in the federal debt; (5) the relatively attractive return on mortgage loans; and (6) the history of safety of mortgage loans.

During the 1920's, the "standard" rate on mortgage loans was 6 per cent over the savings bank territory. Some large loans on business properties were made at lower rates but average rates on the whole portfolio remained close to 6 per cent. Yields on bonds drifted downward during the decade, and after the middle of the period were between 4 per cent and 5 per cent. Generally speaking, 4 per cent was a minimum dividend rate for savings banks, and the trend was upward during the decade. Building was at a high rate, the demand for funds was active, and foreclosures were extremely small. In addition, the use of the guaranteed mortgage spread. These mortgages were guaranteed and sold by mortgage companies and they allowed many country banks to lend on metropolitan properties, income as well as residential.

Another factor leading to increased savings bank lending was the shift of individuals and estates into tax-exempt securities. A large proportion of new loans represented sales of existing properties from which original lenders were withdrawing funds as the properties were refinanced. After 1926, yields on federal obligations were bid down, and it was tempting to switch funds from these investments to mortgage loans. At the same time, however, the demand for mortgage credit also slowed down somewhat, as did the rise in mortgage holdings, and more funds flowed into corporate securities. Public utility and telephone bonds were being accepted as legal investments, and the competition of the late 1920's was leading many bankers to accept lower quality railroad securities for their higher yields.

The end of the prosperous 1920's found the savings banks with nearly $10 billion of assets, largely invested in the private economy, with over half the assets in real estate loans and much of the remainder in railroad and public utility securities. The ensuing decade was to reveal unforeseen weaknesses in the mortgage portfolio and the results of declines in quality standards in the bond portfolio.

Stability of Deposits in the 1930's

The 1930's were characterized by remarkable stability of deposits in the face of the wreckage of the banking system that took place in 1931–33, a sharp decline in the volume of mortgage lending, and the phoenix-like rise of the savings and loan associations in the mortgage field. From 24,970 in 1929, the number of commercial banks dropped to 15,348 in 1934; suspensions of commercial banks in the four years 1930–33 were respectively 1,350, 2,293, 1,453, and 4,000. Deposits in these suspended banks amounted to $6.8 billion out of total commercial bank deposits of $51.3 billion in 1930, and estimated losses borne by depositors came to $1.3 billion.[10] During these same four years, 526 savings and loan associations (out of approximately 12,000) failed with

10. Federal Reserve System, *Banking and Monetary Statistics*, p. 283.

$410.6 million of assets out of an industry total of $8,695.1 million at the beginning of 1930.[11] The corresponding figures for savings banks were eight banks with $28 million of deposits.[12]

TABLE 3-5

ACCOUNTS OPENED AND CLOSED, AND
NEW DEPOSITS AND WITHDRAWALS,
NEW YORK STATE SAVINGS BANKS, 1925–35

(NUMBERS OF ACCOUNTS IN THOUSANDS; DEPOSITS IN MILLIONS)

| | Accounts | | Amounts | |
	Opened	Closed	Deposited	Withdrawn
1925	835	678	$1,191	$1,131
1926	838	704	1,284	1,110
1927	889	738	1,389	1,252
1928	925	767	1,447	1,383
1929	980	822	1,521	1,723
1930	1,038	829	1,492	1,425
1931	1,301	879	1,913	1,646
1932	1,064	991	1,533	1,661
1933	933	934	1,221	1,626
1934	1,019	870	1,247	1,301
1935	941	892	1,220	1,306

Exclusive of interbank and government deposits, commercial bank demand deposits declined from $25.6 billion in 1930 to $16.0 billion in 1933, while time deposits declined from $20.2 billion to $11.7 billion. In contrast, savings bank deposits were $9.1 billion in 1930 and $9.6 billion in 1933. Only in 1933 did deposits decline, by about $300 million. While there was much hoarding of currency, (both gold and paper money) and while the story may have been different had there been no banking holiday in early 1933, it is clear that in savings bank states the

---

11. Josephine Hedges Ewalt, *A Business Reborn* (Chicago: American Savings and Loan Institute Press, 1962), p. 26.

12. The average size of the suspended savings banks was thus $3.5 million. Mergers further reduced the number of savings banks from 598 in 1929 to 565 in 1934.

public regarded the savings banks as safe havens for funds while other institutions were failing in large numbers.

An earlier study shows that only in 1929 had more new accounts been opened in New York State savings banks than were opened in 1933, and in each year of the banking difficulties new accounts exceeded the number of accounts closed except in 1933, when they were virtually the same.[13] The amount withdrawn exceeded the amount deposited in 1929, but not again until the years 1932–34. Dividends credited to accounts, however, maintained the annual increase in deposits in each year except 1933, when deposits fell some $150 million in New York State; this decline was less than 3 per cent. The annual changes in accounts and in deposits are shown in Table 3–5. The large inflow in 1931 is especially noticeable.

The relative stability of the deposits does not lead to the conclusion that the savings banks had no problems as a result of the great depression. This stability precluded the catastrophes that overtook other deposit-type intermediaries, but at the same time there were troubles on the asset side of the balance sheet. Both mortgage loans, which had developed a long record of safety, and bond investments presented serious problems.

Mortgage Loan Experience

The deterioration of mortgage portfolios in the depression was unprecedented. At first, the savings banks reacted as they had in the panics of 1893 and 1907, increasing their mortgage loans in preference to bonds, especially in view of the inflow of deposits. However, the difference between a money panic and a prolonged depression showed up as cumulating delinquencies and rising foreclosures. Like other lenders, the savings banks had succumbed to competitive pressures in the 1920's and had made loans on optimistic appraisals, influenced by rising costs and real estate prices. Under conditions of severe deflation, the supposed margin between loan and value often became nonexistent.

In Massachusetts, foreclosures between 1932 and 1940 amounted to $423.2 million. Mortgage loans did not decline by

13. Welfling, *op. cit.,* pp. 150-51.

this amount, however, as foreclosed properties were typically resold with purchase money mortgages, estimated to have been $281.8 million on these properties.[14] Repayments fell to about half their dollar volume of the 1920's and averaged about 4 per cent of mortgage principal. In other savings bank states also, the banks became reluctant lenders after 1933, making few new loans other than purchase money mortgages and "additional" loans required to rehabilitate properties and keep them in earning condition. In New York State these additional loans were often made by the Savings Banks Trust Co., as they exceeded the loan-to-value restrictions of the savings bank law. Table 3–6 indicates the gravity of the deterioration in New York State. It is evident that 23.8 per cent of the loans, by number, were delinquent in some regard (interest, taxes, in foreclosure, or subject to rent assignment or agreement) in 1935, affecting 41.4 per cent of mortgage principal. The arrears amounted to 9 per cent of the affected principal in 1936 and to 3 per cent of total principal.

TABLE 3-6[15]

MORTGAGE LOANS IN ARREARS,
NEW YORK STATE, 1934–37

| | Per Cent in Arrears | | Arrears, Per Cent of Affected Principal | Arrears, Per Cent of Total Principal |
	Number	Principal		
1934	18.6	32.3	6.0	1.9
1935	23.8	41.4	6.4	2.6
1936	18.3	33.9	9.0	3.0
1937	14.1	28.0	8.8	2.4

Losses from the depression experience with mortgage loans are difficult to measure, not only because they include reductions in anticipated earnings and costs of foreclosure and operating and selling properties, but also because in accounting terms the properties were often written down and losses recognized in later years when earnings would absorb them. Lintner estimated

14. Lintner, *op. cit.*, p. 228.
15. Welfling, *op. cit.*, pp. 74-75.

that gross losses on the real estate mortgage portfolios in Massachusetts amounted to 16.4 per cent of the total mortgage portfolio held in 1931, with subsequent recoveries amounting to not more than 10 per cent of this total.[16] Other real estate climbed to about 14 per cent of total mortgages in New York State by 1937; at this time the total of mortgages plus other real estate approximated the total mortgages held in 1929. To avoid book losses, the banks tended to hold the properties until they could recover the various costs involved in the properties, although late in the decade they disposed of them at prices approximating the new mortgages.

Shifts of Assets

As a result of the depression experience, savings banks lost much of their former interest in mortgage lending. After 1932, total

---

TABLE 3-7[17]

MUTUAL SAVINGS BANKS'
REAL ESTATE LOANS AND "OTHER" ASSETS,
1930–40

(MILLIONS OF DOLLARS)

	Real Estate Loans				"Other" Assets			
	U.S.A.	*N. Y.*	*Mass.*	*Conn.*	*U.S.A.*	*N. Y.*	*Mass.*	*Conn.*
1930	5,635	3,282	1,234	391	229	150	34	8
1931	5,869	3,470	1,255	407	269	171	45	10
1932	5,903	3,536	1,240	409	354	208	69	16
1933	5,752	3,481	1,203	397	496	283	103	27
1934	5,480	3,328	1,151	381	647	377	136	37
1935	5,196	3,173	1,096	361	796	464	168	49
1936	4,956	3,028	1,048	349	922	547	193	57
1937	4,884	3,004	1,023	342	930	545	193	62
1938	4,826	2,978	1,006	340	907	525	188	62
1939	4,812	2,999	989	336	849	478	179	63
1940	4,835	3,040	969	334	784	438	167	58

---

16. Lintner, *op. cit.*, pp. 255-56.
17. NAMSB, *Fact Books.*

loans declined in each remaining year of the decade. The experience was uniform in the various savings bank states. Figures for the combined banks and the three larger states are shown in Table 3–7. Figures for other assets are included as a fairly close measure of foreclosed real estate. During the 1930's, the banks shifted heavily into government obligations, in effect putting all of the increase in assets and the decline in mortgages into this form. The volume of new mortgage lending constituted a very small fraction of the lending being done, with the result that the savings banks' share declined rapidly. As a proportion of their own assets, real estate loans fell from the 55 per cent figure reached at the beginning of the decade to 40 per cent in 1940. More of this drop is accounted for by the decline in loans than by the rise in assets.

During the latter half of the decade total mortgage credit increased, but the savings banks chose not to share in the increase. The reluctance to lend extended to the "new type" of loans consisting of direct reduction loans and Federal Housing Administration loans. The relative shares of the total nonfarm residential mortgages held by savings and loan associations, insurance companies, savings banks, and commercial banks changed as follows during the decade:[18]

	1930	1935	1940
savings and loans	37.8	28.2	29.4
life insurance	17.7	18.8	20.8
savings banks	27.0	34.0	28.2
commercial banks	17.5	19.0	21.6

With the benefit of hindsight, it is clear that the savings banks were refusing to expand mortgage loans at a time when the safest loans were being made and when yields relative to the

18. The HOLC held more mortgage loans in 1935 than did the commercial banks or insurance companies. In these years individuals were the largest lenders on residential mortgages. "Individuals and others" held $11.4 billion out of $27.6 billion of loans in 1930, and $7.6 billion out of $22.2 billion in 1935; savings banks held about $4 billion in 1935.

low yields on government bonds were attractive. However, engrossed as they were with disposing of properties and disenchanted with the net yields being provided by mortgage portfolios, the bankers were shifting assets into government securities. Table 3–8 shows how the increase in holdings of governments exceeded both the net increase in securities and the increase in total assets. "Other" assets were, of course, much higher in 1940 than in 1930, and the banks' response to the banking crisis was still indicated by much higher cash assets—which, in comparison to yields on governments, were less expensive than had been the case in the 1920's.

TABLE 3-8[19]

CHANGES IN SAVINGS BANK ASSETS,
1930–40

(MILLIONS OF DOLLARS)

Asset	1930	1940	Increase
U.S. Government securities	499	3,108	2,609
State and local securities	920	551	(369)
Other securities	2,278	1,588	(690)
Total securities	3,697	5,247	1,550
Loans	5,947	4,917	(1,030)
Cash assets	291	977	686
Other assets	229	784	555

State and local securities were disposed of in some cases because of the decline in quality of these securities, and also because of their greater value to other investors because of tax exemption. Railroad, telephone, and other utility securities were disposed of to a considerable extent because of the deterioration in their credit standing during the depression. Dividends were reduced drastically and, as earnings permitted, losses were taken on these securities. Since securities were openly quoted, and in some states specific bank holdings were open to public scrutiny,

19. *All-Bank Statistics,* pp. 46-47.

the banks were under more pressure to dispose of depreciated bonds than was the case with mortgage loans or foreclosed properties.

New Deal Reforms

If an observer had surveyed the wreckage of the banking and financial system as it appeared in 1934 and speculated on the structure of the system over the next decade or two, he might easily have concluded that the one institution that had come through the crisis of 1931–33 with colors flying was the savings bank. He might be pardoned if he had concluded that savers would avoid savings and loan associations and commercial banks and that a new period of savings bank growth was about to begin, in which the dominant position of the banks in the Northeast would spread throughout the country. For reasons discussed in a later chapter, however, it was not the savings banks but the savings and loan associations that profited from the developments of the mid-1930's. Between 1930 and 1937, time and savings deposits at commercial banks fell by nearly 25 per cent and savings at savings and loan associations by nearly 33 per cent; savings at mutual savings banks rose about 8 per cent. However, legislative and other structural changes that took place in the nation's financial machinery during the days of the New Deal laid the basis for extremely rapid increases in the activity of savings and loans in succeeding years.

Much of the overhauling of the banking system during the New Deal period was concerned with the markets for savings and mortgage financing, as one of the principal objectives was to restore a flow of funds into construction. Foreclosures rose to unprecedented rates. Especially in farm areas, demands arose for moratoria on foreclosures and legislatures met the demands. The existence of these new laws probably reduced the pressure to pay on mortgagors in urban areas, and foreclosure laws were amended in urban states as well. The Reconstruction Finance Corporation was already established (1932), primarily to lend to commercial banks and railroads; it was patterned somewhat after the War Finance Corporation of World War I. Part of its benefits were to enable commercial banks to extend loans to savings banks and savings and loan associations. Savings banks' borrowings rose from $4 million in 1931 to $16 million in 1932 and 1933, while other liabilities rose from $13 to $28 million—small absolute amounts, but significant increases.

Home Owners Loan Corporation

A second agency of considerable importance was the Home Owners Loan Corporation, which was revolutionary in that it made loans of government funds directly to individuals. Essentially, the plan of the HOLC was to exchange government bonds for distressed mortgages with lenders who preferred to do so. The HOLC refinanced the loans at 5 per cent and with 15-year terms, with a moratorium on principal payments for three years. Rarely outside of savings and loan associations were mortgage loans amortized, and the typical mortgage loan was for three to five years, after which it became a demand loan or was renewed for another short term. The HOLC wrote down the loans to 80 per cent of appraisal and offered this amount of bonds in the exchange. The bonds at first paid 4 per cent, later issues 3 per cent (and became fully guaranteed), and later 2.75 per cent and 2.25 per cent. The HOLC ceased lending in 1936, at which time it had disbursed about $2.7 billion in exchange for mortgages plus other sums for modernization, taxes, and similar reasons. The amounts disbursed to different recipients are shown in Table 3–9. Life insurance companies turned over about 9 per cent of their residential mortgages, the savings banks about 12 per cent, savings and loan associations and individual and other lenders about 13 per cent each, and commercial banks about 26 per cent.

Before its liquidation in 1951, the HOLC found it necessary to foreclose on about one fifth of its mortgage portfolio, but these properties were resold with new mortgages. As savings poured into the various institutions during World War II, while mortgage loans were relatively scarce, the HOLC was able to hasten its liquidation by sales of mortgages. Although dealing with an unprecedented distress situation, the HOLC liquidated without a net cost to the Treasury.

TABLE 3-9[20]

DISBURSEMENTS MADE BY THE
HOME OWNERS LOAN CORPORATION

(MILLIONS OF DOLLARS)

To mortgagees:	
Savings and loan associations	770
Individuals	575
Commercial banks	525
Savings banks	410
Mortgage companies	196
Insurance companies	165
Trusts, estates, etc.	110
TOTAL	2,750
To others:	
Taxes and assessments	230
Repairs, etc.	70
Miscellaneous expense	44
TOTAL	340
Total	3,094

Federal Home Loan Bank System

The innovation with probably the greatest impact on the structure of the savings and mortgage finance institutions is the Federal Home Loan Bank System. Late in 1931, the President's Conference on Home Building and Home Ownership considered a proposal from President Hoover that a system of Home Loan Discount Banks be established with government capital, but eventually revert to private ownership in the manner of the Federal Land Banks, and be co-operatively owned by "building and loan associations, the savings banks, and other home loan

20. Federal Home Loan Bank Board data.

agencies."[21] The principal support for the idea came from the savings and loan associations.[22] Opposition arose mostly from insurance company, mortgage company, and commercial bank interests, and the bill establishing the banks was not enacted until the end of the legislative session in July, 1932. The system consisted of (originally) 12 regional Home Loan Banks, supervised by a Federal Home Loan Bank Board of five members. Savings and loan associations, savings banks, and insurance companies were eligible for membership. Members could borrow without security for short terms and on mortgage security for long terms (up to ten years). The original capital subscription from the Treasury was $125 million, and debentures could be sold, secured by mortgages obtained by the regional banks from their members, up to five times the amount of the capital. Members were to purchase stock in their respective Home Loan Banks equal to 1 per cent of their mortgage loans. Enabling legislation was required in the several states, since savings and loan associations, as well as savings banks, were state chartered. An original provision authorizing loans direct from the regional banks to homeowners was repealed and the HOLC, described above, was substituted.

The Federal Home Loan Bank System has always been essentially a savings and loan institution. Many of the first directors of the banks and members of the Federal Home Loan Bank Board were savings and loan people, and the association's principal trade association was instrumental in passage of the legis-

---

21. The failure of savings banks to capitalize on this situation is discussed in Chapter 5.

22. "Herbert Hoover knew more about savings and loan associations and their value to a community than any other person who has ever lived in the White House. He believed in the savings and loan business as a significant, though small, link in the nation's financial system, and he saw some of its potentialities for becoming something greater . . . By one of the more fortunate strokes of chance he was President of the United States when savings and loan leaders saw that something had to be done, and done right away, to assure any real future for their institutions." Ewalt, *op. cit.*, pp. 49-50. And, ". . . without the determined effort of the savings and loan business to get the legislation passed, it probably would have failed of enactment." (p. 53)

lation and in organization of the system. When federal charters for associations were introduced, federal associations were required to belong to the system. At the end of the first year, the system had as members one fifth of the associations, possessing one third of total assets. At the end of 1963 (30 years later), membership consisted of 4,960 associations and 41 savings banks. The associations represented 98.3 per cent of the assets of savings and loans, while the savings banks represented less than 10 per cent of savings bank assets. Since 1959, there have been no insurance company members.[23]

Federal Savings and Loan Associations

Establishment of the Home Loan Bank System thus set the stage for the rapid growth of the savings and loan business during the next period of expanded mortgage lending. Two other aspects of the system were the introduction of federal charters for the savings and loan associations and the system of insurance for savings shares. Federal charters were provided in the HOLC act of 1933 and were the fruit of much effort on the part of some leaders of the savings and loan business. Other segments of the business, as well as some state supervisors and other lending institutions, opposed the movement. Considerable discretion was left in the act to the Federal Home Loan Bank Board, which was ". . . authorized, under such rules and regulations as it may prescribe, to provide for the organization, incorporation, examination, operation and regulation of associations to be known as 'Federal Savings and Loan Associations' and to issue charters therefor. . . ." It was also provided that government funds, up to $100,000, could be invested in such new or converted associations up to the shareholders' investment. In spite of this incentive, during the first half year (to the end of 1933) only one charter had been granted to a converting state association and 58 new charters issued. By the end of 1934, however, 158 conversions and 481 new charters resulted in 639 federal associations. Since then the number of federally chartered asso-

23. United States Savings and Loan League, *Savings and Loan . Fact Book,* 1964, p. 112.

ciations has reached approximately one third of the total (about 2,000 out of 6,000), but the federal associations represent slightly more than half of total assets. Roughly half of the federals represent new charters and half conversions.

Deposit and Share Insurance

Federal insurance of bank deposits and of savings and loan accounts was another innovation brought about by the collapse of the banking system. The idea of insurance of bank deposits was an old one but was generally considered impractical because of the failure of limited state plans in the past. The temper of the times, however, was such that the Congress adopted insurance in 1933 over objections of the banking fraternity. Member banks of the Federal Reserve System were required to join the Federal Deposit Insurance Corporation; thus, national banks were blanketed in, in contrast to their exclusion from earlier state experiments. Insurance was coupled with the authority granted to the Reserve Board to regulate interest payments by insured banks; this situation reduced the interest savings banks may have had in joining the FDIC as nonmember banks. The possibility of insurance providing a competitive advantage for commercial banks, however, led the savings and loan associations to explore a similar measure.[24] Insurance for savings and loan associations resulted in 1934, as part of the Federal Housing Act. Early drafts of this legislation provided for savings bank membership in the Federal Savings and Loan Insurance Corporation, but the banks were left to decide whether or not to accept Federal Deposit Insurance Corporation membership.

Neither the savings banks nor the savings and loan associations embraced insurance enthusiastically. The savings banks felt that the assessments of the FDIC were based on risks in commercial banking and were, therefore, unnecessarily high for savings banks. At the same time, they recognized the competitive

---

24. "Savings and loan leaders moved very cautiously in advocating such a device. They probably would never have pushed the idea at all in their own councils had not the insurance of bank deposits become a successful undertaking." Ewalt, *op. cit.*, p. 92.

disadvantage of not offering deposit insurance. Consequently, while a few savings banks joined the FDIC, the general answer was to establish state systems. In 1932, Massachusetts established the compulsory Mutual Savings Central Fund, Incorporated, which was designed primarily for liquidity purposes. To this was added in 1934 the Deposit Insurance Fund, which insured savings deposits in full. This plan is still in operation; for the few savings banks in the Commonwealth that have joined the FDIC, it insures deposits in excess of FDIC limits.

The two other largest savings bank states established insurance plans also, but in these states the savings banks later moved into the FDIC. The New York plan was terminated in 1943 and the Connecticut plan in 1960. By 1964, 327 savings banks were insured by FDIC (including eight also in the Massachusetts plan), 179 were state covered, and eight were noninsured.[25] In that year, the 1,981 federally chartered, plus 2,482 state-chartered savings and loan associations, totaling over 96 per cent of aggregate association assets, were members of FSLIC.

The remainder of this period reflects, on the one hand, burgeoning deposits in financial intermediaries and, on the other, the predominance of government bonds among the assets during World War II and the rapid increase in mortgage lending in the 20 years 1945–65. These developments are surveyed briefly here, in view of topical discussions in later chapters.

World War II

The key to much of the direction of developments in the 25 years after 1940 is the extent of inflation permitted during World War II. While the government's intention was to finance the conflict as much as possible through taxation, it relied heavily, in fact, on deficit financing. In order to prevent bond prices from declining as interest rates rose, the Treasury and the Federal Reserve System agreed on a pegged interest-rate struc-

25. It is not generally realized that mutual savings banks represent about 40 per cent of all bank assets examined by the Federal Deposit Insurance Corporation. The Corporation does not directly examine member banks examined by the Comptroller of the Currency and the Federal Reserve.

TABLE 3-10[20]

MUTUAL SAVINGS BANKS'
HOLDINGS OF SECURITIES,
SELECTED DATES, 1940–65

(MILLIONS OF DOLLARS)

	1940	1945	1950	1955	1960	1965
Bonds:						
U.S. Government	3,193	10,650	10,877	8,463	6,243	5,485
State and municipal	612	84	96	646	672	320
Corporate and other	1,301	989	2,081	2,738	4,249	3,744
Total bonds	5,106	11,723	13,054	11,848	11,164	9,549
Stocks:						
Bank	118	116	163	330	352	452
Other	10	11	16	331	541	1,020
Total stocks	129	127	179	626[a]	827[a]	1,426[a]
Total securities	5,235	11,850	13,233	12,474	11,991	10,975

[a]These totals are net of reserves and are consistent with the rest of the data except for the breakdowns of stocks in these years which are reported on a gross basis.

TABLE 3-11[27]

LOANS OF MUTUAL SAVINGS BANKS,
SELECTED YEARS, 1940–65

(MILLIONS OF DOLLARS)

	1940	1945	1950	1955	1960	1965
Mortgage loans	4,836	4,208	8,261	17,457	26,935	44,726
1-4 family		1,894	4,312	11,100	18,369	30,190
Multi-family		1,493	2,742	4,468	5,937	10,063
Nonresidential		797	1,164	1,831	2,575	4,428
Farm		24	44	58	54	45
Other loans	82	62	127	211	416	862

ture, which naturally was a reflection of the very low rates that had come about during the 1930's. The yield curve for government securities was pegged at a bill rate of three eighths of one

26. NAMSB, *Fact Book,* 1966, p. 21, and earlier editions.
27. NAMSB, *Fact Books.*

per cent and rose to 2.5 per cent for long-term securities. About
$68.5 billion of governments were purchased by commercial
banks, leading to corresponding increases in their deposits, and
to subsequent increases in monetary incomes. While governmental controls retarded the increase in prices, the newly created
funds tended to lie idle longer in inactive demand deposits, but
they also flowed through financial intermediaries in large volume.

Since there was little demand for funds except from the government during the war, competition for time deposits was not
severe. While demand deposits (other than interbank and government) rose from $34.9 billion in 1940 to $75.9 billion in
1945, time and savings deposits at commercial banks also
doubled—from $15.7 billion to $30.2 billion—but not as the
result of active solicitation by the banks. The public was buying
large quantities of United States Savings and other bonds of the
Treasury—holding $44.2 billion of savings bonds in 1945—but
in addition had idle funds to be held available for postwar
purchases. Much the same situation characterized business
corporations. Individuals and businesses held unusually large
cash balances, but also let some of these balances spill over into
time and savings deposits at their commercial banks, even
though the interest returns offered made little difference.

The public was also building up liquid assets in other forms.
Savings bank deposits rose by nearly one half, from $10.6 billion
to $15.3 billion; savings and loan shares rose from $4.7 billion to
$8.5 billion; and life insurance reserves rose from $29 billion
to $41.7 billion. Thus, in a period of little competition for
funds, when rates being paid by financial intermediaries reflected primarily the returns they were getting from pegged rates
on government securities, the multiplicity of commercial bank
offices tended to command the lion's share of the increase in
liquid saving other than savings bonds. Of the four leading
financial institutions, commercial banks increased their share of
the time and savings deposit market in this period from 26.1 per
cent to 31.6 per cent, while savings banks fell off from 17.7 per
cent to 16.0 per cent and life insurance reserves declined from

48.4 per cent to 43.5 per cent; savings and loan shares increased from 7.8 per cent to 8.9 per cent.

The savings banks had roughly five billion more dollars to invest in 1945 than they had in 1940. This amount and more went into government obligations (see Table 3–10). All other principal categories of assets declined, as government bond holdings rose to $10.7 billion and constituted 63.5 per cent of total assets. At this point, mortgage loans reached a low of 25.9 per cent of assets, and amounted to $4.2 billion.

Postwar Developments

After World War II the postponed housing demands of the 1930's and 1940's were able to make themselves felt, as consumers held large quantities of liquid assets and lenders had huge holdings of government securities they could liquidate at pegged prices to make mortgage loans. In addition, inflated incomes resulting from the postwar inflation, based partly on the building boom itself, resulted in additional inflows of funds for the intermediaries to put to work.

The combination of monetary and other influences on the economy in the 20 years 1945–65 resulted in very large flows of financial savings and very rapid growth for the system of financial intermediaries. (The drastic shifts in 1966 are described in Chapter 4.) Taking savings and loan shares, savings bank deposits and individuals' commercial bank time and savings deposits alone, the total increased from $52.6 billion in 1945 to $292.7 billion at the end of 1965, an increase of more than 500 per cent. This growth resulted in a considerable rearrangement of the financial structure. This rearrangement can be shown by a comparison of the shares of financial saving held in various forms. Table 3–12 shows the percentages held by commercial banks, savings banks, and savings and loan associations, of two different totals.

The increase in the relative share of the savings and loan associations is striking—a more than two-fold increase with regard to the leading deposit-type institutions and a more than four-fold increase with regard to all the forms of saving listed. The increase in savings held at savings and loan institutions during this period was from $7.4 billion to $110.3 billion. Estimated savings of individuals at commercial banks increased from $27.8 billion to $130.0 billion and total time deposits to $146.7 billion, while deposits at savings banks were rising from $15.3 billion to $52.4 billion.

TABLE 3-12[28]

PERCENTAGE SHARES OF SAVINGS IN
DIFFERENT FORMS, SELECTED YEARS

	Per Cent of Total of Three Forms			Per Cent of Total of Eight Forms		
	Commercial Banks	Savings Banks	Savings and Loans	Commercial Banks	Savings Banks	Savings and Loans
1945	56.8	29.1	14.1	21.9	11.2	5.4
1955	43.5	26.4	30.1	19.7	11.9	13.7
1965	44.4	17.9	37.7	27.4	11.0	23.2

The geographical restriction of the savings banks to 18 states, and their historical position as leading depositories in considerably fewer states, however, distorts the conclusions to be drawn from national data. In all three of the leading savings bank states, deposit gains between 1950 and 1964 were greatest for savings banks. In New York State the savings banks' gains were approximately equal to the combined increase of commercial banks and savings and loans—about $17 billion. In Massachusetts, the savings banks' gains were nearly twice those of the others combined, and the same was true in Connecticut. For all the savings bank states the total gains were surprisingly similar, being between about $30 billion and $33 billion for all three. For the ten New England and Middle Atlantic states, however, the savings banks' gains were substantially larger than either of the other two.

28. The three forms are commercial bank time and savings deposits, savings bank deposits, and savings and loan shares. The eight forms are these plus life insurance reserves, U.S. savings bonds, credit unions, postal savings, and investment companies.

In the national savings market, the share of the commercial banks declined for a time after the war because of these banks' ability to shift funds from government bonds to business and other loans. The constant rise in their demand deposits, generated by their own loan activity, provided sufficient funds, based on rising reserves from the Federal Reserve System, without requiring aggressive competition for time deposits. Other financial intermediaries were also able to dispose of government securities, but any growth in deposits naturally had to be of the time deposit variety. Thus, other intermediaries grew at the expense of the commercial banks' share of the market for savings.

After the Accord of 1951, in which the Treasury and the Federal Reserve reached a measure of agreement permitting the latter to unpeg government security prices, bank reserves grew at a less rapid pace, demand deposits also grew less rapidly, and commercial banks returned to the interest in time deposits that they had shown in the 1920's. During the 1950's, with temporary interruptions, demands for loanable funds were great, causing a rise in interest rates. Managers of corporate, municipal, and other funds became more acutely aware of the costs of holding idle cash, and demand deposits were pared to the minimum required for operations. In order to retain funds, it appeared that the commercial banks would have to recapture as time and savings deposits what they were losing on the other side of the lobby.

Intertwined with these considerations was rising interest on the part of commercial banks in higher-yielding assets, particularly consumer loans and mortgage loans. By 1956, competition for funds had raised average rates paid by savings and loan associations, savings banks, and commercial banks in each year of the decade. As a result, the commercial banks were bumping the ceiling imposed on them by the Federal Reserve's Regulation Q (governing the rates banks may pay). Near the end of 1956, the rates allowed by Regulation Q were raised. Following this development, commercial banks more aggressively sought time money, causing their time deposits to become more heavily weighted with corporate deposits and less with those of individuals. The creation of a market for negotiable certificates of deposit was an important step in this direction. Following this measure, taken in 1961, commercial banks branched out into new ways of seeking time deposits or similar funds. Their methods included savings bonds, notes, and debentures.

As a consequence of these changes in the competition for financial savings, the asset structure of financial intermediaries also changed. Savings and loan associations, naturally, continued to make mortgage loans, but for a period of time were able to dispose of government securities in order to raise funds. Their key role in the mortgage market and the building boom of the postwar period, along with their widespread geographical location, led to extremely rapid growth of savings at these institutions. The commercial banks followed suit, to a degree, by rapidly expanding their holdings of mortgage loans, as well as consumer loans. As the pressure of rising interest rates continued into the 1960's, the commercial banks also shifted a considerable part of their government bond portfolio into municipal securities.

Growth of Mortgage Lending

The savings banks responded to the new climate by allocating more than the net increase in assets into mortgage loans. All types of mortgage lending were expanded. By 1964, mortgage loans represented three fourths of total assets. A tabulation of sources and uses of funds by savings banks for the period 1950–65 shows total uses and sources of $42.9 billion, with mortgages accounting for $38.1 billion of the uses; corporate and other securities, $3.2 billion; and all other, $1.5 billion. The sources were $33.4 billion of net deposit gains; sale of government securities, $5.9 billion; and all other, $3.6 billion.[29]

In the great expansion of mortgage loans in this 20-year period, each type of institution tended to carve out a position in a special field of mortgage lending. The savings and loan associations continued to specialize in conventional loans and the savings banks concentrated on FHA and Veterans' Administration loans; the commercial banks tended to show more diversity.

29. NAMSB, *Annual Report,* May 1966, p. 11.

An important factor in this development was the geographical limitations of the savings banks. Limited in their ability to make mortgage loans in their home states equal to the resources available, they turned to out-of-state lending, which required the use of guaranteed mortgages.[30] By 1964, savings banks had made two fifths of their mortgage loans out of state, and of these three fourths were in non-savings bank states. These out-of-state loans were about equally FHA and VA loans. Throughout the period, the savings banks' share of federally underwritten mortgage debt rose constantly, and in 1965 it reached 31 per cent of the total. As a result, savings banks were the largest holders of this type of mortgage debt, with $25.7 billion of a total $84 billion in 1966.

At the close of the third half-century of savings bank history, one is struck by the similarity of problems that have existed for most of the first 150 years of savings banking. The essential nature of the savings banks as financial intermediaries has persisted, but it has altered with the enormous changes in the economy. Originally oriented toward philanthropy, the savings banks have responded to rising affluence and industrialization by serving the public generally rather than the lowest income groups alone. Growth brought the assets of the system past the $60 billion mark in 1966. On a national basis, the savings banks were thus about half as large as the combined savings and loan associations. Yet in the northeast corner of the nation, where the savings banks are concentrated (New England and Middle Atlantic states), their holdings of savings exceeded those of savings associations by a margin of more than two to one.

This growth has brought with it continuing pressures for expanded powers. In most states, security investments have been restricted to assets on legal lists. Over the years these lists have been expanded to bring in new types of assets (railroad, utility, and other corporate bonds, and common stocks), and restrictions on loans have been reduced. Still, when economic factors have so dictated, the banks have concentrated their assets heavily in certain areas, as witness the postwar rise of mortgage loans. This

---

30. Massachusetts was an exception because of tax treatment of assets other than local mortgages.

shift, in turn, would have been difficult or impossible without the development of federally guaranteed loans. At the same time, the inter-industry competition among different kinds of financial institutions has made commercial banks, as well as savings and loan associations and insurance companies, major factors in mortgage and savings markets. The reverse side of this movement has been pressure for expanded loan powers of savings banks in areas such as personal loans, traditionally handled —if at all—by other institutions in most savings bank states.

The key role of savings banks in mortgage markets was not exploited in the 1930's, partly because of their geographic limitations. Other institutions assumed the role nationally that savings banks still perform in New England and New York State. While few new savings banks were established either in savings bank or other states, the growth of the system within savings bank states has been reflected in pressure to open branch offices. In 1965, of the 506 savings banks, 247 had branches that exceeded in total the number of head offices (716); thus there were 1,222 savings bank offices. In the ten largest mutual savings bank states in mid-1965, there were 1,174 offices of savings banks, 7,178 offices of commercial banks, and 2,678 offices of savings and loan associations. One result of the restricted number of savings banks has been larger average growth of these institutions than in the case of commercial banks or savings and loans. At the end of 1966, the assets of the average savings bank exceeded $120 million, while the average commercial bank had $29 million and the average savings and loan association $21.5 million. Naturally, the average figures conceal much dispersion in all three cases; the largest commercial banks are considerably larger than the largest savings bank.

Resurgent interest in savings banking has recently led to efforts to expand the industry, both through permissive chartering legislation in states not having such laws and through the introduction of federal chartering. Statehood for Alaska was quickly followed by legislation and chartering of the first savings bank in that state (Anchorage, 1961); a second was established in Fairbanks in 1965. In 1964, the Commonwealth of Puerto Rico authorized formation of mutual savings banks by a law

permitting new charters. Such legislation has also been introduced in other states. In addition, efforts have been made to
incorporate new banks in counties of savings bank states where
no savings bank exists; such a bank was established in Rockland
County, New York State, in early 1965.

Federal charter legislation was introduced in 1957, and has
been reintroduced regularly since that time, with administration
and bipartisan support. Extensive congressional hearings were
held in 1963, and further hearings were held in 1966 and 1967.
The subject of federal chartering is discussed at length in Chapter
5. These developments, as well as numerous activities of both
individual banks and trade association groups, indicate the growing
importance of financial intermediaries in general and increasing
interest in mutual savings banks specifically.

II | Savings Banks in Savings and Capital Markets

CHAPTER 4

Savings Deposits

THIS chapter and the following one deal with the operations of mutual savings banks in the savings market. This chapter concentrates primarily, although not exclusively, on characteristics of savings bank deposits, while Chapter 5 takes up broader considerations of the role of these banks in the savings market, the case for extending the geographic range of mutual savings banking, and related issues.

Concepts of Saving

A variety of statistics is available for measuring the importance of the mutual savings banks in the savings market. The basic data on savings flows are provided by the national income statistics of the Department of Commerce, the flow of funds data of the Federal Reserve System, and the savings statistics of the Securities and Exchange Commission. All are useful in different ways. The income (or income and product) data of the Department of Commerce visualize the economy as an aggregate and relate total output (gross national product) in dollar terms to incomes received by principal segments of the economy. Conceptually, what the aggregate economy produces for investment rather than for consumption is the economy's gross saving for the period. The saving may be done by persons, businesses, or governments, or the saving of any segment may be negative.

Thus, in the national income accounts, personal saving is the residual obtained by subtracting consumption expenditures from disposable personal income.

The flow of funds accounts agree with the national income accounts, with one major and some minor differences of definition. The major difference is that the flow of funds accounts include expenditures on consumer durable goods as gross saving, rather than as consumption expenditures. Minor differences, in terms of dollar amounts, are in the treatment of government insurance and pension claims as household saving in the flow of funds accounts. The basic utility of the flow of funds accounts is to show the flow of money and credit from one sector, such as households, to other sectors, such as business, and the extent to which the accompanying claims are direct or through intermediaries.

An illustration of the differences in concept and treatment is provided by the annual data for 1965. Gross national product

Chart 4–1

Personal Saving as Percentage of Disposable Personal Income

1947—66

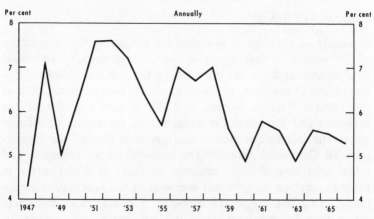

Source of data: U.S. Department of Commerce, Office of Business Economics

Chart 4-2

Gross Saving

1947– 66

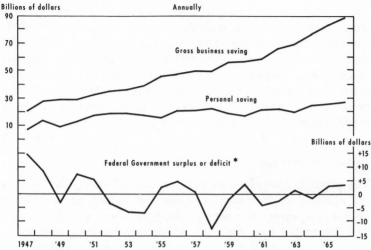

*National Income Accounts
Source of data: U.S. Department of Commerce, Office of Business Economics

was $681.2 billion, which, after deductions for capital consumption and comparable allowances, represented a national income or output of $559 billion. Persons did not receive retained corporate profits, but did receive interest, dividends, and transfer payments, making personal income $535.1 billion. Personal tax and nontax payments reduced this figure to disposable personal income of $469.1 billion. Personal outlays, consisting of consumer expenditures, interest, and transfer payments to foreigners, of $443.4 billion left personal saving of $25.7 billion. Personal saving, as a percentage of income, is shown in Chart 4–1.

In the flow of funds accounts, the $25.7 billion total is increased to a figure of $45.3 billion by the treatment of increased credits in government insurance and by the net increase of consumer durables after capital consumption. Putting back capital consumption of durables and housing into gross income provides a figure for gross saving of $105.1 billion.[1] Gross saving is shown in Chart 4–2.

The Securities and Exchange Commission statistics are more direct measures of financial assets and liabilities and changes therein. They deal with individuals and nonprofit organizations and show annual savings in terms of net acquisitions of financial assets, as well as total holdings of financial assets. For purposes of comparing financial institutions in the markets for financial assets, the Securities and Exchange Commission data provide more direct measures. For placing the financial assets in a broader concept of saving, the other types of data are useful.

Forms of Savings

The popular, spur-of-the-moment concept of saving is that it is the opposite of spending; spending and saving are commonly used as antonyms. The act of saving, however, usually involves spending money for some asset. Other than hoarding money, the act of saving requires the saver to acquire some asset thought of as capital rather than as an item of consumption. The question of what assets properly to include as savings presents many semantic and definitional problems.

In the early days of savings banks these problems were not diverse or difficult. A saver did one of very few things: He accumulated money, usually cash itself; he acquired a savings deposit at a savings bank; or he accumulated business property, including farm property. In the earlier decades of this country, the accumulation of real assets represented the major form of diverting output to saving. The property was often produced directly by the saver rather than being purchased. As the economic development of the country went on, more of the population settled in urban areas and became dependent upon money incomes. Indeed, this development was a major one leading to the establishment of mutual savings banks, as community leaders sought some means of providing an instrument through which low-income groups could make provision for their own financial emergencies.

---

1. See *Federal Reserve Bulletin*, January, 1967, pp. 147-51.

Thus it came about that, for the "common man," saving was thought of primarily in terms of the "rainy day." Before the modern era, the hazards of illness and accident and the loss of income with old age posed not only serious but often tragic problems of maintaining income for basic consumption. A "nest egg" in the savings bank for emergencies and some capital to live on in old age, plus insurance for one's family in case of earlier death, represented the principal motives for saving. The spread of income between the rich and the poor led to a distinction, broadly speaking, between the rich who saved and invested in family and corporate businesses and the poor whose savings were mostly savings bank deposits and insurance policies.

With the income revolution of the last few decades, the nature of saving has again changed. Disposable personal income has risen constantly since the great depression of the 1930's, and since World War II has climbed from $160 billion (1946) to $505.3 billion (in 1966). In terms of constant 1958 dollars, the increase is from $227 billion to $451.6 billion, very close to a doubling in 20 years. While the rise in income per capita is considerably slower (about 43 per cent in real terms), over a period of a generation the degree of discretion in disposing of personal income has increased tremendously. Contrary to the Keynesian fears of the 1930's, the public has not found it difficult to spend a fairly constant fraction of this income for consumption, while at the same time the fraction devoted to nonconsumption has produced a constantly rising source of funds. In terms of the Department of Commerce national income data, the proportion of disposable income saved has run fairly consistently around 6 per cent, with, however, readings as high as 7.6 per cent and as low as 4.9 per cent since 1950, and with an apparent downward drift in the 1950's and 1960's except for 1967.

With the higher level of income now enjoyed—as well as higher levels anticipated more or less consciously as a result of decades of experience—and with considerably more protection against the proverbial rainy day in the form of unemployment and health insurance, pension plans, and greater private insurance coverage, the public has had a wider choice in its disposition of income. Acquisition of durable goods has become a significant measure of this disposition; in other words, the choice is not simply between goods and services for immediate consumption versus rainy day assets; it is, rather, a three-fold choice among current consumption, liquid assets, and other assets. The other assets in turn are divisible into real assets that provide enjoyment in some manner and income-producing assets. In the category of real assets are the numerous durable goods such as automobiles, television sets, boats, recreation equipment, and many others, as well as housing, which has always been considered a form of saving. In the second category are pension funds and marketable securities of a variety of forms, generally distinguished from liquid assets. Investment in higher education is another form of income disposition that might be classified in either category.

TABLE 4-1[2]

PERSONAL CONSUMPTION, IN
1958 PRICES, SELECTED YEARS

(BILLIONS OF DOLLARS)

	1936	1946	1956	1966
Personal Consumption	138.4	203.5	281.4	415.5
Durable goods	14.5	20.5	41.0	70.8
Nondurable goods	73.4	110.8	136.2	185.9
Services	50.5	72.1	104.1	158.7

In contrast to the attitudes of the 1930's and earlier years, the acceptance of these real assets as forms of saving has become fairly general. In both accounting terms and the general language, it is recognized that these things are forms of wealth. In a balance sheet sense, a family may have a large net worth represented by durable goods, ranging from a piano and Picassos to ping pong tables, as well as by stocks and bonds or the family farm. A corollary of this acceptance is the further recognition that credit extended for the acquisition of these goods, or educa-

---

2. *Economic Report of the President, 1967,* p. 214.

tion, may be justified in the modern economy. It is now an accepted custom not only to "save up" for these expenditures but to buy them with consumer credit and to save for them through repaying the credit.

Durable goods represented 11.7 per cent of consumption expenditures in 1929, fell to 7.3 per cent in 1933, and recovered to 11.5 per cent in the defense-boom year of 1941. The Korean War year of 1950 saw the proportion rise to 15.1 per cent. Since then it has remained consistently higher than it was in the boom years of 1929 and 1941, with the low point coming in 1952 at 12.8 per cent. During the durable-goods boom of 1955 the percentage reached 15.8 per cent, after which it remained above 14 per cent except in the slump of 1958, and in 1963 to 1966 was over 15 per cent. Thus, durable goods appear to represent roughly a one-third larger proportion of total consumption spending than was the case prior to the great depression.[3]

Total consumer credit was small at the end of World War II because of lack of durable goods and because of controls on production and credit. At the end of 1945 total consumer credit was only $5.7 billion, but it increased rapidly during the catch-up period thereafter and has trended upward since, passing the $80-billion mark in 1965. "The persistency of the rise is the result of many factors, but it reflects mainly the fact that more and more people are using installment credit for more and more purposes. Faced with the choice of buying services or buying durable goods to provide the services, consumers have increasingly demonstrated their preference for the latter."[4] Because of rising incomes, the proportion of income devoted to repayment of consumer debt has not risen with the same speed as has consumer debt in total dollars. During the long expansion beginning in 1960, consumer debt repayments required approximately 13 per cent of disposable personal income in the years 1960–62 and then rose to 14 per cent in 1964 and slightly higher

---

3. A discussion of short-run factors influencing spending on durable goods may be found in "Consumer Income, Spending, and Saving," *Federal Reserve Bulletin*, April, 1965, pp. 519-29.

4. "Developments in Consumer Credit," *Federal Reserve Bulletin*, June, 1965, p. 795.

in 1965. Consumers' holdings of liquid assets, however, greatly exceeded their consumer debt, rising from $400 billion in 1960 to $600 billion in 1966.

Recent Trends

Extension of recent trends suggests a very large volume of personal saving in the near future. Since a relatively large part of total saving is done by those with relatively high incomes, it is quite possible that the volume of saving may rise considerably as more and more families attain what are now considered high incomes. On the other hand, of course, this expectation was equally possible 20 years ago, but the proportion of income saved, other than by purchase of durable goods, has not risen. Still, the figures are suggestive. Recent research has shown that the top fifth of families in income save 20 per cent or more of their incomes, while the bottom fourth tend to save not more than 8 per cent; in dollar figures, the top fifth tend to save over $2,500 while the bottom fourth tend to save less than $250.[5]

TABLE 4-2[6]

PERCENTAGE DISTRIBUTION OF FAMILIES AND INCOME BEFORE TAXES,
BY INCOME LEVEL, 1950, 1963, AND 1975

	Families			Income		
	1950	1963	1975	1950	1963	1975
Under $3,000	31.0	18.5	12.0	11.5	5.0	2.0
$ 3,000- 5,000	31.0	17.5	13.0	24.5	10.0	5.0
5,000- 7,000	19.0	21.5	13.5	22.5	18.0	8.0
7,000-10,000	12.0	22.5	22.5	20.5	26.5	18.5
10,000-15,000	5.0	14.5	23.5	12.0	24.0	27.0
15,000 and over	2.0	5.5	15.5	9.0	16.5	39.5
ALL FAMILIES	100.0	100.0	100.0	100.0	100.0	100.0

---

5. George Katona and others, *1963 Survey of Consumer Finances,* Monograph 34, Survey Research Center, University of Michigan, Ann Arbor, 1964.

6. *Loc. cit.*

National Industrial Conference Board projections indicate that more than 15 per cent of American families will receive $15,000 and over in 1975, in terms of 1963 dollars.[7] The Board's tabulation of families and incomes for 1950, 1963, and 1975 is reproduced in Table 4–2. Even if national income continues to rise at a fairly stable rate of around 4 per cent per annum and if the proportion of personal income saved remains roughly the same, there will be a constantly increasing increment of funds devoted to saving, simply because the percentages apply to rising amounts of income.

Financial Assets

The preceding historical chapters have indicated that the savings banks have suffered a serious decline in relative importance. However, the data are subject to different types of arrangements and interpretations. For purposes of comparison, the most relevant data deal with savings accounts and other liquid assets, but the definition of financial assets that are competitive with savings bank deposits may also include life insurance reserves, pension fund claims, and credit and equity market instruments. While the relative importance of savings banks on a national basis is obviously less than it has been in the past, this fact is necessarily colored greatly by their limited geographical area of operations. Even if the savings banks had grown as rapidly as their competitors in savings bank states, they would have lost ground nationally simply because they could not grow where they did not exist.

As a quick benchmark by which to measure changes in financial asset holdings of individuals in the postwar savings markets, Table 4–3 shows the amounts and percentages of change of several financial claims.[8]

The obvious characteristic of these rates of growth is their diversity. The great difference between the rates of growth of savings banks, life insurance companies, and commercial banks,

---

7. National Industrial Conference Board, *Economic Potentials of the United States in the Next Decade,* New York, 1965.

8. Unless otherwise noted, statistics quoted in this discussion are based on the Securities and Exchange Commission estimates of savings.

on the one hand, and of savings and loan associations and credit unions, on the other, suggests that the former should be thought of as mature industries, while the latter, at least for this period of time, should be thought of as new or developing industries. While this classification of savings and loan associations—which trace their ancestry nearly as far back in this country as do the savings banks—may seem strange, it is also true that in many respects the savings and loan business became a new system during the 1930's, with federal charters, insurance of accounts, and the Federal Home Loan Bank System. Savings and loan associations grew with extreme rapidity after World War II, along with the high level of construction and mortgage lending that followed the lean years of both the depression and the war. The high rate of growth of credit unions is, of course, a reflection of the small base from which they started. Savings bonds were primarily a wartime phenomenon and are the only form of financial asset not at a historic high at the end of 1966, having exceeded $50 billion in the mid-1950's.

TABLE 4-3

FINANCIAL ASSETS OF INDIVIDUALS,
1947 AND 1966

(BILLIONS OF DOLLARS)

	1947	1966[p]	Percentage Change
Savings bank deposits	17.7	55.0	210.7
Savings and loan capital	9.7	113.9	1,074.2
Commercial bank time and savings	34.7	145.4	319.0
Credit unions	.5	10.0	1,900.0
Life insurance reserves	43.8	127.9	192.0
U.S. Savings bonds	46.2	50.2	8.7

[p]—Preliminary

The rates of growth of the savings banks, commercial banks, and life insurance companies are roughly comparable, especially when considered as average annual rates of growth. Respectively, the compound annual rates for this period are 6.1 per cent, 7.8 per cent and 5.8 per cent. The rates for savings and loans and for credit unions are 13.9 per cent and 17.1 per cent.

If credit and equity market instruments are included in the financial assets of individuals, the rapidly rising holdings of stocks in the postwar period greatly change the relative proportions of the different institutions. In 1966, common and preferred stock holdings, including those of investment companies, amounted to $516.3 billion and had risen from $285.9 billion in 1956. All of this rise is accounted for by the rising dollar values of these equities, as the annual amount of savings from current income used for this purpose tends to be negative. However, the depressed market in 1966 lowered the proportion from its 1956 level. The relative proportions of different assets, including credit and equity instruments, are shown in Table 4–4.

TABLE 4-4

AMOUNTS AND PROPORTIONS OF FINANCIAL ASSETS,
1956 AND 1966

(BILLIONS OF DOLLARS)

	1956		1966	
	Amount	*Per Cent*	*Amount*	*Per Cent*
Mutual savings bank	30.0	5.0	55.0	4.9
Savings and loan	37.1	6.2	113.9	10.2
Commercial bank	48.5	8.1	145.4	13.0
Credit union	2.9	.5	10.0	.9
Life insurance	78.1	13.1	127.9	11.4
Stocks	285.9	48.6	516.3	46.0
Marketable bonds	60.4	10.1	104.0	9.2
Savings bonds	50.1	8.4	50.2	4.4
TOTAL	593.0	100.0	1,122.7	100.0

Thus, the other types of financial assets that lost ground in terms of market shares over this ten-year period are savings bank deposits (slightly), life insurance reserves, and marketable and savings bonds.

Another type of financial claim—omitted from the tabulation because it is not of the same nature of liquidity—is the reserves of pension funds. Contributions to these funds have grown rapidly in the postwar environment, and in 1966 alone the reserves of insured, noninsured, and governmental funds increased by over $13 billion to $167.1 billion. They thus exceed each of the categories tabulated above, except common and preferred stock holdings. They have grown by 83.4 per cent since 1956.

By the end of 1966, financial asset holdings of individuals exceeded $1,350 billion, against which existed financial liabilities of mortgage, consumer, and security debt of $307 billion, leaving net equity of individuals of over $1,000 billion.

Regional Importance of Savings Banks

When viewed in the geographical areas in which mutual savings banks exist, the competitive position of these banks is much more important than it is nationally. Taking all of the 18 mutual savings bank states, deposits in these banks, savings and loan capital, and time deposits of commercial banks aggregated $153.2 billion at the end of 1965, which represented slightly over half (51.6 per cent) of the savings held in these three forms nationally. In this half of the deposit-type savings market, the savings banks held $52.4 billion (34.2 per cent), commercial banks held $59.4 billion (38.8 per cent), and savings and loan associations held $41.4 billion (27 per cent). Thus, in the 18 states in which they are chartered, savings banks held approximately the same volume of time deposits as did commercial banks and significantly more than savings and loan associations.[9] In these 18 states, which of course represent 100 per cent of savings bank deposits, 41 per cent of commercial bank time deposits and 36.3 per cent of savings and loan capital.

The regional importance of the savings banks is further emphasized by confining similar comparisons to the three major savings bank states, New York, Massachusetts, and Connecticut. On a relative basis, savings banks are as important in some

9. The measure of commercial bank deposits here is the time deposits of individuals, partnerships, and corporations. This figure overstates considerably the savings of individuals in this form. "Business-type" time deposits approximated $16 billion in 1965.

other New England states, but these three states have roughly 80 per cent of all savings bank deposits, with over half of the total in New York State. In these three states, as of the end of 1965, savings banks held $42.5 billion of deposits, compared to $23.6 billion for commercial banks' time deposits and $10.4 billion for savings and loan associations. Thus, the savings banks held more than the other two intermediaries combined.

In spite of these more favorable comparisons, the position of the savings banks has eroded somewhat even in the mutual savings bank states. In the decade from 1955 to 1965, commercial banks increased their time deposits more rapidly than did savings banks in each year except 1956, while the savings and loan associations increased by greater amounts in the first but not the second half of the decade. Taking the longer period 1950–65, savings banks gained $33.4 billion, commercial banks $42 billion, and savings and loan associations $34.6 billion in these states. In the three major savings bank states, however, the increases in deposits were $26.8 billion for savings banks, $18.6 billion for commercial banks, and $8.4 billion for savings and loan associations. While the proportion of new savings flows captured by the savings banks remained below the proportion of savings deposits already held, the trend during the 1960's suggests that the erosion of their position may be approaching an end. The proportion of new savings flow captured by the savings banks in the 18 savings bank states rose constantly after it dipped to 22.9 per cent in 1960 from 25.7 per cent in 1959. In the years 1961–64, the proportion rose each year—23.5 per cent, 25.4 per cent, 28.1 per cent, and 32.5 per cent—but it fell back to 23.7 per cent in 1965 in the face of rising yields and aggressive commercial bank competition for funds and lower subsequently.

In the savings bank states, as well as nationally, the first half of the current decade witnessed a considerable rise in the proportion of new savings flows going into deposit-type institutions. In the savings bank states, gains of savings banks, commercial banks, and savings and loan associations in the aggregate exceeded $5 billion for the first time in 1957; they reached a temporary high point of $7.1 billion in 1958. After two years of lower figures, deposit gains reached $8.2 billion in 1961 and climbed to $15.2 billion in 1965. Nationally, the flow of funds into the assets included in the Securities and Exchange Commission data on saving increased from $21.6 billion in 1960 to a high of $57.5 billion in 1965; from the boom year of 1959 the increase was from $32.9 billion. Gross financial saving declined to $46.1 billion in 1966, about the same as in 1963. Between 1959 and 1965, savings in these forms increased 74.7 per cent, while the flow of savings into savings deposits and shares rose 130 per cent. Fluctuations in the flow of credit and equity market securities have been significant, as may be seen in Table 4–5. This flow reached $10.1 billion in 1959, the year of the "magic fives" and historically high market yields, while the following year the net flow was negative. In the turbulent markets of 1966 direct investment in securities reached a record $15.7 billion. Contractual savings of the insurance and pension type rose at a relatively stable pace.

TABLE 4-5[10]

FLOWS OF SAVINGS, 1959–66

(BILLIONS OF DOLLARS)

Year	Time and Savings Deposits and Shares	Pension Reserves	Life Insurance Reserves	Currency and Demand Deposits	Securities	Total
1959	10.7	8.6	2.9	.6	10.1	32.9
1960	13.1	8.5	3.6	−2.5	−1.0	21.6
1961	18.3	8.7	3.8	.4	1.1	32.2
1962	24.8	9.3	4.3	2.8	−.4	40.8
1963	23.3	10.2	4.5	6.8	1.6	46.4
1964	23.6	9.5	4.8	7.0	7.0	53.9
1965	22.6	12.7	5.3	10.0	4.9	57.5
1966	16.4	13.0	4.4	−3.3	15.7	46.1

10. Based on Securities and Exchange Commission data. Time and savings deposits and shares include savings banks, commercial banks, savings and loan associations, and credit unions. Pension reserves include private insured and noninsured and governmental. Securities include savings bonds.

Savings Flows

These data suggest that the relative flows are responsive to a variety of influences. The total flows appear to be responsive to changes in the level of income, while the relative flows respond to the attractiveness of competing assets. This latter relationship is illustrated in Chart 4–3.

Savings bankers have long recognized the sensitivity of deposit inflows to competitive factors. Until the prolonged recovery beginning in early 1961, absolute amounts of deposit gains could be plotted with the spread in yields between (for example) three- to five-year Treasury securities and savings bank interest rates with a high degree of correspondence. During the five years 1960–64, however, deposits and annual gains trended upward persistently, while the yield spread did not decline on balance as had been the typical development in preceding recoveries. (More recent developments are discussed later.) During this period heavy deposit inflows into deposit-type intermediaries kept downward pressure on market rates, except for the shortest-term rates. Competitive pressures, including increases in rates permitted under Regulation Q, kept upward pressure on dividend rates. The rise of deposit gains during the recovery raised the question whether such gains did not now depend more upon income than on yield differentials.

However, if deposit gains are thought of as percentage, rather than absolute, increases for the year, a high correspondence between such gains and the yield spread is apparent for the whole period 1947–66. Deposit changes as percentages of deposits at the beginning of the year are plotted with the spread between the average rate on three- to five-year Treasury securities and dividends paid in Chart 4–4 (see page 134). In only two years do the directions of the curves diverge. In both 1951 and 1964 the yield spread decreased, but deposit gains were larger than they were the year before. In both years incomes were unusually high and the yield spread was rather small. Also, by immediately preceding historical standards, interest rates were considered to be relatively high. In 1964, the reduction of personal income tax

Chart 4–3

Net New Money, Deposit Change, and Yield Spread

1947 – 66

Mutual Savings Banks

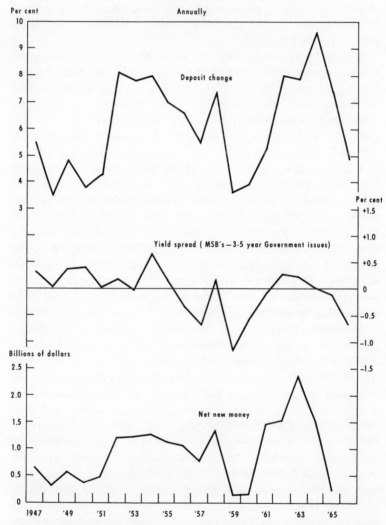

Sources of data: National Association of Mutual Savings Banks and Board of Governors of the Federal Reserve System

rates and the maturity of the "magic fives" were additional factors.

If the effect of interest credited to accounts is eliminated by considering only the net new money (difference between amounts deposited and amounts withdrawn), great variations in the amount of net new money are found. The smallest amount was $137 million in 1959, when withdrawals were greater than in any previous year and were exceeded by new deposits by only this amount. In that year, deposits grew primarily because of $1.095 billion of interest credited. Prior to 1959, the largest inflow of new money had been in 1958, when new deposits were virtually as large as in 1959 but withdrawals were considerably less. After 1959, net new money increased each year until 1964, when it reached $2.3 billion, with records in both deposits and withdrawals. Although the absolute amount of net new money has fluctuated greatly, and in a few years has barely been a positive amount, the direction of change in every year was the same as that of total deposit gains, with a small exception in 1956. Interest credited has risen every year in the 1947–66 period; in seven years, including 1965 and 1966, net deposit gains were smaller than in the preceding year. In each of these seven years net new money was also smaller and caused the decline from the preceding year. Only in 1956, when there was a slight decline in net new money, did interest credited lead to a deposit gain slightly larger than that of the preceding year. Thus, fluctuations in net deposit gains are primarily the result of variations in net new money.

1965 and 1966

The unusually tight money market of 1966 and its development beginning in 1965 further illustrate some of these relationships. There is a measure of coincidence in the fact that the most restrictive conditions to characterize money and capital markets since the Great Crash of 1929 came in the sesquicentennial year of the savings banks. The high rates brought about in securities markets by the restraining actions of the Federal Reserve System in early and mid-1966 led many holders of savings funds to bypass intermediaries and to invest directly. This process went so far as to lead to the coining of the term "disintermediation" to describe it. Flow of funds data indicate that financial intermediaries supplied less than 30 per cent of total funds raised in 1966, in contrast to their share of more than 50 per cent throughout the long recovery period.

Credit flows reached record levels in the first half of 1966, and were maintained in the face of restrictions imposed by the Federal Reserve with increasing severity after late 1965.[11] Business demands for external financing expanded rapidly as a result of investment in fixed assets and inventory build-up and because of accelerated tax payments. At the same time, government demands for funds expanded and were evidenced by sales of both Agency obligations and certificates of participation. From a level of $76.7 billion in 1965, credit and equity funds were flowing at an annual rate of $85.4 billion in the first half of 1966. Although flows declined in all other segments of the market, increases in corporate and federal borrowing accounted for the increase.

The great demands for funds, pressing on supplies limited by Federal Reserve actions, forced interest rates up to levels above those reached in the early 1930's. A liquidity climax was reached in August and September, 1966, when securities markets were clogged by corporate borrowers and commercial banks seeking funds for loan expansion and deposit losses. The market yield on three-month Treasury bills averaged 3.95 per cent in 1965 and rose to 5.36 per cent in September, 1966; three- to five-year issues went from a 1965 average of 4.22 per cent to a September, 1966, figure of 5.62 per cent; long-term Treasurys reached 4.80 per cent in August and Báa corporates averaged over 6 per cent from September through December.

Federal Reserve actions were marked by use of Regulation Q as a weapon of monetary restriction during this period. The Federal Reserve System aimed particularly at reducing the volume of funds flowing to business and succeeded in reducing the proportion of total credit and equity funds supplied by commercial banks from more than one third, the average for 1961–65, to

11. See Board of Governors, *Annual Report for 1966*, pp. 43 *et. seq.*

less than one fourth. Throughout the expansion, Regulation Q ceilings had been raised as necessary to permit commercial banks to remain competitive for time deposits and certificates. The fourth increase came in December, 1965, when banks were permitted to pay 5.5 per cent for time accounts other than savings deposits, an increase from 4.5 per cent (4 per cent for those of less than 90 days). At the same time, the discount rate was raised from 4 per cent to 4.5 per cent. While there are suggestions that the Board of Governors may have thought they were virtually eliminating the ceiling by raising it to 5.5 per cent, new offering rates moved up to the new ceiling over the first half of the year. In the first quarter commercial banks were obtaining funds sufficient to expand bank credit at a rate of 9 per cent. Restrictions on expansion of bank reserves led member banks to increase their borrowing from the Federal Reserve System, and net borrowed reserves reached $250 million by April.

Credit demands continued to mount, bank credit continued to expand, and the Federal Reserve System became more restrictive as summer approached. In June the Board of Governors indicated a desire to discourage competition for time deposits by raising slightly the reserve requirements for time deposits—from 4 per cent to 5 per cent on those deposits in excess of $5 million at each member bank. By this time, the competition from commercial banks paying 5.5 per cent was leading to greatly reduced inflows of funds at savings banks and savings and loan associations, with accompanying shortages of funds for mortgage loans. In August the Board announced a further increase in the reserve requirement to 6 per cent to take effect in September. Shortly thereafter (September 1) the presidents of the reserve banks sent publicized letters to the member banks, requesting the banks to restrict the expansion of business loans rather than continuing their sales of municipal securities and offering relaxation of the usual rules at the discount window to those banks that complied.

The final steps were taken in late September when the Board reduced the Regulation Q ceiling on certificates of less than $100,000 to 5 per cent. This reduction followed a considerable increase in the issuance of "consumer-type" certificates by commercial banks as they met increasing difficulties in selling larger corporate certificates in the face of market rates at or above 5.5 per cent. These smaller certificates largely replaced regular savings deposits at commercial banks, but they at least permitted the commercial banks to maintain their total deposit levels while funds were being diverted from savings institutions either to commercial bank certificates or directly to market securities. Enabling legislation was passed at this time to permit the Board, the Federal Home Loan Bank Board, and the Federal Deposit Insurance Corporation to establish for the first time interest rate ceilings for commercial banks, savings and loan associations, and savings banks. With certain regional exceptions, where savings institutions had been paying higher rates, the ceiling rate on deposits became 5 per cent except for the 4 per cent rate on regular savings deposits at commercial banks.

, Definite signs of slowing of the expansion late in the year reduced credit demands. Funds supplied to credit and equity markets, which had been at an annual rate of $85.4 billion in the first half of the year, fell to a rate of $62.9 billion for the second half. Although the Treasury sold $5.1 billion of direct obligations, sales of Agency obligations and participation certificates fell considerably more, and private and municipal demands also decreased. For the full year, the net flow of funds was $73.4 billion, down from $76.7 billion in 1965. In conformity with these developments interest rates began to recede rapidly, and by the year-end rates offered by commercial banks and savings institutions were again competitive.

Savings Bank Deposits in 1966

Several aspects of the behavior of deposits at savings banks during the year of spectacular monetary restraint are notable. As may be seen from Table 4-6, the net deposit gain for the year was nearly $2.6 billion in spite of the rate pressures on savings institutions. The gain was considerably less than the record gain in 1964 and also well below the gain in 1965. Net new money virtually disappeared for the year as a whole and at $224 million was reminiscent of the 1959 and 1960 figures. Inflowing deposits, however, did at least exceed amounts withdrawn in spite of the attractions of commercial bank certificates and market yields. The larger amount of interest credited in 1966 accounted for the bulk of the deposit gain. This amount reflected both higher interest rates and a higher deposit base. The surprising aspect of the deposit figures is that amounts deposited—$16 billion—reached record heights. Amounts withdrawn—$15.8 billion—were also at record levels. It appears that while some depositors were withdrawing funds in large volume for placement elsewhere the general competition for funds was attracting deposits to the savings banks in equal volume.

TABLE 4-6

DEPOSIT CHANGES, 1963–66

(MILLIONS OF DOLLARS)

Year	Amounts Deposited	Amounts Withdrawn	Net New Money	Interest Credited	Net Deposit Gains	Per Cent Gain
1963	12,230	10,691	1,539	1,716	3,255	7.9
1964	14,165	11,847	2,319	1,918	4,237	9.6
1965	14,587	13,063	1,525	2,057	3,582	7.4
1966	16,018	15,795	224	2,333	2,557	4.9

Table 4–7, showing monthly changes in deposits, suggests reasons for the timing of some of the changes. The excess of withdrawals over new deposits in April, 1966, was another record and followed the crediting of interest at the end of March for which depositors presumably waited before making withdrawals. Withdrawals usually are heavy in April for income-tax payments. This experience led the banks to raise dividend rates, especially in New York City, as of July 1. Following this increase the situation improved, although both amounts deposited and amounts withdrawn monthly tended to be above the levels of 1965 in such a way that net new money remained smaller than in 1965. However, the gain in December, 1966, exceeded that of December, 1965. It is notable that the improvement began prior to the peak of market rates in August and September, and although there was a net outflow in September it was relatively

small. With the benefit of interest credited, December established the largest monthly deposit gain on record consisting of
$101 million of new money and $559 million of interest.

TABLE 4-7

MONTHLY DEPOSIT ACTIVITY, 1965–66

(MILLIONS OF DOLLARS)

| | 1965 | | | 1966 | | |
	Amounts Deposited	Amounts Withdrawn	Net New Money	Amounts Deposited	Amounts Withdrawn	Net New Money
Jan.	1,607	1,319	287	1,814	1,670	144
Feb.	994	783	211	1,103	925	179
Mar.	1,155	986	169	1,198	1,235	− 37
April	1,347	1,480	−132	1,363	1,820	−457
May	1,009	854	155	1,141	1,060	81
June	1,171	1,118	53	1,153	1,342	−189
July	1,515	1,377	138	1,983	1,875	108
Aug.	1,075	887	188	1,237	1,107	130
Sept.	1,056	992	65	1,126	1,187	− 61
Oct.	1,334	1,273	60	1,570	1,560	10
Nov.	1,120	879	241	1,150	934	216
Dec.	1,205	1,115	90	1,180	1,079	101
TOTAL	14,587	13,063	1,525	16,018	15,795	224

While amounts deposited in 1966 exceeded those of 1965 by
about 10 per cent, amounts withdrawn exceeded the 1965 level
by more than 20 per cent. As has been noted in previous periods
of heavy withdrawals, it might be expected that the outflow of
large deposits would lower the average deposit remaining, but
again it did not do so. During the year there was a net gain of
384,000 accounts out of 2.8 million new accounts opened, or 10
per cent more than in 1965. The average size of deposits rose
from $2,349 for all accounts and $2,888 for regular accounts in
1965 to $2,436 and $2,966 respectively at the end of 1966.[12] In
the absence of other activity, dividends would increase the average account by 4.50 per cent in 1966, or the average deposit

12. Total accounts include club, school, and other accounts.

from $2,888 to $3,018. Since the increase was actually $78 rather than $130, it does appear that the deposit and withdrawal activity taken by itself reduced the average deposit.

The ability of the savings banks to raise rates, at least to a limited degree, during 1966 and to offer the same 5 per cent rate for passbook savings as the ceiling rate on consumer-type certificates in the latter part of the year made it possible for deposits to grow by 4.9 per cent. The gain achieved by savings and loan associations nationally was only 3.3 per cent. The inflow to savings and loan associations was reduced more sharply and for a longer period than at savings banks.

Seasonal Variations

Savings bank deposits have pronounced monthly and quarterly variations. Both amounts deposited and withdrawals tend to rise in the quarterly months of January, April, July, and October. The amounts deposited presumably relate to the interest-crediting periods immediately preceding, to announcements of anticipated rates, and to receipts of income such as corporate dividends. Withdrawals relate to tax payment dates and to expenditures for holidays, vacations, and automobiles. Chart 4–5, showing quarterly data, indicates a strong tendency for amounts deposited to rise and fall in alternate quarters; that is, to rise in the first and third quarters and to fall in the second and fourth quarters. Withdrawals characteristically rise through the first three quarters, or at least the first half year, and fall in the fourth quarter. The practice of crediting interest in December (whether at other times or not) probably influences this pattern.

Cyclical Variations

Growth in deposits depends on the excess of new deposits over withdrawals plus the amount of interest credited. Net new money is shown in Chart 4–5 both as the difference between amounts deposited and withdrawn and as a separate curve at the bottom of the chart. That curve, plus that for interest credited, provides the curve for net gains in deposits. This chart indicates the sources of deposit gains after 1954. The effects stemming from the recessions of 1957–58 and 1960–61 are apparent, as are those related to monetary conditions in 1966.

It is clear that deposit gains in these recessions resulted more from smaller withdrawals than from amounts deposited. Withdrawals declined significantly in the fourth quarter of 1957 and rose only moderately in the first quarter of 1958. The recession covered roughly the second half of 1957 and the first quarter of 1958. During the recession amounts deposited were not drastically different from what they had been for more than a year, although they were somewhat higher. Net new money rose principally because of the decline in withdrawals and fell again when recovery set in.

The recession in 1960–61 shows a similar pattern. Amounts deposited quarterly were relatively stable, with the usual seasonal pattern, for the three quarters before and the three quarters after the beginning of the recession. In the last quarter of the recession they rose, as they had in 1958. During the recession, however, withdrawals fell considerably. Indeed, they had been above new deposits throughout the 1959 boom but fell well below them during the recession. In the latter half of the recession both new deposits and withdrawals rose rapidly but with a net inflow. In the first quarter of recovery in 1961 the net inflow disappeared temporarily.

Thus, savings deposits rose in these periods of recession, as they had in the two earlier postwar recessions not described here. During the recovery of 1958–59, net gains in deposits declined steadily, with the exception of only one quarter. Withdrawals rose much more rapidly than did amounts deposited during the recovery and boom, and by the second quarter of 1959 they began to exceed amounts deposited. Thus, net new money was negative for the four quarters ending with the third quarter of 1960.

The pattern for deposit growth prior to the long recovery that began in 1961 was consequently that savings deposits grew in recession, largely because of smaller withdrawals, and grew much more slowly in recovery as withdrawals increased relative to new deposits. It is notable that in the subsequent long recovery withdrawals continued their upward trend, but amounts deposited rose even faster, providing increasing amounts of net new money and net deposit gains through 1964, after which deposit gains grew smaller.

Annual Changes

The behavior of deposits both before and after 1960 seems to be explainable by fundamental and traditional influences as well as by random occurrences. Net gains in deposits have fluctuated between 3.6 per cent (1959) and 9.1 per cent (1964—and higher only in 1946). These gains are based on average deposits for the year; gains from year end to year end are correspondingly higher (see note to Table 4–8). While these annual changes fluctuate over a wide range, they result from relatively much smaller changes in amounts deposited and withdrawn. Table 4–8 shows that amounts deposited have ranged from a high of 30.9 per cent of average deposits to a low of 26.9 per cent in 1960, or a difference of only 4 per cent of deposits. Amounts withdrawn have ranged between 29.7 per cent in 1966 and 24.8 per cent in 1958, a range of only 4.9 per cent. Sometimes the two variables have moved in the same direction, minimizing the effect on net new money. Equally often they have moved in opposite directions, resulting in more significant changes in deposits. Net new money has been as much as 5.6 per cent of average deposits in 1952 and 5 per cent in 1954 and 1964, and as little as about one half of one per cent of average deposits in 1959, 1960, and 1966.

Defined broadly, saving has fluctuated with income. Households have tended to devote relatively stable fractions of income to consumption and saving. The assets acquired with savings, however, tend to change with business prospects and relative yields. During periods of recession, market yields tend to be driven down by monetary policy measures, while deposit-type intermediaries still hold assets acquired in preceding years of higher interest rates. As a result, yield differentials move in

Chart 4-4

Rate of Change in Deposits, Average Yield on 3-5 Year Government Issues.
and Average Mutual Savings Bank Interest Rate

1947—66

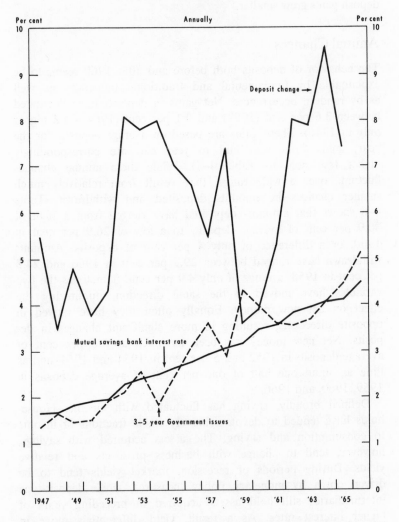

*Sources of data: National Association of Mutual Savings Banks and Board of Governors
of the Federal Reserve System*

favor of intermediaries. In periods of recovery yields on marketable securities rise, while earnings and rates paid by intermediaries lag because of the long-term nature of their assets. Yield differentials shift in favor of marketable securities.

Chart 4-5

Quarterly Deposit Data
1955– 66

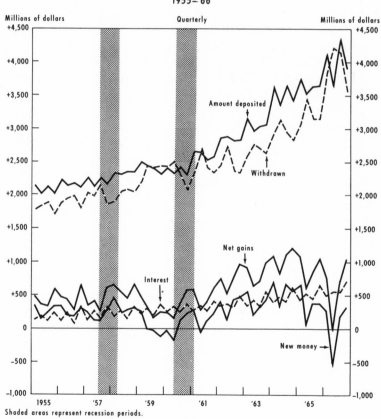

Shaded areas represent recession periods.

Source of data: National Association of Mutual Savings Banks

During periods of unemployment and weaker markets for consumer durable goods, some savers are tempted to emphasize liquidity. For the more sophisticated, common stocks become less attractive and marketable bonds are higher in price. The data on savings bank deposits suggest that such savers do not increase their deposits with new funds so much as they postpone withdrawals. When recovery takes place, market yields improve, common stock prices advance, and withdrawals are stepped up to make purchases of consumer durables and securities. In terms of dollar amounts it might appear that this pattern was broken after 1960, but in terms of amounts relative to existing deposits this conclusion is not obvious. Net new money has risen, but it bears about the same relation to deposits as in previous recoveries. The high ratio in 1964 was exceeded in the prosperous years of 1952 and 1953.

Chart 4-6

Number of Regular Accounts and Average Size

1955—66

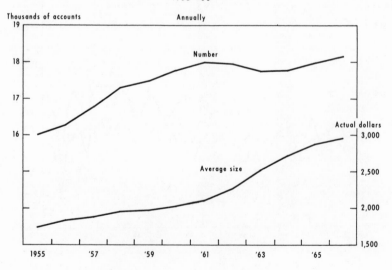

TABLE 4-8[13]

RATIOS OF DEPOSIT ACTIVITY,
REGULAR ACCOUNTS, 1947–66

	Amounts Deposited	Amounts Withdrawn	New Money	Interest	Net Gain
1947	29.8	26.1	3.7	1.7	5.4
1948	28.8	27.0	1.8	1.6	3.5
1949	28.1	25.2	2.9	1.7	4.7
1950	29.0	27.1	1.9	1.8	3.7
1951	29.1	26.6	2.5	1.8	4.2
1952	30.7	25.1	5.6	2.2	7.8
1953	30.6	25.4	5.2	2.3	7.5
1954	30.4	25.4	5.0	2.6	7.7
1955	30.9	26.8	4.1	2.6	6.7
1956	30.1	26.4	3.7	2.7	6.4
1957	28.9	26.4	2.5	2.8	5.4
1958	28.9	24.8	4.1	3.0	7.2
1959	28.3	27.9	.4	3.2	3.6
1960	26.9	26.4	.5	3.4	3.9
1961	28.1	26.5	1.6	3.6	5.2
1962	28.9	25.2	3.7	3.9	7.7
1963	28.7	25.1	3.6	4.0	7.6
1964	30.6	25.6	5.0	4.1	9.1
1965	29.0	26.0	3.0	4.1	7.1
1966	30.1	29.7	.4	4.5	4.8

Note: Ratios of annual totals to averages of beginning-of-year, mid-year and end-of-year deposits. The ratios thus differ from those based on deposits at the beginning of the year. The percentage for net gain was taken from basic source of data and may not add exactly to the sum of new money and interest because of rounding.

One would assume that the response to changes in yield spreads would be mainly by larger depositors. It is no doubt true that large deposits of individuals and nonprofit organizations are more sensitive to alternatives than are most small deposits. However, changes in the numbers of accounts and of accounts opened and closed do not reflect this fact. If it were true that only the large accounts caused the declines in withdrawals in 1957–58 and 1960–61 and the increases in 1958–59

13. NAMSB, *Fact Books.*

and 1966 it would follow that average balances would decline when large accounts were withdrawn. However, since there has been in no full year a complete lack of net new money and since interest credited increases deposits each year, a smaller number of accounts is necessarily reflected in higher average balances. In fact, with the popularity of deposit-type assets in the 1960's, average savings account balances have risen very rapidly. The number of accounts rose constantly until 1961, after which there was a small two-year decline. The principal cause of this decline was apparently the income tax reporting requirements then going into effect. Other factors that may infrequently affect the number of accounts are occasional mergers of savings banks with commercial banks, conversions of savings and loan associations to savings banks, and opening of new branches. The data on number of accounts, however, are not such as to permit much analysis, because a single household may have several accounts in the same or in other banks. A decline in the number of accounts may reflect consolidations of family accounts as well as fewer people being served. The trends of number of accounts and average deposit are shown in Chart 4–6. It is clear that the average deposit has risen persistently, and most rapidly when the number of accounts remained fairly constant.

If the large accounts are the more volatile—an opinion that is supported by general observation—the annual growth in average deposits has nevertheless been persistent. However, the data on deposit activity also suggest that the bulk of savings bank depositors are not highly sensitive to rates and yield spreads. Although some reaction is observable, amounts deposited and withdrawn do not fluctuate wildly but remain within fairly narrow bounds. There have been instances, such as in October, 1959 and during 1966, when withdrawals were very heavy for purchases of marketable securities. Even so, amounts withdrawn were 27.9 per cent of average deposits in 1959 and 29.7 per cent in 1966, while the average withdrawal rate for the whole period 1947–66 was 26.2 per cent. Needless to say, it is on such marginal shifts that long-run deposit growth depends, and as in any market these shifts determine the price. However, compared to shifts of time deposits, particularly corporate, in and out of commercial banks, changes in savings bank funds are considerably less volatile.

Such volatility as there is also reflects the fact that the bulk of savings bank deposits is in financial centers. About 82 per cent of savings bank deposits were in 20 standard metropolitan areas in 1966.[14] In eight of these, savings banks held over half of the savings in commercial banks, savings and loan associations, and savings banks, ranging from 65.7 per cent in the Portland, Maine, area to 54.3 per cent in New York City. In four others, savings banks were the major holders of such savings. The susceptibility of savings bank deposits to pressure from monetary policy actions is suggested by the fact that in 1959 deposits grew only 2.5 per cent in New York City, while the growth in upstate New York was 5.1 per cent. The decline in deposit growth from 1958 to 1959 was very largely accounted for by the behavior of deposits in New York City particularly and other metropolitan areas in general.

Moreover, the sensitivity of savings bank deposits to financial market conditions was apparently greater in the 1966 situation than it was earlier. Areas other than New York City were less insulated from the effects of tight money in 1966 than they had been in 1959. In a majority of the major savings bank areas deposit growth declined more in 1966 than it had in 1959. Paradoxically, the larger percentage growth in 1966 as compared to 1959 and 1960 was made possible largely by the ability of the New York City savings banks to compete effectively by raising rates in mid-year, especially when commercial bank rates on certificates were later rolled back to the same level. Net deposit gains declined by 66 per cent in 1959 but by only 16 per cent in 1966 in New York City; industry-wide the decline was 47 per cent in 1959 and only 29 per cent in 1966, in spite of the fact that declines were larger in most areas outside New York City. This shift is further reflected in the fact that, while the savings banks in total had a slight deposit inflow in both 1959 and 1966, about 40 per cent of the banks had net outflows in 1966 as against about 30 per cent in 1959.[15] Savings and loan accounts, relatively unaffected in 1959, were also much more active in 1966.

14. NAMSB, 1967 *Fact Book*, p. 38.
15. NAMSB *Annual Report*, 1967, pp. 10-11.

Regression Analysis of Deposit Changes

Further analysis of changes in savings bank deposits suggests that the effects of factors influencing deposits are concealed in aggregating data. For example, it is clear that when a single savings institution raises its deposit rate it tends to draw funds from its competitors in the community. If all competitors raise their rates at the same time, however, the change in the total inflow for all may be rather small. Similarly, if commercial banks raise their rates ahead of an increase by savings institutions the total inflow may rise, but it may slow down for the savings institutions. When time and savings deposit growth for commercial banks and savings institutions is aggregated, a relationship between growth rates and yield spreads with three- to five-year Treasurys is apparent, as in Chart 4–7.[16] However, the

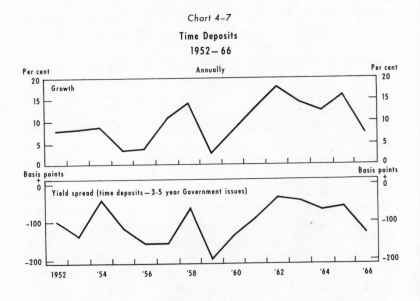

Chart 4–7

Time Deposits

1952– 66

Source of data: Board of Governors of the Federal Reserve System

16. "Monetary Policy and Economic Activity," *Federal Reserve Bulletin,* May, 1967, p. 707.

combined growth rate slowed down for 1964, which was the record inflow year for savings banks, and increased in 1965, when savings bank growth slackened.

Regression equations have been calculated to measure the relationship between changes in income and changes in deposits for the period 1947–65. During this period the average quarterly net deposit inflow at savings banks was $238.3 million, and the average disposable income at seasonally adjusted annual rates, $298.3 billion. The resulting equation is $Y = -29 + .895X_1$, where Y is net new money in millions and X_1 is income in billions. The simple correlation coefficient is .42 and the explained variation (R^2) is only 18 per cent. This low figure presumably reflects the fact that the income data are national, while the deposit data are regional and, in fact, largely local. Allowance for seasonal adjustment factors growing in proportion to the growth of disposable personal income yields the following equation:

$$Y = -17 + 1.18X_1 - .71X_2 - .39X_3 - .19X_4 \text{ where:}$$

When Y is first quarter data, X_2 through $X_4 = 0$;

when Y is second quarter data, $X_2 = $ disposable personal income;

when Y is third quarter data, $X_3 = $ disposable personal income; and

when Y is fourth quarter data, $X_4 = $ disposable personal income.

The multiple correlation coefficient is .60 and the explained variation is 36 per cent, or twice that when disposable personal income alone is used. The seasonal adjustment factors are also important in absolute size. Their effect is to change the apparent relationship between income and net inflow each quarter in the following fashion: From the first to the second quarter, instead of $1.18 million of deposit inflow being associated with $1 billion of income change, the deposit inflow is $.47 million; from the second to the third quarter, the change is from $.47 million to $.79 million; from the third to the fourth quarter, from $.79 million to $.99 million; and from the fourth to the first quarter, from $.99 to $1.18.

Over the period considered, surprisingly little relationship is

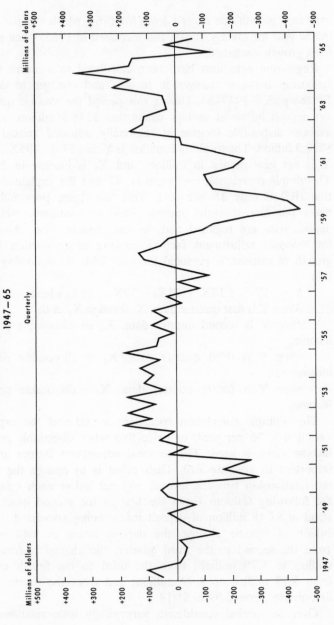

Chart 4-8

Deviations of Actual from Expected Deposit Gains

1947–65

Quarterly

found between deposit changes and the yield spread after consideration is given to seasonal factors. The apparent reason is that increases in deposit rates have frequently gone into effect in the first quarter, and consequently the yield spread has been high at the time of a seasonal net inflow. Frequently the yield spread has been high in the first quarter and declined through the other quarters. Since the net inflow tends to be large in the first quarter even when this yield spread relationship has not existed, the seasonal influence obscures the influence of the yield spread.

Chart 4–8 has been prepared to compare the actual with the expected net deposit inflow on the basis of income after adjustment for seasonal effects, the expected flow being the zero line. In the three years 1947–49, the expected and actual net inflows were close together except for the third quarter of 1948. In 1950 and 1951, actual net inflows were below expected inflows, but remained above them until the tight money situation in 1956–57. The inflow in 1958 and the outflow of 1959, previously described, are clearly discernible. The relatively rapid growth of 1962–64 is also apparent; reasons for this actual level of net deposit inflow above that expected on the basis of disposable personal income have been suggested earlier. These divergencies suggest that the impact of factors other than income affecting deposit flows is substantial. While the effect of the yield spread is reduced over a long period of time, as a matter of statistical measurement, it remains true that a substantial spread tends to have a substantial impact. The situations in 1959 and in 1966 (the latter subsequent to the material shown in Chart 4–3) clearly indicate that funds flow out when marketable securities are sufficiently attractive and return when the spread diminishes and security holders have perhaps taken capital gains.

CHAPTER 5

Savings Banks
in the Savings Market

During their 150-year history in the American economy, mutual savings banks have become the dominant institution in the savings market, have experienced a tremendous relative decline in importance nationally and a significant relative decline regionally, and, in recent years, have shown many signs of a dramatic resurgence. The broad perspective of these changes was traced in the first three chapters. In the developments traced there, can be found some of the reasons for the rise and decline of the industry and for its current efforts to regain its former importance.

Decline in Market Share

The philanthropic origin of savings banking—basic to the later developments of the institution—is not synonymous with other characteristics, such as the mutual principle and trustee control, but was consistent with and determined them in the early days. Since the first savings banks were founded for the purpose of providing the industrious poor with a means of amassing some protection against poverty, they were naturally organized in a manner similar to other philanthropic institutions. The civic leaders who established the first savings banks in the eastern seaboard cities were the same citizens who established hospitals, orphanages, and other eleemosynary institutions such as the

American Philosophical Society in Philadelphia and the Society for Prevention of Pauperism in New York.

As the center of industrial activity spread westward, the reasons that had been behind the founding of savings banks in the East did not exist in the newly expanding areas. With a few notable exceptions, new savings banks were not founded outside the original area, while in the older section those established before or shortly after the Civil War were adequate. Well before 1900, the philanthropic motive for establishing a new savings bank was no longer the compelling one, and the few established after the Civil War were motivated more by prestige, opportunities for employment, or relationship to other financial institutions. In newer sections of the country these motives, coupled with the need for mortgage credit, more often led to the formation of building and loan associations, which were sometimes organized by those primarily interested in the construction business.

Thus, prior to the expansion of commercial banking into the savings account market, mutual savings banks had little competition in the cities and towns of New England and New York; in the rest of the country, however, where liquid savings were small, they were handled by state banks and trust companies and building and loan associations. At that time roughly two thirds of the savings account business was in the hands of the savings banks. The establishment of the Federal Reserve System and the distinction for reserve purposes between demand and time deposits, as well as relaxation of prohibitions on mortgage lending by commercial banks, brought about a rapid increase in the commercial banks' share of the savings market. Furthermore, in the decades from 1890 to 1930, many new building and loan associations were formed.

It was a natural development that some of the trustees of the savings banks did not look upon these developments with alarm. Although new savings banks were not being formed for philanthropic purposes and the number of savings banks was gradually shrinking, there was still a strong residue of philanthropy in the attitude of the trustees. While the statement would be too strong to be universally true, there was undoubtedly a feeling among many of the leading citizens who served on boards of trustees that as other institutions grew up to serve the saver there was no reason for savings banks to resist the trend toward a decline in their relative importance. As Professor Roger Murray has pointed out,[1] the same citizens who acted as trustees of hospitals and orphanages would welcome a decline in the need for these institutions and would see similar progress in the declining relative need for the savings banks. The general conservatism with which savings banks were managed—whereby, for example, bonds purchased at premiums were immediately written down to par—and the long-standing pride in the safety record of the banks are consistent with this unaggressive attitude. Furthermore, it was sometimes the case that a savings bank trustee was, as well as a trustee of other philanthropic organizations, a director of a commercial bank and could not, therefore, be expected to be alarmed over the relative rise of commercial banks in the thrift field.

Nevertheless, it is the nature of a savings institution to grow by at least as much as the interest credited from year to year, so that the decline of the savings banks was relative as measured by their share of the market. Consequently, while other institutions grew much faster, it is still true that the savings banks attained assets of $10 billion by 1930, although their holdings of time and savings deposits had fallen below one third of the total. They were still dominant in their historical region. A New England trustee, therefore, had little reason to think of attempting to establish a savings bank in the Middle West; his institution was performing its historic function, but the need was not apparent elsewhere.

The continuation of the past was evident also in the relatively passive approach of savings banks to expanded powers of lending or branching. Innovations came from time to time but apparently as much from the impetus of borrowers (as, for example, railroads and public utilities) as of the banks. The sad state into which the insurance industry fell and the public interest aroused by the Armstrong investigations in New York State did not impel the savings banks to offer a substitute on a wide scale.

1. In lectures to students at the Graduate School of Savings Banking.

The efforts of Justice Brandeis led to permissive legislation in Massachusetts, but New York State savings banks did not obtain the right to sell savings bank life insurance until many years later.

Opportunities in the 1930's

The depression of the 1930's presented to the savings bank industry an opportunity that, for reasons that were then controlling, it did not grasp. While failures were widespread among commercial banks and building and loan associations, they were amazingly rare among mutual savings banks. The long record of conservatism and safety of the savings banks stood them in excellent stead during the hectic days before the banking moratorium, and their deposits actually rose each year during the 1930's, with the exception of 1933, when they fell only slightly. Many savings banks were in serious difficulties; railroad and other bonds were in default and low in price, while delinquent mortgages and foreclosed real estate rose to unprecedented heights. Some savings banks merged with others, but the general lack of liquidation of savings bank deposits permitted the banks to continue to operate.

One of the most severely depressed areas of the economy in the 1930's was the housing industry. It was therefore natural for the federal government to seek ways to restore construction and a flow of mortgage funds. It was also natural to look to the mutual savings banks as the logical instrument for attaining this goal, because they were in the soundest condition of any of the banking institutions. Just what steps were taken prior to the introduction and passage of the Home Loan Bank legislation are difficult to document, but it appears that the eventual plan to establish new thrift institutions with federal charters and to stimulate mortgage flows through deposit insurance would have been built on the structure of the 518 savings banks then existing had they so desired.

The home mortgage system of the country was prostrate. It became a matter of administration direction to the Chairman of the Federal Home Loan Bank Board that something should be done about it;

some vehicle should be created to revive the home mortgage market throughout the country. The mutual savings bank industry was first approached to see whether it would be interested and would sponsor the development of a system of Federal mutual savings and mortgage institutions. They were not interested. Then the savings and loan associations had their opportunity. Up to then, the idea of a dual system in financial systems was, of course confined to the commercial banking system.[2]

Other factors bearing on the attitude of the savings bankers at the time include the fact that savings and loan association executives were also, by and large, not favorably inclined to a federal system. Recommendations for a system of federal home loan banks and for federal charters for savings and loan associations were rejected by those attending a national conference in Philadelphia in 1931. Further, it is pertinent that in those days savings bankers considered themselves closely related to commercial bankers and were generally members of and active in The American Bankers Association. The general withdrawal of savings bankers from the association, leaving it as the spokesman primarily for the commercial banking segment, occurred as a result of disagreement over taxation of mutual institutions in the late 1950's. Consequently, it was not surprising that savings bankers generally concurred in The American Bankers Association opposition to the proposed Home Loan Banks.[3]

Reform of Savings and Loan Business

Actually, the plight of the savings banks was not so serious that it overcame the natural reluctance to accept federal regulation, while the building and loan associations, with many institutions closed and with a widespread problem of liquidity, felt greater

2. Speech by A.D. Theobald, President, First Federal Savings and Loan Association, Peoria, Ill., at the 16th Midyear Meeting, National Association of Mutual Savings Banks, New York, December 4, 1962. Mr. Theobald was a member of the staff of the United States Savings and Loan League at the time he mentions.

3. Savings bankers generally belonged to their state and national associations of savings banks while they were members of The American Bankers Association.

pressure to seek support from this source. As described in Chapter 3, the principal support for this legislation, predating the New Deal but expanded as part of the New Deal program, therefore came from the associations, as well as from real estate groups. In the three years 1930–32, more than 400 associations, with total liabilities of about $200 million, failed; in 1933, the number of failures dropped to 88, but their liabilities in that year were $215 million. In addition, there were many "frozen" institutions which, while not closed, were unable to pay out funds to shareholders or to make loans because of lack of liquidity.

On the other hand, the savings banks escaped the liquidity problem sufficiently to stay open because of the public acceptance of the savings banks and because financial conditions in New England and New York State were less disrupted than elsewhere. In those areas there were also many fewer frozen savings and loan associations. The savings bankers consequently favored rehabilitation of their own institutions by their own efforts. They were also strongly influenced by a desire to protect the reputation of the savings banks by preventing association in the public mind with other thrift institutions that were more vulnerable to withdrawals. They benefited from relatively strong surplus positions and their ability to absorb losses. They hoped to maintain the image of the savings bank, which could have been blurred if they were lumped together in supporting, and thus suggesting the need for, the Home Loan Banks.

A bulletin distributed to savings banks by their national association after the President's Conference on Home Building and Home Ownership remarked that

. . . throughout the entire conference in Washington, considerable emphasis was placed by various speakers on the fact that building and loan associations and "savings" banks are in an "alarming" condition and that something should be done to better that situation. No attempt was made to distinguish between "mutual" savings banks and other savings banks. It is proposed, therefore, that our Association be represented at the hearings on the bills which have already been introduced in Congress, and prepare a statement for incorporation in the records to the effect that "mutual" savings banks are different from other "savings" banks, that we have no interest in the plan, and that we want to make clear the fact that "mutual" savings banks are not the institutions being referred to. . . .

The bulletin further noted: "We are of the opinion that the plan is not economically sound, since it appears to be based on a further extension of credit and the country has been suffering from an excess rather than a deficiency of credit."

The position taken by savings banks at this time is understandable in the light of their relative condition and contemporary attitudes. To experience virtually no failures while commercial banks and savings and loan associations were experiencing unprecedented difficulties necessarily created an impression of self-sufficiency in spite of the real difficulties being faced. These difficulties, however, could be met through state organizations set up to provide mutual assistance among savings banks themselves. In the climate of the mid-1930's, the opinion that the "excess of credit" that had led to the depression would have to be "worked off" before recovery could proceed was orthodox thinking. To have foreseen the postwar growth of savings institutions and mortgage markets 10 years before it began would have required clairvoyance. Both the savings banks and savings and loans were motivated by the necessity of conserving their institutions, but the condition of the savings banks did not require as drastic measures as did that of the savings and loan associations.

Postwar Revival of Savings Banking

The resurgence of the savings and loans after World War II, taking them to the $100 billion mark in savings by 1964, along with more aggressive competition from commercial banks in the savings market, created a postwar situation in which the mutual savings banks changed from a passive institution oriented toward its philanthropic past to one convinced of its role in the future. The requirements of the 1930's brought into savings banks' management new and capable people, who were less imbued than their predecessors with the tradition of passively accepting deposits and providing depositors with a "satisfactory return consistent with safety." The decline in the relative position of savings banking led to a declining ability to speak with authority before legislatures and thus to an accelerating disadvantage in the competition for savings. Even if there had been no ambition to evolve and progress with the rapidly changing postwar economy, a more dominant position was required to prevent the industry from being overwhelmed by the competition and faced with an absolute as well as relative decline when other kinds of savings media were offered to the public. The survival and well-being of the savings banks required a resurgence of activity, which in turn has required a reassessment of the role of savings banks in the modern economy.

The efforts to extend the industry, after decades during which the number of savings banks gradually declined, faced severe obstacles. The national association took an early step when it commissioned a firm of management consultants to evaluate the savings banks and their functions and to recommend changes in the operation of the banks and their association.[4] State associations commissioned studies of the banks and their prospective roles in the economy.[5] Additional studies were undertaken by the staffs of the national and state associations, including the monograph *Mutual Savings Banking,* prepared by the research department of the national association for the series written for the Commission on Money and Credit. Underlying these developments was the development of an active and capable national association. ". . . The rebirth of the national association has added a new dimension to mutual savings banking."[6] The association has provided a vehicle for the unification, strengthening and extension of the savings bank industry through the various programs adopted in the postwar period.

As a result of the Booz, Allen, and Hamilton report, the national association was restructured and redirected toward ex-

4. Booz, Allen, and Hamilton, *General Survey,* National Association of Mutual Savings Banks, 1956.

5. One example is John Lintner, *Mutual Savings Banks in the Savings and Mortgage Markets* (Cambridge, Mass.: Harvard Graduate School of Business, 1948). Other studies were made at various times in New York State and elsewhere.

6. Roger F. Murray, "Prospects for Savings Banking in the United States Economy," Address to the 46th Annual Conference of Mutual Savings Banks, Philadelphia, May 16, 1966.

pansion and modernization of the industry. Dr. Grover W. Ensley was selected as Executive Vice President, following his service as Executive Director of the Joint Economic Committee of the Congress. During the following decade the association assumed a role of leadership in developing programs for expanding depositor services, savings bank life insurance, investment and loan powers, management development, government relations, economic research, and geographic extent of the savings bank system. Impetus for the establishment of new savings banks under state charter and for federal charter legislation has stemmed largely from the national association.

The realities of politics being what they are, competitors of the savings banks have tended to resist expansion of savings bank powers granted by the several legislatures. In addition, extension of the number of savings banks runs into the problem that savings bank laws exist in only 18 states (including Alaska, which adopted such a law in 1960) and the Commonwealth of Puerto Rico (which passed a savings bank law in 1964).[7] In view of inevitable and natural opposition, the possibility of persuading the remaining states to pass chartering laws faced serious difficulties. This situation provided impetus to the revival of the idea of federal charters, although the possibility of adding new banks where state law permits has continued to receive attention.

Exercise and Expansion of Existing Powers

Certain steps have been open to the savings banks within the existing legislative framework. Additional branches, as permitted by legislative restrictions, have been opened. By mid-1966, the number of savings banks having branches had increased to 250 (out of 506 banks), with 729 branches, for a total of 1,235 offices. At the end of 1945, 85 banks had 143 branches. A considerable degree of adaptability is inherent in savings bank investment powers, which can be exploited to maximize income consistent with

7. Furthermore, a few states where savings banks exist have no provision for chartering new ones. Even in New Hampshire, charters were granted by legislative enactment rather than administrative action prior to 1965.

other objectives. The drastic increase in mortgage loans in recent years is an example, and the over-all industry figures conceal a minority of savings banks that have not conformed to the average increase. On the deposit side, it has been possible to compete more effectively with innovations such as notice accounts (on which higher interest is paid in return for imposition of notice before withdrawals can be made) and bonus accounts (which qualify for a higher rate when a program of deposits has been completed). Such classification of deposits, however, required legislative approval in most instances.

Amendments to savings bank laws have been sought aggressively in recent years. Although there is a general pattern of deposit, loan, and investment powers, provisions do vary from state to state in important respects.[8] These differences, plus those existing between savings banks and other institutions, provide incentive and argument for further change. Any detailed description here would probably soon be out of date. In general, savings banks are often restricted in deposits by limitations on the amount that can be accepted from an individual (a flat amount or percentage of deposits) and by restricting depositors to individuals and nonprofit organizations. Borrowing is restricted, sometimes to the sole purpose of paying deposits but otherwise to percentages of deposits and time limits. Restrictions on lending vary; some ten states permit unsecured personal loans, but New York State does not at the time of writing.[9] Where permissible, such loans are limited in amount and maturity. Mortgage loans are defined in terms of loan-to-value ratio, maturity, and location of property. Amendment of the New York law in 1966 brought to ten the number of states that permit savings banks to make conventional mortgage loans on out-of-state properties, although FHA and VA loans may be made in

8. As of the dates of their publication, these provisions are summarized in *Comparative Regulations of Financial Institutions,* Subcommittee on Domestic Finance, Committee on Banking and Currency, House of Representatives, 88th Congress, November 22, 1963, and *A Profile of State-Chartered Banking,* National Association of Superintendents of State Banks, Washington, D.C., 1965.

9. Maryland and Delaware follow the prudent-man rule rather than specifying assets legal for savings banks.

other states. In some states there are also ceilings on the proportion of assets that may be represented by mortgage loans, including guaranteed loans.

Similar provisions cover investments, which are generally specified by types and within types restricted to securities that meet a variety of tests. Ceilings generally prevail on the proportion that may be invested in each type. Provisions for a small proportion of assets to be held in forms left to the discretion of the banks are common. Similar provisions apply to preferred and common stocks, but the statutes vary; for example, Massachusetts permits investment in bank stocks, but New York State does not.

Provisions covering branching vary from prohibition to permission for restricted state-wide branching. In New York State branches are permitted under a complicated formula that provides for a restrictive ceiling on the number of branches and gives weight to population, location, and other factors.[10] Some states provide capital requirements for branches, and of course FDIC regulations apply when a bank seeks permission to branch. FDIC requirements are also a major factor in establishing a new bank.

Many of these provisions have been eased or modernized in recent years, and the likelihood that others will also be relaxed is great. The purpose in seeking revisions is primarily to permit the savings banks to adjust to new competitive conditions and to keep step with their competitors in offering the public products in demand as well as to generate the income necessary to pay attractive rates of interest to depositors. Specific circumstances affect individual amendments. For example, the New York State savings bankers anticipate a shortage of funds for personal loans in their state. Experience with out-of-state mortgages through FHA and VA programs has led to an interest in following with conventional loans, which is increased by the imbalance be-

---

10. In early 1966, this provision was relaxed to some extent in a general revision of banking laws precipitated by the conversion of the state's largest bank to a national bank in 1965. As part of the "package," the savings banks obtained powers to make limited out-of-state conventional mortgages and to create some additional branches.

tween deposit inflows and demands for mortgage credit. Pressure for additional branching powers often stems from population movements to suburbs outside the branching area permitted by older laws.

New Savings Banks

While branching is an obvious device to extend the scope of the savings banks, creation of new savings banks provides a different kind of problem. An existing bank, with adequate surplus, is naturally in a position to direct its growth through a branch rather than through its head office. However, the mutual type of institution faces another situation when beginning *de novo*. As noted above, no new savings bank was established for many years, since the original motivation had long since disappeared. The motivation today must stem from the existing industry collectively, in the absence of unusual circumstances, rather than from individuals motivated primarily by philanthropy. In contrast to an enterprise with capital stock, a savings bank cannot be started by investors seeking profit on their investment. The original capital funds cannot gain in value as can the stock of a new commercial bank. These funds cannot be withdrawn until retained earnings replace them. This situation has led to new industry efforts to establish new savings banks. In addition, a small number of savings and loan associations have converted to mutual savings banks.[11]

It is noteworthy that one solution to the problem of raising capital for new savings banks was provided by European experience. The Central Industry Fund was established in 1961 as a nonprofit membership corporation, and an arm of the National Association of Mutual Savings Banks, with a charter from the State of Delaware. It was modeled on similar funds in the Scandinavian countries and Great Britain. Savings banks become

---

11. There has been a very small, but interesting, reshuffling of charters. Some few savings banks have merged into commercial banks, and one fairly large savings bank, converted to a national bank. Recently a few savings and loan associations have become national banks. Where the stock type of savings and loan exists, it is more logical to convert to a commercial bank.

members by responding to requests for pledges for specific purposes. The first activity of the Fund was to assist in the formation of the Alaska Mutual Savings Bank in Anchorage. One of the first pieces of legislation adopted after Alaska became a state was a law permitting chartering of mutual savings banks. The shortage of capital there led a group of citizens familiar with savings banking to seek a charter. The FDIC estimated the potential deposits to be about $3 million after three years of operation and set a figure of $250,000 (about 8 per cent) as the required amount of capital funds; the Alaska Department of Commerce concurred in this figure. Local citizens raised half of this amount, and the Central Industry Fund provided the other half. These funds came, in turn, from 250 other savings banks.[12] Estimates of potential deposits turned out to be on the low side. The bank opened in December, 1961; it had deposits in excess of $4 million a year later and of more than $11 million at the end of three years. By the end of 1965, deposits exceeded $16 million. This deposit growth was not at the expense of existing savings and loan and bank competition, and in spite of high interest payments by usual standards, the existence of the bank brought lower mortgage loan rates in the area. In order to maintain adequate surplus accounts, it was necessary for the Alaska Mutual Savings Bank to issue debentures, which have thus become another potentially useful instrument in expanding the savings bank system.

Other developments within the confines of state charters have included the establishment of a new bank in New York State. The lack of new banks and the lack of banks in some counties of even such a strong savings bank state as New York offered savings bank competition an argument that there is no need or demand for additional savings bank facilities. The new bank in Rockland County, established in 1965, was the first savings bank in that county and the first new savings bank in the state in 35 years. In this instance a fund sponsored by the state association provided some of the original capital funds. A second savings

---

12. Additionally, savings banks contributed furniture and equipment, as well as technical assistance, and the furnishings of the bank's board room were a contribution from the savings banks in Sweden.

bank has been chartered and opened in Alaska, this one in Fairbanks. In Puerto Rico a 1964 law authorizing charters was followed by establishment of a bank in 1966. Debenture financing was used by the last named two banks. On the other side of the ledger, a small savings bank established by Danish settlers in the Virgin Islands in 1881 has recently discontinued operations as a mutual savings bank. In 1965, a bill was introduced in West Virginia to permit formation of savings banks there. Finally, as mentioned earlier, there have been a few conversions of savings and loan associations, which then merged with existing savings banks; this development has taken place mainly in the Northwest.

Efforts to Obtain Federal Charters

The difficulties of obtaining legislation in the states not now providing for savings banks, however, points to the likelihood that long strides in extending the scope of savings banking will require passage of federal chartering legislation. Thus, the opportunity available to the savings banks in the mid-1930's is now one they seek aggressively. Where the forces of adversity were insufficient, the resurgence of the savings banks has reversed their position.

Efforts directed toward federal chartering and "dual banking" for mutual savings banks began with the introduction in 1957 of a bill entitled "The National Mutual Savings Bank Act." Representative Abraham J. Multer (D, N.Y.) was the sponsor of this bill. Under its provisions, the Comptroller of the Currency was empowered to charter and regulate mutual savings banks. An important provision permitted federal and state savings and loan associations to convert to savings banks.

The National Mutual Savings Bank Act proposal was succeeded in 1960 by another bill introduced in the House by Congressman Multer and in the Senate by Senator Bush of Connecticut and Senator Sparkman of Alabama. While this bill met objections to placing authority in the office of the Comptroller, it was criticized for establishing a new three-man Federal Mutual Savings Bank Commission, which was to regulate the newly chartered institutions jointly with the FDIC. Like the original bill, it provided for conversion of savings and loan associations and for expanded powers of savings banks.

Objections to the original proposal arose from the Federal Home Loan Bank Board on grounds that funds could be diverted from mortgage markets if savings and loan associations converted to savings banks with wider investment powers. Consequently, new drafts of legislation in 1961 and 1962 shifted to the Federal Home Loan Bank Board the power to charter and to supervise, and provided that the Federal Savings and Loan Insurance Corporation—to be renamed the Federal Savings Insurance Corporation—would take over from the FDIC insurance of deposits in the new institutions.

The principal hearings on this legislation were held in 1963, when the Subcommittee on Bank Supervision and Insurance of the House Committee on Banking and Currency considered the bill introduced at that time.[13] The savings banks presented their case fully, and their arguments are summarized subsequently. The federal charter bill was opposed by the representatives of commercial banks, principally The American Bankers Association, and by the savings and loan interest, which proposed that essentially the same powers as envisioned for federal savings banks be incorporated in new legislation covering savings and loan associations.

At this time the growing competition in the savings market between commercial banks, on the one hand, and both savings banks and savings and loan associations, on the other, and political reflections of this competition in such matters as controversy over the taxation of mutual institutions, led to a drawing together of the thrift institutions. The "money crunch" of 1966

---

13. Hearings on H. R. 258, Eighty-eighth Congress, First Session, October 29, 30, and 31, 1963. Earlier in the year the full committee held preliminary hearings. Subsequent hearings were held by the Subcommittee on Bank Supervision and Insurance, especially in early 1966 (Eighty-ninth Congress, Second Session; H. R. 11508), but these were less extensive and largely reviewed the 1963 hearings.

also pointed up the desirability of broader loan and investment powers for both types of thrift institutions. By 1967, the United States Savings and Loan League had redrafted a proposed new savings and loan law, and it was apparent that this bill had much in common with the current version of the savings banks' federal charter bill. Consequently, Congressman Multer, then Chairman of the Subcommittee on Bank Supervision and Insurance, proposed that the two bills (the Federal Savings Association Act and the Federal Savings Bank Act) be merged into a single law providing for federal charters for institutions into which both savings banks and savings and loan associations might wish to convert. The resulting bill, the Federal Savings Institutions Act, stemmed from this amalgamation carried out by the National Association of Mutual Savings Banks, the United States Savings and Loan League, the staff of the Subcommittee, and the staff of the Federal Home Loan Bank Board. This bill was reported favorably by the Subcommittee and by the Banking and Currency Committee to the House in late 1967. Its provisions are summarized after the discussion of the savings banks' case for federal charters presented mainly at the 1963 hearings.

During the development of this legislative history, support for federal chartering arose from several quarters. In 1961, the Commission on Money and Credit made several specific proposals aimed at promoting economic growth and stability.[14] The Commission stated that "These recommendations stress greater mobility for investment and greater equality of opportunity for financial institutions to offer services they now provide. They would enable the financial institutions to become less specialized in investment, if they so desired." It pointed out:

A multitude of regulations promulgated by the states and the federal government now govern the kind and amounts of assets that commercial banks, savings banks, and savings and loan associations may hold. The restrictiveness of these regulations and their unequal application have handicapped these institutions in directing their

14. Commission on Money and Credit, *Report (Money and Credit; Their Influence on Jobs, Prices, and Growth),* (Englewood Cliffs, Prentice-Hall, N.J.: 1961). The quotations that follow appear on pp. 159-64.

lending into areas and uses where more profitable opportunities exist. The regulations also often discourage initiative and competition, which in turn reduce [sic] the contribution of the private financial institutions to economic growth.

Recommendations included the following:

. . . that the regulatory authorities be authorized to permit greater flexibility to savings banks and savings and loan associations to acquire a wider range of suitable long-term debt instruments. Commercial banks should be allowed the same flexibility in investing their time and savings deposits . . . that restrictions on financial institutions which prevent or impede lending over a wider geographical area than at present should be liberalized. . . .

Specifically, on the question of federal charters, the Commission noted:

At present commercial banks and savings and loan associations may obtain federal charters. Since only 17 states now provide for the establishment of savings banks, it is not possible to establish savings banks in two thirds of our states. Federal charters for savings banks would permit operation in any state, and this would stimulate competition and enterprise among financial institutions, improve the banking facilities in some communities, and perhaps encourage greater conventional mortgage lending activity in all areas.

In 1963, the Committee on Financial Institutions appointed by the President reported to him that:

Both [savings banks and savings and loan associations] perform the basic economic function of providing a relatively liquid earning asset to individual savers and investing in long-term relatively illiquid obligations, mainly residential mortgages. As financial intermediaries, these institutions are more than mere middlemen between savers and borrowers. They hold assets which savers would for the most part be unwilling to hold directly, and their liabilities have a degree of liquidity which individual borrowers would be unable to provide directly.

In attracting funds, mutual savings banks and savings and loan associations compete not only with each other but with commercial banks as savings institutions. But mutual savings banks are concentrated in the northeastern part of the country, whereas savings and loan associations and commercial banks are found in the 50 states. Charters for mutual savings banks are available in only 18 states.[15]

After reviewing the arguments of the proponents of federal charters, the Committee concluded:

The Committee is generally disposed favorably toward measures that would enhance the mobility of savings in response to investment needs, where consistent with other important objectives. Whether the establishment of new Federal mutual savings banks or the conversion of existing institutions to that form would make a major contribution to such mobility is unclear, but it would presumably tend in that direction. To the extent that the availability of Federal charters led to increased competition for savings, the public would benefit from more favorable returns on amounts saved. Moreover, although an excessive multiplication of savings institutions could threaten the solvency of existing and new institutions, this danger seems remote in view of the chartering standards that now exist. . . .

Mutual savings banks have wider investment powers than savings and loan associations and are in a better position to respond to changes in the composition of investment needs. It is argued that the opportunity to establish additional mutual savings banks, either by the chartering of new, or the conversion of existing, institutions, would provide a desirable safeguard against excessive specialization in mortgage financing by savings institutions. . . . Furthermore, savings institutions would be better able to adapt, and less vulnerable, to a relative decline in the demand for residential mortgage funds, for with broader investment powers they could supply funds for other productive uses.

The Committee concludes that voluntary Federal charters should

---

15. The Committee, sometimes called the Heller Committee, consisted of the Chairman of the Council of Economic Advisers, the Chairman of the Board of Governors of the Federal Reserve System, the Administrator of the Housing and Home Finance Agency, the Chairman of the Federal Deposit Insurance Corporation, the Director of the Bureau of the Budget, the Chairman of the Federal Home Loan Bank Board, the Comptroller of the Currency, and four members of the Cabinet: the Attorney General and the Secretaries of Agriculture, the Treasury, and Health, Education, and Welfare. This quotation is from the Committee's *Report*, p. 34.

be available for mutual savings banks, subject to adequate supervisory standards and safeguards.[16]

In January, 1966, President Johnson specifically endorsed federal savings bank legislation in his Economic Report to the Congress and recommended adoption of federal charters. He based his recommendation on protection of the public's savings, equitable regulation of financial institutions, and improved flows of funds to borrowers. The Subcommittee on Bank Supervision and Insurance held hearings again in February and March, 1966, and subsequently reported the bill favorably to the full House Committee on Banking and Currency. In his Economic Report of January, 1967, the President repeated his recommendation for "provision of Federal charters . . . to enlarge and strengthen our system of thrift institutions,"[17] and again in his Economic Report of February, 1968. The bills did not come to a floor vote during these developments, but it appeared that a significant number of Congressmen favored the legislation and that it was supported by real estate interests, most of the savings and loan business, and governmental agencies, while the principal opposition was the commercial banks.

Savings Banks' Case for Federal Charters

Legislation is proposed, defended, and opposed almost universally on the high grounds of public interest. By some peculiar coincidence the public interest, as seen by those most concerned, just happens to be concurrent with their own. Traditionally, seekers of tariff protection are motivated by their concern for employment, contractors and cement manufacturers see great public benefits in new highways, and the users of and producers of silver were in disagreement over the new silverless coins only because of their concern for a sound coinage. Thus, in the tradition of American politics, savings bankers have necessarily—and properly—presented the case for federal charters primarily in terms of benefits to the public. It does not prejudge the problem to state that an impressive case has been made. Representative Moorhead remarked at the

16. *Loc. cit.*
17. *Economic Report of the President,* January, 1967, p. 22.

conclusion of the presentation of the industry's case by Mr. Morris D. Crawford, Jr., "In the nearly five years that I have served on this committee this statement that you have made is the most scholarly, thorough, complete, and helpful statement that has ever been made to the committee." Clearly, the savings bank proponents of federal charters are convinced of the public interest in their position.[18]

The industry's case for federal charters rests primarily on the grounds of equity and fairness of regulation under dual banking, the equity and advantages to the public in permitting savings banks to compete where they are now effectively barred, and on specific claims of improved savings flows, mortgage flows, and resource allocation. Mortgage-market weaknesses in 1966, forecasts of large future demands, and introduction of the Federal Savings Institutions Act shifted emphasis to long-run mortgage flows.

Equity Argument

Equity toward the savings banks, as well as toward the public, has been argued as follows:

The federal charter effort was launched only after searching exploration revealed it to be the only feasible vehicle for achieving equality of competitive opportunity, consistent with basic industry objectives and national economic goals. . . . Simple equity requires that the benefits of dual chartering be extended to mutual savings banks. . . . In most States the weight of entrenched local competitive opposition has frustrated attempts to establish mutual savings banks. It is a fact of business life that local institutions do not generally welcome new competition. Even in the new State of Alaska, where the need for new savings facilities was patently clear, the organization of one mutual savings bank required a two-year effort . . . the draft legislation is permissive; it does not require that savings banks be established automatically whenever applications for new institutions are submitted, but at least it does enable applications to be submitted for acceptance or rejection on their

18. See the address of Dr. Grover W. Ensley to the National Savings Conference of The American Bankers Association, March 14, 1967.

merits. This would seem to be an elementary right in a competitive society, all the more so since it is a right available to all of the principal competitors of mutual savings banks.[19]

The necessity for federal charters, if mutual savings banks are to be able to expand in number and continue to modernize their powers, was suggested by Chairman Horne of the Federal Home Loan Bank Board in later testimony. After referring to the limitation of savings banks to 18 states and to the location of savings and loan associations, commercial banks, and credit unions in all states, he noted:

> The widespread distribution of these other financial intermediaries is due at least in part to the fact that they can be chartered by either Federal or State authorities. The dual system is an accepted principle in these other major areas. In this connection the truly pertinent consideration is not the desirability of the dual system in the abstract, but the fact that mutual savings banks are the only comparable group of institutions that currently do not have the option of organizing and operating under Federal jurisdiction if they wish to do so.[20]

Public Interest Arguments

The public interest argument is bolstered by specific claims of benefit from extension of the savings bank system. The conviction rests "on the record of unparalleled safety and uniquely useful service to the public achieved by the savings bank industry in nearly a century and a half of operation in this country."[21] Five areas of improvement were cited during the 1963 hearings:

    1. an increase in the volume of savings accounts in local communities and a better distribution of savings throughout the nation;

    2. a broad choice of savings facilities and greater rewards for the public's thrift;

19. *Hearings, op. cit.,* (1963) Statement of Mr. Crawford, pp. 46-47, 70, 119.
20. 1966 *Hearings,* p. 29.
21. 1963 *Hearings,* p. 47.

3. a greater flow of mortgage credit, improved efficiency of mortgage markets, and reduced costs to mortgage borrowers;

4. strengthening of the dual system of federal and state charter and supervision and improved competitive opportunity in financial markets;

5. broadened investment powers for savings institutions to enhance their flexibility of operations and lead to more efficient resource allocation in the community.

Stimulus To Thrift

Specific evidence was marshaled to support each point. The evidence cited to support the claim for a larger and better distributed flow of liquid saving was diverse.[22] "The existence of mutual savings banks stimulates thrift among individuals, both because these institutions are dedicated entirely to this purpose, and because their activities provide a competitive incentive for other types of institutions." Data suggest that savings accounts are greater, both on a per capita and on an income basis, where savings banks compete for savings. A summary of such data for 1962 submitted to the subcommittee is shown in Table 5–1. From this table it appears that holdings of savings accounts are 60.2 per cent of personal income in the ten main savings bank states and 38.1 per cent in the non-savings bank states. Per capita holdings of savings accounts are virtually double those of non-savings bank states.

TABLE 5-1

SAVINGS ACCOUNTS AND PERSONAL INCOME, 1962

Area	Total Savings Accounts (millions)	Personal Income (millions)	Per Cent	Per Capita Savings Accounts	Per Capita Personal Income
10 main m.s.b. states	$ 80,058	$132,893	60.2	$1,639	$2,720
18 m.s.b states	107,600	199,000	54.1	1,401	2,590
Non- m.s.b. states	91,035	238,924	38.1	835	2,192
United States	198,635	437,924	45.4	1,069	2,357

---

22. *Ibid.*, p. 82 *et seq.*

A study prepared for the Savings Banks Association of the State of New York showed that in 1958 per capita savings accounts ran much higher in those counties of New York State that had savings banks than in other counties. The median per capita savings account in savings banks and savings and loan associations and time deposits of commercial banks was $975 in the 28 counties having savings banks and $430 in the 27 counties without savings banks.

There are, obviously, reasons for higher rates of liquid savings in savings bank states other than the mere presence of savings banks. It appears reasonable, however, to assume that the presence of competing institutions tends to increase the volume of this disposition of income. The commodity offered by a savings institution competes for consumer dollars with commodities offered by other business establishments. It is doubtful that the propensity to save is so strong or so fixed that savings flows would be the same regardless of the existence of depositories. Where savings banks have existed for many years the public has become accustomed to using them, much as people use other available business establishments. Competition, both between savings banks themselves and between them and other intermediaries, must have at least marginal effect on the use of personal income.

Evidence supporting this view has been presented by a study conducted at the University of Chicago, which concludes that the financial structure of a community strongly influences the rate of personal saving.[23] This study found that in 13 of the leading states in terms of income and wealth, local savings were higher in the four states with mutual savings banks than in the other nine states and that the difference was significant over the 30-year period studied (1929–59). Similar conclusions followed from comparisons of metropolitan areas of similar income characteristics. The actual ratio of savings to personal income in six leading savings bank cities was 55 per cent, as compared to 40 per cent in other cities with similar income characteristics. In

23. Irving Schweiger and John S. McGee, *Chicago Banking: The Structure and Performance of Banks and Related Financial Institutions in Chicago and Other Areas*, Graduate School of Business, University of Chicago, 1961.

the savings bank cities, saving was higher than that expected on the basis of income, in terms of regression analysis, while in the other cities it was lower (in each case with minor exceptions).[24] This study concluded that ". . . the major effect of the presence of mutual savings banks was apparently to increase the total of savings in local institutions." A similar conclusion followed from study of areas where commercial banks were in competition with savings and loan associations: ". . . the increase in local savings with commercial banks in multiple office areas was not accomplished, on the average, at the expense of the local savings and loan institutions but rather from a joint realization of a greater part of the savings potential of the area."[25]

Consumer Choice and Reward

The second argument, that the public would have a wider choice of thrift institutions and be better rewarded, is supported by competitive reactions to changes in Regulation Q covering maximum rates that may be paid by commercial banks. On December 6, 1965, commercial banks were authorized to pay up to 5.5 per cent on time deposits, an increase from 4.5 per cent although the ceiling of 4 per cent on regular savings deposits was not changed, coincident with an increase in the discount rate from 4 per cent to 4.5 per cent. At this time commercial banks had begun to extend the use of certificates of deposit— originally introduced primarily to compete for large corporate balances—to smaller denominations usually called savings certificates.[26] Some commercial banks, especially in the New York City area, immediately increased the rates offered on these smaller certificates. A survey of savings bank reaction covering the period through January, 1966, showed that 141 savings banks, or 29 per cent of the 485 respondents (out of 506 banks, total), had raised rates paid at that time. Of these, 54 had prior intentions of raising rates, and 87 may be said to have acted

24. *Ibid.*, p. 45.

25. *Ibid.*, p. 50.

26. In the Midwest and South some banks had offered small certificates for many years.

defensively. Twelve of the banks raising rates did so by intro-
ducing special categories of accounts, which had recently been
authorized in Connecticut. Of the 126 banks raising rates on
regular accounts, 65 went from 4.25 per cent to 4.50 per cent,
and 37 went from 4 per cent to 4.25 per cent. Slightly over half
of the banks that increased rates were in New York State—44 in
New York City and 21 upstate—and 56 of these 65 banks went
to 4.50 per cent.

Earlier reactions to changes in Regulation Q led to increases
in rates, with the defensive reaction often on the side of commercial banks. A study made by the Federal Reserve Bank of
Cleveland at the end of 1965 concluded that ". . . the number
and importance of competing financial institutions are likely to
have played a major role in influencing the decision of bankers
to adjust rates offered to depositors."[27] This study was ad-
dressed primarily to examining the effect of bank size on rate
changes, and it covered an area where there are few savings
banks. Other Federal Reserve surveys suggest closer relationships. One published following the change in Regulation Q of
December, 1961, concluded that ". . . wide geographic differences in the proportion of banks raising rates on savings deposits
. . . may be due in part . . . to differences in the extent and
intensity of competition for savings from other financial institutions."[28] A study made by the Federal Reserve Bank of Boston
at about the same time explained that banks in Vermont did
not generally go to the full 4 per cent permitted because "most
other savings institutions (mutual savings banks and savings
and loan associations) in Vermont presently have a 3.75 per cent
rate on regular savings [and] a 3.5 per cent rate by commercial
banks is competitive."[29] In New Hampshire many banks did go
to 4 per cent. "The competition for savings deposits in New
Hampshire has been led in general by savings banks which aver-

---

27. "Survey of Changes in Interest Rates on Savings and Time Deposits,"
Economic Review, Federal Reserve Bank of Cleveland, December, 1965.

28. "Interest Rates on Time Deposits, Mid-January 1962," *Federal Reserve Bulletin,* February 1962, p. 147.

29. "Interest Rates Paid on Savings," *New England Business Review,*
Federal Reserve Bank of Boston, March 1962.

age the highest rate paid by mutual savings banks in New England." And in Maine, "Almost three fourths of the commercial banks in the Augusta area are at 4 per cent while no commercial banks in the Aroostook and Bangor area are above 3 per cent . . . the Augusta area has a heavy concentration of savings banks and savings and loan associations and the commercial banks were following their rate lead."

Mortgage Credit

A third argument for federal charters is that the flow of mortgage credit would be improved. By September, 1966, savings bank holdings of mortgages on properties in non-savings bank states had reached $13.6 billion, having increased from about $2 billion in 1954. The bulk of this increase was in federally underwritten loans, as out-of-state conventional mortgage lending was restricted, and took place in spite of other restrictions such as higher taxes on assets held in this form.[30] Very nearly all of the net gain in deposits since World War II has appeared on the asset side as mortgage loans. By the end of 1964, mutual savings banks held more FHA and VA mortgages than any other lender, and held about 30 per cent of the total in 1966 as shown in Table 5-2.

TABLE 5-2

FEDERALLY UNDERWRITTEN MORTGAGE DEBT,
BY MAIN TYPES OF HOLDERS, 1966

(MILLIONS OF DOLLARS)

	FHA	VA
Savings banks	14,394	11,340
Commercial banks	7,830	2,634
Life insurance	12,411	6,209
Savings and loan	5,266	6,150

The savings bank argument for expanded mortgage loan powers in the proposed federal charter bill, however, was not based

30. NAMSB, *Fact Book,* 1967, p. 46 and *passim.*

simply on the increase in their holdings of mortgage loans. The argument was that savings bank investment powers have been sufficiently flexible to permit this channeling of funds into the mortgage market as supply-demand relationships and yield spreads dictated, while a decline in the need for mortgage financing relative to supplies of funds could be met by slowing down the rate of mortgage lending and diverting funds to other productive uses. After 1966 the savings banks' position also includes the argument that expanded powers would lead to a larger and more stable flow of mortgage credit. Savings and loan associations are restricted mainly to residential mortgages and may take marginal loans or low-yield securities in periods of slack mortgage demands. Savings banks also have a more diversified portfolio of mortgage loans, including more multi-family and nonresidential loans. Authorization to make nationwide conventional loans would increase the flexibility of savings bank lending and improve the flow of funds to borrowing regions.[31]

In this connection, a study of the Federal Reserve Bank of Atlanta is relevant. It concluded:

Despite the apparent tendency for Southerners to spend a smaller proportion of their incomes and to save a larger part than in the past, it is unlikely that the South will be able to rely immediately

---

31. The evolution of regulation is well illustrated by a question and answer at the 1963 hearings (p. 225):

"Mr. Multer: Now, what is the reasoning behind the limitations in many states as we have it in New York, which would prohibit a savings bank from making a conventional mortgage outside of its home State except in a State that is contiguous to the home State?

Mr. Crawford: I think there is very little reasoning behind this, Congressman. I think it is a matter of evolution. Indeed when the FHA and VA loans were first authorized, New York did not permit savings banks to make those loans outside the State of New York. Then they permitted them to be made through a trustee, and finally they permitted them to be made on a nationwide direct basis.

Now, in conventional loans we have gone from similar restriction to the confines of the State of New York to now adjoining States, and I certainly hope that before too long our legislature would permit us to go nationwide on a direct basis."

(Mr. Crawford might have added that in the earlier history of the banks, the geographical lending area was less than statewide.)

solely upon its own savings to finance its capital investment. The rate of savings in the South is still below that of the rest of the United States, despite its recent upward trend. In 1964, the lower savings rate combined with the lower per capita income out of which to save thus meant that per capita holdings in the Sixth District states increased only $106, compared with a national increase of $164.

The prospect of the South's catching up completely with the rest of the nation in its level of savings thus depends upon its continued income growth, as well as upon an increase in its rate of savings. However, a rising rate of savings, insofar as it provides for capital investment, may help stimulate that income growth.

A similar observation applies to the California mortgage market:

The interregional mobility of funds would be improved if proposed legislation before Congress for the granting of federal charters to mutual savings banks were adopted. Among other things, the legislation provides for nation-wide acquisition of conventional mortgage loans on a participation basis with other lenders. At the present time, mutual savings banks can acquire California mortgages only if they are FHA-insured or VA-guaranteed.[32]

Dual Charter System

The remaining arguments—strengthening the dual charter system and improving resource allocation—overlap the others and have been touched upon. The argument based on strengthening the system of dual charters is essentially that when financial institutions have a choice of charters, both chartering agencies are stimulated to keep regulations up to date and to seek legislative improvements, while in the absence of choice the attention of regulatory authorities tends to be concentrated on those institutions that have a choice, and it is more difficult to reach the ear of the legislature. The history of both the commercial banks and the savings and loan associations that tend to have roughly the same proportion of assets in state and federal sys-

32. Leo Grebler and Eugene F. Brigham, *Savings and Mortgage Markets in California;* (Pasadena: California Savings and Loan League, 1963), pp. 179-80.

tems over the years suggests that neither system tends to dominate the other. An additional facet of the argument is that a
system of savings institutions, operating primarily in capital
markets, should be protected from absorption into the commercial banking system and that a dual charter system would help
to provide this independence. A related facet—that the mutual
type of institution merits encouragement—is discussed at a later
point.

Resource Allocation

The argument relating to resource allocation is essentially that
an intermediary with wide and flexible investment powers is
better able to react to relative demands for long-term credit
from different sectors of the economy in response to market
signals of yield spreads.

On this point, Chairman John E. Horne's testimony in 1966 is
illustrative:

> Turning first to geographic impediments, I call attention to the fact
> that the bill would provide for a system of financial institutions
> having reasonably broad authority to invest outside their local
> areas. This would improve the interregional flow of funds within
> the country and tend to reduce interregional interest-rate differen-
> tials.
>
> On the second point, the bill would provide greater freedom of
> choice among alternative forms of investment. The savings banks
> established under the bill would have broader investment authority
> than savings and loan associations, the bulk of whose investments
> outside the liquidity area is generally confined to residential mortgage
> loans.[33]

The history of savings banks, of course, provides many examples of this shifting of assets among mortgages, private securities,
and government obligations.

This point raises an obvious question, whether the same objective could not be attained as well by granting savings and
loan associations investment powers similar to those already existing for savings banks or proposed for them in the federal

33. 1966 *Hearings*, p. 30.

charter bill. This possibility apparently has to be answered on the grounds of the different characteristics of savings and loan associations and savings banks. A savings and loan association with the full investment powers of a savings bank would be *de facto* a savings bank and might more consistently take the name as well. In addition, legal differences in the relationship between the savings bank depositor or the account holder with their institutions would need to be reconciled. According to tradition and to the law of savings bank states, the savings bank depositor is a creditor of the bank; mutuality refers to the fact that the banks are operated for the benefit of depositors rather than to an ownership relationship.[34]

The question of whether the objectives of the federal charter bill might not more efficiently be obtained by broadening the powers of existing savings and loan associations to equal those of proposed federal mutual savings banks, as strongly suggested by the savings and loan trade association, was not specifically debated in the hearings prior to 1967. There were, however, implications that supervisory authorities preferred to maintain a degree of control over the number of institutions granted the expanded powers, both through their powers of permitting the conversion of existing savings banks from federal to state charters and of savings and loan associations to federal savings banks. The associated implication is that it was not considered desirable to grant the expanded powers broadly to all currently existing savings and loan associations.

No charter could be so issued unless the Board determined among other things that the operation of the Federal savings bank would not cause undue injury to existing institutions, including commercial banks, that accept funds from savers on deposit or share accounts. In conversion cases there would also have to be a determination that the history of the converting institution had been of a character

---

34. The Committee on Financial Institutions appointed by President Kennedy apparently preferred conversion of savings and loan associations into mutual savings banks over broadening of the formers' powers: "The existence of such a (federally chartered mutual savings bank) system would provide an alternative for savings and loan associations that desired to engage in more diversified lending and investing under appropriate supervision and safeguards." *Report*, p. 30.

commensurate with the superior standards of performance expected of a Federal savings bank.[35]

The same position appears in the attitude of the Treasury Department. "The Treasury worked closely with the Federal Home Loan Bank Board in developing and drafting the regulatory and supervisory standards and safeguards which have been incorporated in H.R. 11508 to assure that the new Federal savings banks will adhere to the high standards of performance appropriate for mutual savings banks. . . ." The Treasury statement continues:

> The breadth of investment powers to be granted to Federal savings banks makes it imperative that such banks make ample provision for liquidity, that such banks not rely on the home loan banks as a source of investment funds (thereby exhausting one potential source of liquidity), that such banks not become heavily dependent upon potentially volatile sources of funds attracted in large aggregates from depositors highly conscious of small interest rate differentials, that the soundness of the widely varied assets of such banks be subject to particularly careful scrutiny through examination, and that those carrying the burdens of management of such banks be held to a high standard of fiduciary responsibility. Many of the specific provisions included in the bill serve this safeguarding purpose. However, statutory ratios and rules can never themselves fully substitute for the prudent judgment of responsible management and alert surveillance by supervisory authorities.

> In this regard, also, the Treasury Department feels that only those existing institutions with exemplary records of past performances should be permitted to convert to Federal savings banks. An institution which has merely met minimum standards of performance under another charter should not, therefore, be qualified for a Federal mutual savings bank charter, especially if prevailing standards of operation in that industry are not comparable to those standards expected of Federal mutual savings banks.[36]

---

35. Statement of Chairman John E. Horne, Federal Home Loan Bank Board, 1966 *Hearings,* p. 30. In the original, "character" appears as "charter," an apparent typographical error.

36. Letter to the Subcommittee from General Counsel Roy Englert, 1966 *Hearings,* p. 33.

In any event, one solution to the problem has been suggested by the introduction of the Federal Savings Institutions Act in 1967, under the terms of which savings and loan associations would not convert to savings banks, but both could convert to the new type of savings institution modeled essentially after savings banks.

Federal Savings Institutions Act

The principal significance of the new bill to authorize federal charters introduced in 1967 is, of course, that it creates a united front to persuade the Congress to modernize the savings and loan law and to provide federal charters for savings banks. As this book goes to press it does not seem likely that the bill will be enacted in the immediate future, but the slowly gathering strength behind the federal charter bill and its annual progress through the legislative machinery, combined with the unified support for the new version, suggest that the chances for eventual passage of such a bill are greatly enhanced. A milestone was reached when the House Banking and Currency Committee reported out the bill, H.R. 13718, to the House of Representatives on November 29, 1967. Since future rewritings and amendments still remain likely, the provisions of the bill are summarized here rather than detailed. These provisions may be classified as general provisions, those relating to deposits and sources of funds, and those relating to loans and investments.

A major factor in the progress of the Federal Savings Institutions bill was the mortgage credit crisis of 1966, in which saving flows at thrift institutions, mortgage flows, and housing all declined sharply. This development emphasized changes in financial and savings markets that had gradually emerged since the late 1950's, the long-run implications of these changes for the flow of mortgage credit, and the question of the ability of savings institutions to compete for savings and mortgage funds. The House Banking and Currency Committee's *Report* on the bill clearly indicates the importance of these developments:

Two related developments have created a radically different savings market in recent years, endangering continued progress toward national housing objectives. These developments are: (1) the long-run uptrend in interest rates since the Treasury–Federal Reserve "accord" in 1951; and (2) the strong commercial bank shift to savings deposits as a major source of lendable funds. The latter, in turn, came in response to the slow and irregular growth in commercial bank demand deposits, caused by rising interest rates and other factors which reduced the relative level of demand deposits, and by the exercise of a flexible, contracyclical monetary policy by the Federal Reserve, which all too often has had the effect of allocating credit to the detriment of the housing industry.

The adverse implications of this new environment for the future cost and adequacy of mortgage credit are clear. The result of a shift in savings from savings institutions is a diversion of funds away from the mortgage market. This is so because savings and loan associations and mutual savings banks channel almost all of their funds into home mortgage loans. Together, during the postwar period, they have accounted for almost three-fifths of the total growth in residential mortgage credit. Commercial banks, by contrast, have placed substantially less than half of their savings growth into home mortgages in recent years. . . . .

The crucial point here is that savings institutions can lend in mortgage funds only what they can attract in savings. If they attract only a dwindling share of the public's saving, housing will suffer. On the other hand, if their long-run ability to attract savings is strengthened, home buyers, builders, and the economy in general will benefit for years to come.[37]

The Committee approved the bill and reported it to the House in the belief that it would contribute to an increased and more stable flow of mortgage credit in three interrelated ways:

First, it would increase the total flow of financial saving by strengthening thrift institutions throughout the Nation;

Second, it would increase the share of saving channeled into mortgage credit by redressing the current competitive weakness of mortgage-oriented thrift institutions; and

Third, it would promote a more stable flow of mortgage funds

---

37. *Federal Savings Institutions, Report of The Banking and Currency Committee on H.R. 13718,* House of Representatives, 90th Congress, 1st Session, December 13, 1967, pp. 6–8.

over the business cycle by providing needed investment flexibility for thrift institutions.[38]

With regard to the first point, the Committee cites the conclusions of the University of Chicago study mentioned above, and of a later study conducted by economists of the Federal Reserve Bank of Chicago:

. . . the local pool of liquid savings is significantly influenced by the relationship between commercial banks and near banks in the area. The greater the importance of near banks to commercial banks, the greater is the overall pool of savings in the area. Part of the enlarged local pool of savings may be attributed to new savings stemming from greater availability of savings facilities and increased competition among savings institutions, while the remainder of the enlargement may be attributed to a repatriation of current savings from outside the area and from other forms of savings.[39]

With regard to the second point—increasing the share of savings flowing to housing—the Committee *Report* notes the importance of flexible deposit and investment powers, and the need to provide important financial services required by the increasingly important younger age groups of the population.

Increased investment flexibility—for example, through provision of limited consumer loan authority—would be one of the most effective means of strengthening the long-run ability of mortgage-oriented savings institutions to compete for savings and generate funds for housing. Such flexibility would strengthen their long-term earnings and hence their ability to pay attractive rates of return to savers—essential in a high-interest-rate environment. It would also enable thrift institutions to tap important segments of the savings market now served primarily by non-mortgage-oriented commercial banks, particularly the younger age groups of the population.[40]

Finally, the Committee *Report* states that the Federal Savings Institutions bill would help stabilize the flow of mortgage funds:

In this regard, it is important to remember that, while the major

---

38. *Ibid.,* p. 8.

39. George G. Kaufman and Cynthia M. Latta, "Near Banks and Local Savings," *The National Banking Review,* Vol. 3, No. 4 (June 1966), pp. 539-42.

40. *Ibid.,* p. 10.

recent and prospective problem is the question of serious mortgage scarcity, the major problem earlier in the 1960's was an abundance of savings relative to available mortgage outlets that led to widespread concern over deterioration in the quality of mortgage credit in some areas. More flexible lending and investing powers for savings institutions would be one of the most effective means of correcting the wide swings in the mortgage market between periods of scarcity and overabundance.

During periods when savings inflows are large relative to mortgage demand, excess funds could be channeled into short-term investments and other alternative assets. Savings institutions would no longer have to choose between the alternatives many faced in the early 1960's of discouraging savings growth, on the one hand, or of accepting increased mortgage lending risks, on the other. With increased flexibility, savings could be encouraged continuously, lending risks reduced, and liquidity increased. In later periods of reduced savings growth or relatively strong mortgage demands, savings institutions would be able to convert nonmortgage assets into mortgage loans. This would supplement their declining savings inflows, thereby cushioning the reduction in the overall supply of mortgage funds.[41]

The House Banking and Currency Committee was also strongly impressed by the 1966 experience, noting that:

The importance of flexible powers for the flow of mortgage credit was further shown by the relative performance of mutual savings banks and savings and loan associations in 1966. Reflecting their relatively broader powers, mutual savings banks were better able to compete for savings and to maintain a comparatively stronger volume of mortgage lending, particularly in local markets.

Saving flows declined by 29 per cent at savings banks in 1966, only about half as great as the 57 per cent decline at savings and loan associations. Because of their stronger savings experience, savings banks were able to channel a substantially larger volume of funds into the mortgage market during each of the 8 months between July 1966 and February 1967 than savings and loan associations, despite their much smaller aggregate size and geographic limitation to little more than one-third of the country. Due to their lesser need to restore

41. *Ibid.,* pp. 12–13.

liquidity positions, moreover, savings banks were able to provide stronger support to the recovery in housing activity that got underway in late 1966 and early 1967.

The stronger savings bank mortgage lending performance during 1966 not only reflected their relatively smaller savings decline, but also the fact that they were able to provide additional funds for mortgage lending by liquidating nonmortgage assets. Thus, savings banks channeled an amount equivalent to 108 per cent of their savings growth into mortgages during 1966, while savings and loan associations were able to channel only 89 per cent of the combined increase in their savings and borrowings into mortgages.[42]

The general provisions of the proposed bill cover chartering and conversion of existing institutions. Another set of provisions spell out types of deposits that may be accepted and other sources of funds. A third group of provisions relate to loan and investment powers.

The Federal Savings Institutions Act provides for "federal savings associations" under the supervision of the Federal Home Loan Bank Board. Federal savings and loan associations, state-chartered associations, and savings banks may be approved for conversion by the Federal Home Loan Bank Board. The Board is to have, in general, the same supervisory powers as it now has, but legislative provisions covering the fiduciary responsibilities of directors, uses of proxies, and related matters are more specific. In addition, the Board is to have authority to require associations to maintain liquid assets within the statutory range of 4 per cent to 10 per cent and, if thought desirable, an additional "special" requirement of 5 per cent. As in previous drafts of bills, the re-named Federal Savings Insurance Corporation would insure deposits, and insured savings banks transferring to the new system would bring with them a "dowry" from the FDIC.

Other general provisions specify the fiduciary relationship of directors and set a limit of three years for the duration of proxies given by depositors for the conduct of general business and six months for special purposes, such as consideration of mergers. The bill provides for the savings and loan system of

---

42. *Ibid.,* p. 13.

elected directors but permits a converting savings bank to maintain its system of trustees. The savings and loan system of payment of withdrawals in rotation in cases of difficulty is permitted, but only in cases approved by the Board. The bill makes the specific provision that branching must conform to state law, as in the case of commercial banks.

Although the general term for the new institutions is "federal savings associations," converting mutual savings banks may maintain their old names, including "bank," "society," and other such designations. In addition, converting savings and loan associations may, beginning in 1973, adopt the name "bank," the delay being designed to allow state legislatures time to consider making this change in state laws. Also, in the new institutions savers' funds are to be called "deposits" and as such earn "interest."

Powers to seek deposits are broadened over those generally open to savings banks or associations. Savings deposits continue to be accepted from nonbusiness concerns, and time deposits to be accepted from businesses for not less than six-month periods or from others for not less than 91 days. Certificates of deposit may be employed, and a certain rate of interest on deposits may be promised in advance, not merely "anticipated" as at present. An important provision authorizes federal savings associations to sell mutual fund shares to depositors.

Federal savings associations are authorized to borrow and to issue debt securities of various kinds. They may also serve as trustee or custodian under the terms of the Federal Self-Employed Individuals Tax Retirement Act of 1962 (Keogh-Smathers Act) and for other qualified retirement plans. The associations may also accept public deposits.

On the loan and investment side, federal savings associations would have broader and more flexible powers, while at the same time they would be intended to serve primarily as mortgage lenders. In a departure from the approach of the present savings and loan law, the bill authorizes a variety of loans and investments rather than permitting these as exceptions. In general, associations are required to hold mortgage loans equal to at least 60 per cent of assets other than liquid assets. Aside from this requirement, associations may make loans secured by: pass-books, collateral eligible for direct investment, cash value of life insurance policies, and mobile homes. They are also authorized to make home improvement loans, education loans, and any loans insured by a federal agency. Significantly, they may make unsecured consumer loans up, although the bill reported to the House in late 1967 provided a ceiling of only $1,000. The savings and loan concept of a primary lending area of 100-mile radius for mortgage loans would be retained.

Investments authorized by the bill include obligations of the Treasury and of federal agencies, general obligations of states and municipalities, corporate bonds, limited amounts of bonds of Canada and the Provinces, and debentures issued by other insured thrift institutions. In addition, the lesser of 5 per cent of assets or 50 per cent of surplus accounts could be invested in corporate stocks.

This general survey of the loan and investment powers proposed for federal savings associations suggests that the more flexible provisions of various state savings bank laws have been imitated, and that these powers would be much broader than those now enjoyed by federal savings and loan associations.

The discussion in the preceding pages leads to questions concerning the role of mutual institutions in the capital markets, in a presumably free-enterprise, profit-oriented economy. Similarly, any consideration of mutuality leads to further comparison of the trustee arrangement that is traditional in savings banking and the usual arrangement in savings and loan associations—in which shareholders are members and are offered a voice in selection of management. Further consideration of these matters makes possible a broader view of the role of mutual banks. A review of the development and practices of savings banks in other countries provides additional background for such a view. Consequently, discussion of the mutual and trustee concepts is postponed until after Chapter 8, which sketches some international comparisons of savings banks.

CHAPTER 6

Savings Bank Life Insurance

THE savings banks found themselves in the life insurance business as a result of demands for reforms stemming from the scandals in the insurance business in the first decade of this century. Life insurance was not immune to the effects of the industrial development of the country, which brought about the conditions exposed by the muckrakers. Theorists such as Bellamy and Veblen, journalists such as Steffens and Tarbell, and political figures such as Roosevelt, Pinchot, and Bryan attacked the sources of monopoly power and exploitation that characterized the American economy around the turn of the century. The beef, coal, whiskey, oil, sugar, banking, and other "trusts" became household words and favorite subjects of articles in popular magazines such as *McClure's, Collier's,* and *Everybody's.*

Life Insurance Difficulties

The specific situation that brought troubles in the life insurance field to public attention was the internal maneuvering for power among top executives and holders of the limited number of shares of stock of the Equitable Life Insurance Company.[1] In

---

1. This situation is detailed in Alpheus T. Mason, *The Brandeis Way* (Princeton, N.J.: Princeton University Press, 1938), pp. 83-96, and in R. Carlyle Buley, *The American Life Convention, 1906-1952* (New York: Appleton-Century-Crofts, 1953), pp. 199-209. Contemporary magazines carried many articles on the subject. See, for example, *World's Work,* various issues in 1905.

brief, James Hazen Hyde, first vice-president, was a conspicuous social spender, and was the object of an attempt by James W. Alexander, president and one of three trustees of Hazen's inherited majority stock, to oust him from his office. The controversy attracted much public attention and resulted in the directors appointing a committee headed by Henry Clay Frick to straighten out the matter. Frick's committee recommended the removal of all of the top officers, and it resigned when its report was not adopted. Hyde offered to dispose of his shares, which he did by selling them to Thomas Fortune Ryan for $2.5 million. Ryan placed the stock in the hands of three trustees, all outstanding citizens: Grover Cleveland, George Westinghouse, and Morgan J. O'Brien. The trustees selected new directors and management.

The difficulties at the Equitable were far more complex than a mere struggle for power. Many charges of self-dealing, diverting of funds, improper lending and investing, and waste and inefficiency were sensationally aired in the press. The New York State Superintendent of Insurance discovered that the company had been guilty of much mismanagement that his department had somehow overlooked in prior years. Other states' superintendents and legislatures took renewed interest in the insurance companies that did business in their states. Well over a half million Equitable policyholders were apprehensive about the soundness of their policies. Although nearing the end of its session, the New York State legislature established an investigating committee, the famous Armstrong Committee, named for its chairman, William W. Armstrong. This committee engaged Charles Evans Hughes as counsel.[2]

The Armstrong Committee

Although the proceedings of the Armstrong Committee were not conducted in a sensational manner, the results were damaging to the public's image of the life insurance business. Testimony

---

2. The results of the investigation are contained in *The Armstrong Committee Record: Testimony, Exhibits, Report* (New York State, 1906). Shepard B. Clough, *A Century of Life American Insurance: A History of the Mutual Life Insurance Company of New York* (New York: Columbia University Press, 1946), and several insurance texts describe the committee's investigations.

of the executives of the large companies revealed numerous transgressions. These included secret political contributions not shown in the records of the companies, payments of more than a million dollars to a lobbyist in Albany, extravagant salaries, widespread nepotism, diversion of commissions to officers, personal loans from companies to officers of other companies at nominal rates of interest, window dressing, and conflicts of interest in syndicate operations. The combination of nepotism and high salaries resulted in some very high combined incomes; the president of one large company and his son were paid more than the salaries of all the governors of all the states and territories combined. Window dressing was accomplished by selling inferior securities to interlocked banks at inflated prices prior to statement dates and repurchasing them soon after. It was common practice for directors of insurance companies to join underwriting syndicates that sold securities to their companies and to retain large profits from the transactions.

Industrial insurance, the kind whose shortcomings led most directly to the establishment of savings bank life insurance, was not emphasized at the hearings. It was brought out, however, that costs were very high because of the collection of weekly premiums and that the agents selling and collecting for this kind of insurance earned very small incomes.

Corrective legislation resulting from the Armstrong Committee hearings was passed in New York State in 1906. The new laws, comprising more than a hundred printed pages, limited expenses, amounts of new business companies could obtain, and surplus accumulations. They also provided for standard policy forms, restricted investments, forbade syndicate underwriting, and resurrected chartering of mutual insurance companies. Other provisions covered executive compensation, policy dividends, and other provisions, such as lapse penalties and information to be printed in the policies.

Interest of Louis D. Brandeis

These developments led to the involvement of Louis D. Brandeis and to the establishment of savings bank life insurance. As a result of the difficulties at the Equitable, a group of Bostonians formed a New England Policy-Holders' Protective Committee "for the purpose of advising themselves as to the condition of the Company," and retained Brandeis as counsel. He was already so interested in the problems of the insurance business that he preferred to accept the post without fee, in order to be free to pursue his own conclusions as to the public interest in the matter.

Brandeis' attention centered on the problems of industrial life insurance. He early concluded that correcting the waste and inefficiency disclosed in the insurance business would still leave industrial insurance too expensive and uneconomical to serve the general public. In his article "Wage-Earners' Life Insurance," appearing in *Collier's* in 1906 and based on his investigations for the New England Committee, he pointed out that the average life expectancy of a man aged 21 was 40.25 years. An accumulation of 50 cents a week in a Massachusetts savings bank for that length of time would amount to $2,265.90 at 3.5 per cent interest (less than the average rate paid in the decade 1896–1905). The same amount paid for a typical industrial insurance policy would provide $820.00 of insurance protection. If, after 20 years, the savings bank deposit were withdrawn, it would have grown to $746.20, while the insurance policy would provide about $165.00[3]

Proposal For Savings Bank Life Insurance

Industrial insurance was sold house-to-house and generally provided for weekly premiums of five or ten cents and multiples thereof, the benefits varying with age and other factors. Naturally, the collection of weekly premiums in such small amounts created very high collection costs. Brandeis found that two stock companies and one mutual—Metropolitan, Prudential, and John Hancock—sold about 94 per cent of all industrial insurance and that management costs exceeded 40 per cent of pre-

3. Louis D. Brandeis, "Wage-Earners' Life Insurance," *Colliers*, September, 1906, p. 16.

mium income. This cost suggested a comparison: Management costs of savings bank deposits made during 1905 were 1.47 per cent, or about one twenty-fifth as much. The widespread use of industrial insurance was indicated by the fact that out of about 21 million policies in force, nearly 16 million were of the industrial type.

The inefficiencies of industrial insurance resulted in premiums about double those of ordinary insurance, and the methods of selling led to a high lapse rate. About two thirds of these policies were abandoned in the first three years. Not only was there complete loss to these policyholders, but there were also added costs for others. Only one policy in twelve was carried to maturity. Collection costs alone amounted to a fifth of the premiums. Thus, Brandeis concluded that the evils brought out by the Armstrong Committee and journalists were minor in explaining the high cost of this type of insurance.[4] He reported to the New England Committee: "Neither the profits wrongfully diverted nor mere substitution of other officers, however scrupulous and efficient, can afford an adequate remedy for the evils disclosed. The interests of present and future policyholders demand that there be more radical changes in the system."[5] In comparing life insurance companies with the Massachusetts savings banks, he remarked, "I do not say that the income returns of the great companies manned by the great financiers were unreasonably low, but merely that the small banks with their low-salaried officers earned more."[6]

In the *Collier's* article Brandeis went to the heart of the problem in these words:

The sacrifice incident to the present industrial insurance system can be avoided only by providing an institution for insurance which will recognize that its function is not to induce working people to take insurance regardless of whether they really want it, or can afford to

4. "The real cause of these meagre results to the insured from industrial insurance is not financial depravity or extravagance, but the extraordinary wastefulness necessarily attendant upon the present system of supplying life insurance for working men." *Ibid.*, p. 17.

5. Mason, *op. cit.*, p. 91.

6. Louis D. Brandeis, *Business—A Profession* (Boston: Small, Maynard & Co., 1914), p. 132.

carry it, but rather to supply insurance upon proper terms to those who do want it and can carry it—an institution which will recognize that the best method of increasing the demand for life insurance is not eloquent persistent persuasion, but, as in the case of other necessaries of life, is to furnish a good article at a low price.[7]

Letting people come to purchase insurance and making savings banks the place to come appealed to Brandeis for a variety of reasons. He saw a close correspondence in the existing functions of savings banks and his proposed insurance departments. He noted that adding insurance would require only three new functions: "Fixing the terms on which insurance shall be given, the initial medical examination, and verifying the proof of death."[8] He noted that the banks already required the third in order to identify deceased depositors, that the second would cost no more for a savings bank than for an insurance company, and that the first is the work of an actuary, as available to the banks as to others. He listed as further advantages of savings bank operation:

1. Management would be by trustees and officers trained to recognize a "quasi-public trust which should be conducted as a beneficent and not as a selfish money-making institution."

2. Management was already "trained to the practice of strictest economy."

3. There need be "no large increase of clerical force or incidental expense, except such as would be required if the bank's deposits were increased. Until the insurance business attained considerable dimensions, probably the addition of even a single clerk might not be necessary."

4. The holders of "the 1,829,487 savings bank accounts, a number equal to three-fifths of the whole population of the state, would at once become potential policyholders."

5. ". . . house to house collection of premiums could be dispensed with. The more economical monthly payments of premiums could also probably be substituted for weekly payments." In addition, Brandeis cited several advantages that

---

7. *Collier's,* September, 1906, p. 17.
8. *Loc. cit.*

would follow from cooperation among participating savings banks.[9]

The Armstrong Committee had suggested, almost in passing, a similar idea. Its report included the comment:

A great reform could be accomplished if the expense of solicitation and collection could be avoided by the establishment of branch offices where insurance might be obtained by the thrifty poor who desire it. But the opinion of those connected with the companies is that such a plan would be impracticable and the committee is without information which would justify an attempt to compel its introduction.[10]

Since the Committee devoted relatively little of its attention to industrial insurance and because the major witnesses were insurance executives, most of the testimony was in the direction of explaining the necessity of high costs in this field.

The adoption of savings bank life insurance in Massachusetts was a monument to the enthusiasm and persistence of Louis D. Brandeis. While circumstances were favorable in the sense of great public interest in the problem and dissatisfaction with the old and large companies, Brandeis faced reluctance and in some cases opposition from savings bankers themselves. In addition, of course, forceful and effective opposition from the insurance companies was to be expected.

The reluctance of the majority of savings bank trustees and officials stemmed from a variety of reasons. Some did not think that the savings banks should embark in another field, which seemed to them to add risks to the banks and which in any event was under a cloud. Others were associated with insurance companies and not only were subject to divided loyalty but believed that the insurance companies were doing as good a job as could be done. Simple conservatism motivated others, while still others had no ambition to take on new problems. One banker in Boston remarked that "We have trouble enough as it is now, from depositors who are hardly able to write their names, and if an insurance department were to be added here I

---

9. *Ibid.,* p. 28.

10. *Report,* Assembly Document No 41, X, 445; quoted in Mason, *op. cit.,* pp. 113-14.

don't see how we could find time or floor space to handle it. . . ." A more cogent reason was cited by another: "It appears to me that the average savings bank cannot well conduct an insurance business because the bank is a local institution only. The machinery of insurance would be costly even if there were a central association to keep us in touch with our policyholders in other parts of the state."[11] Interest in the Brandeis proposal was even less evident in other savings bank states; in the other states there was the possibility of waiting to see how developments worked out in Massachusetts.

Adoption in Massachusetts

Brandeis' genius as an organizer is evident in his management of the campaign to obtain a savings bank insurance law. Realizing the futility for the time of expecting leadership from savings banks as a group, he concentrated on building up pressures from civic and other outside groups, while converting a few savings bank trustees at a time. He established the Massachusetts Savings Bank Insurance League as the official body to promote the reform and obtained the services of two former governors, one Republican, one Democrat, as president and vice president. Former governor W. L. Douglas, a prominent shoe manufacturer and president of the People's Savings Bank of Brockton, offered to provide the initial $25,000 guaranty fund for his bank to enter, should a law be passed. The League included leaders in all important occupations—industrialists, financiers, clerics, educators, and members of labor organizations. Brandeis also engaged the son of Elizur Wright, Walter C. Wright, as consultant.

"The main barrier in the campaign was the ultra-conservatism of savings bank officials themselves. Therefore Brandeis and his aides centered on getting as many savings bank men as possible into the League. . . . Vague apprehension prevailed lest insurance departments thus engrafted on savings banks should

---

11. These comments are quoted in Mason, *op cit.,* pp. 154-55. Of course, savings bankers later recognized the value of this service to depositors and to the banks.

somehow impair the latter's integrity." Brandeis consequently stated, "I am convinced that if we are to overcome the ultra-conservative views of the savings bank treasurers, we must in the main work, not directly upon the treasurers, but through the trustees of the banks. . . ."[12] While far from all savings bankers were converted, some influential ones were, and representatives of nearly half of the banks were affiliated with the League by early 1907.

In 1906, Massachusetts appointed a Joint Special Recess Committee to study the insurance laws. As in several other states, this development was a reflection of the events in New York State, and the Committee surveyed the whole life insurance business. The proposal for savings bank life insurance was thus only one recommendation before the Committee. The Committee's hearings featured testimony by insurance company experts deriding the Brandeis proposal and adverse testimony from some representatives of savings banks. Much of the argument was not germane to the issues, but attempted to deride the proposal as visionary and impractical. The response of Brandeis and his supporters was, on the one hand, to provide all the available facts and, on the other, to step up the pressures from outside groups. As he had done from the beginning, Brandeis also argued that his proposal was actually a conservative one in that reform was inevitable and that the alternative to savings bank life insurance was government insurance. Early in his study of insurance, he had told the Commercial Club of Boston, ". . . whatever and however strong our convictions against the extension of governmental functions may be, we shall inevitably be swept farther toward socialism unless we curb the excesses of our financial magnates." In fact, the Governor of Missouri foresaw the time "when the state would insure her own citizens at a far less cost and with far more safety to those who need that protection."[13]

Originally opposed to the proposal for savings bank life insurance, the Joint Special Recess Committee was gradually con-

12. *Ibid.*, p. 165.
13. *The Literary Digest*, October 14, 1905. Wisconsin did establish a State Life Fund in 1913.

verted by Brandeis' unremitting efforts and unanimously reported in favor of the measure in early 1907. Governor Guild supported it in his inaugural address of January, 1907. The measure was then successfully piloted past pitfalls and obstacles in the legislature; it was voted by the house on June 24 and by the senate on June 25, and it was signed by the Governor on June 26, 1907.

The bill provided for maximum policies of $500 and annuities of $100. Premiums could be paid from depositors' savings accounts. All but 4 per cent of the premiums were invested by the savings banks, the 4 per cent going to a guaranty fund. Supervision was supplied by seven trustees of the General Insurance Guaranty Fund, who were appointed by the Governor. These trustees offered a great deal of voluntary and uncompensated service in the early years.

Slow Beginnings

As the opponents of savings bank life insurance had predicted, it was not an immediate success. Delays were encountered in obtaining the services of a competent actuary, such people being scarce at the time, and a well-known actuary, S. H. Wolfe, served as unpaid consultant for some time. Time was consumed in drawing up policy forms, engaging a medical director and local examiners, and in drawing up their rules and regulations. It was necessary for each interested savings bank to raise a guaranty fund of $25,000 and to obtain the approval of the state commissioners of insurance and banking. Delay in obtaining this approval slowed the expected inauguration of the plan by the People's Savings Bank of Brockton, and the Whitman Savings Bank set up the first plan in June of 1908. Predictions were also borne out in that few policies were sold. The next step, therefore, was establishment by the Boston Chamber of Commerce of the Wage Earners' Committee on Insurance, with the assistance of E. A. Filene. This committee publicized savings bank life insurance and the fact that offices to accept applications could be set up by employers, unions, credit unions, welfare agencies, and similar organizations. Wage earners were informed through lunch hour lectures and folders placed in pay envelopes. As a result, the demand for policies began to rise.

By 1912, only four banks had opened insurance departments, and 13 banks were operating as agencies without having their own departments. There were still only four banks operating departments in 1922, when there was $20 million of insurance in force. This total grew to $58 million ($46 million of ordinary insurance and $12 million of group) by 1928, and in 1929 the movement received considerable impetus when the largest savings bank in Massachusetts, the Boston Five Cent Savings Bank, opened a department. There were in all ten banks by the end of 1929, when insurance in force amounted to $68 million, and 23 banks in 1935, when the amount reached $110 million. Since 1934, the insuring banks have repaid the state's appropriation for the system. The progress of the system is summarized in Table 6–1. In recent years, 36 banks have operated insurance departments. Nearly all of the remaining banks, however, serve as agencies for the operating banks, so that insurance is available at virtually any savings bank. A feature of the Massachusetts system is the additional agencies operated by others; many employers and some institutions provide this service, the Associated Industries of Massachusetts being a supporter of this development.

TABLE 6-1[14]

MASSACHUSETTS SAVINGS BANK LIFE INSURANCE, SELECTED DATES

(MILLIONS OF DOLLARS)

		Insurance in Force		Number of Policies	Insurance Purchased
	Ordinary	Group	Total		
1945	247.6	16.4	264.1	291,706	19.7
1950	360.7	31.9	392.6	423,312	33.1
1955	496.7	47.1	543.8	488,931	41.4
1960	669.8	68.7	738.5	538,874	61.3
1965	947.5	124.4	1,072.0	621,207	90.3
1966	1,006.3	145.5	1,151.7	643,533	91.2

14. NAMSB figures, tabulated from state reports as of October 31.

In addition to the policies listed in Table 6–1, more than 8,000 annuity contracts represent annual payments of over $1 million. Surrenders and lapses are low. In 1963, 8,246 policies were surrendered, representing $10.123 million and 4,400 were lapsed, prepresenting $13 million.[15]

Adoption in New York State

The story of the opposition to adoption of savings bank life insurance in Massachusetts largely explains the slowness with which it was adopted in other states. New York State approved savings bank life insurance in 1938 and Connecticut in 1941.

Shortly after the beginnings of the system in Massachusetts, proponents of the movement introduced bills, in 1909 and 1910, in the New York legislature. Support for these measures was weak, however, and the Superintendent of Insurance did not favor them. The legislature received no further bills on the subject for two more decades. Thereafter, in the 1930's, development of the idea was remarkably similar to its earlier history in Massachusetts. A bill providing for limited amounts of non-medical insurance was introduced without success in 1932. Shortly thereafter the daughter of Justice Brandeis, Susan Brandeis, who was practicing law in New York City, formed a group to promote savings bank life insurance. Associated with her were William L. Grossman, who authored an article on the subject for *The Nation,* and Norman Hapgood, who had published Brandeis' article in *The Nation* in 1906. Their efforts led to the introduction of another unsuccessful bill in 1934, at which point Justice Brandeis himself became active in the movement. As a result, the Savings Bank Life Insurance League was founded to promote educational and legislative activities. The interest of Governor Lehman was aroused by this group, and he became a strong supporter of permissive legislation. Bills died in committee again in 1935 and 1937, but Governor Lehman strongly supported legislation in his annual message of 1938.

---

15. *Annual Report of Commissioner of Banks, 1964, Section C,* p. 116.

Following the gubernatorial endorsement, bills were introduced in the senate and the assembly (the Livingston-Piper bill). As in Massachusetts, savings bankers were largely apathetic, and the position of the state association was that the banks should not support the bill. On the other hand, some individual savings bankers favored it, and at least the official attitude of representatives of the insurance companies was that they did not object. While very critical of the Massachusetts system, the president of the Metropolitan Life Insurance Company, Leroy A. Lincoln, stated that:

> . . . (T)he position of this company has been uniform and consistent in maintaining only that any legislation should impose the same legal requirements; the same taxation, and require the business to be subject to the same supervision as applied to life insurance companies. . . .
>
> The legislation pending in the State of New York . . . does now for the first time meet the criticisms which have existed against proposals in other years, and, so far as the Metropolitan Life Insurance Company is concerned, there is no more reason why we should take exception to the presence of this proposed institution in the life insurance business than would be the case if it were any other legitimate competitor, always assuming that the same comparative status continues to exist.[16]

There was, nevertheless, strong conservative opposition to the proposed bills. Savings bank reluctance to support the movement was based partly on the slow development in Massachusetts and on the awkward organization there, with the system divided among the banks, the Savings Bank Life Insurance Council, and the General Insurance Guaranty Fund. Consequently, the savings banks favoring the adoption of insurance proposed that in New York there should be a central agency to hold a guaranty fund and issue policies. In the end, the efforts of Governor Lehman and the Savings Bank Life Insurance League resulted in the passage of the Livingston-Piper bill in

---

16. Quoted from *National Underwriter*, January 28, 1938, by Donald R. Johnson, *Savings Bank Life Insurance* (Homewood, Ill.: Richard D. Irwin, 1963), pp. 33-34.

1938, which provided a system roughly comparable to that in Massachusetts but with a maximum at that time of $3,000 of insurance.

The system grew considerably more slowly in New York than its proponents had hoped. However, insurance in force passed the $100 million mark in 1947, $200 million in 1952, $300 million in 1956, $400 million in 1960, and $500 million in 1962. By the end of 1966, insurance in force amounted to just over $1 billion and was represented by more than 300,000 policies. In 1964, New York State savings banks for the first time sold more insurance (over $140 million) than did those in Massachusetts. In that year, the New York State savings banks had nearly 9 million regular savings accounts, and the annual gain was 85,200; savings deposits amounted to about $28 billion and the deposit gain for the year was $2.5 billion. Recently there have been 57 banks with insurance departments and 47 acting as agencies, a total of 104 banks out of 125.[17]

Organizational Structure

In form of organization the Massachusetts and New York systems have several resemblances. At the top of the Massachusetts system are three central organizations. The Division of Savings Bank Life Insurance is part of the Commonwealth's Division of Banking and Insurance, which also has divisions of banking and insurance. The Division is tied to the General Insurance Guaranty Fund in that the latter consists of seven trustees (appointed by the Governor with consent of the Governor's Council), one of whom is appointed to serve as president of the Fund and as commissioner of savings bank life insurance. The trustees appoint a deputy commissioner, who must be approved by the Governor and the Council. He then becomes a salaried state employee, but is supervised by the trustees of the Fund. The Division also contains the system's actuary and medical director plus other staff. The expenses of the Division are reimbursed by the insurance system. In addition to the Fund and the

17. *Report of Superintendent of Banks, 1964, II,* 40. In early 1967, 106 banks wrote policies.

Division, the Savings Bank Life Insurance Council was organized in 1938 and made an official part of the system in 1947. This arm provides many housekeeping functions in the issuance of policies and collection of premiums, advertising and public relations, research, and related matters.

In New York the administration of the system is more centralized. The Division of Savings Bank Life Insurance created by the original act became the Savings Bank Life Insurance Fund in 1940, at which time the General Insurance Guaranty Fund and the individual banks' guaranty funds were merged into this organization. This Fund is also supervised by a board of seven trustees, who are appointed by the Superintendent of Banks. Each is unpaid, as in Massachusetts, may not be connected in another capacity with the insurance business, and may serve not more than two four-year terms.

Adoption in Connecticut

Adoption of savings bank life insurance in Connecticut followed a path strongly reminiscent of those taken in Massachusetts and New York. It was characterized by impetus from a source outside savings bank circles, several legislative failures (as in New York), opposition from insurance and conservative groups, apathy on the part of most savings bankers, support from a sympathetic governor, and eventual adoption. In the modern environment of savings banking, the original apathy has changed to a wider recognition that, in the provision of "thrift" services rather than narrowly conceived deposit services, savings bankers have a natural interest in at least some areas of life insurance, and some of the recent steps in this direction have taken place in Connecticut.

The outside impetus in this instance came from a Bridgeport newspaper, *The Sunday Herald,* and its editor, Leigh Danenberg, who was, as might be assumed, an admirer of Justice Brandeis. Largely through his efforts, legislation was introduced, beginning in 1937, that would have provided a system modeled after that in Massachusetts. Four years later, after support had been provided by Governor Robert A. Hurley, a bill drawing on experience in both New York and Massachusetts was approved.[18] The plan went into effect in early 1942 and, as has been the case in the other two states, its coverage has been small in terms of total insurance coverage, but it is growing at respectable average annual rates. Coverage reached $50 million in 1958 and $99.9 million in 1966, of which ordinary insurance was $56.1 million and group insurance the remainder. Recently, 11 banks have issued policies and 34 others have acted as agency banks. In addition to these amounts of coverage, the development of a life-insured mortgage plan offered on a voluntary basis by 64 of the 71 banks in the state, and which is sold jointly with a private company, brought the total of group insurance to nearly $100 million at the end of 1964.[19]

The Connecticut system has also become the vehicle for potential expansion of savings bank life insurance to other states. Outside of Massachusetts, New York, and Connecticut the savings banks have been handicapped by their small numbers, which tend to make difficult actuarial soundness of a state plan. In addition, the overhead expenses of a central organization for actuarial and medical supervision and determining premiums and dividends could not be spread sufficiently thin. In order to provide these services to out-of-state savings banks in the event the latter succeed in obtaining franchises to write insurance, the Savings Bank Life Insurance Fund of Connecticut obtained authorization to adopt the Inter-State Plan of Savings Bank Life Insurance and to convert to The Savings Bank Life Insurance Company. This new company was chartered to serve savings banks only and is owned only by them. Participation currently involves only savings banks in Connecticut. The company reinsures risks written by the savings banks. It provides an actuary and a medical director; calculates premiums, reserves, and dividends; and provides forms and prescribes standards of health and insurability. As savings banks in other states obtain authorization to issue or sell policies, these services can be extended to them. This plan is largely a reflection of the more important role of the National Association of Mutual Savings Banks in

18. The details of these plans are described in Johnson, *op. cit.*
19. *Annual Report of the Bank Commissioner, 1964*, p. 24.

recent years, as the association was instrumental in promoting and developing the plan.

TABLE 6-2[20]

LIFE INSURANCE IN FORCE, BY TYPES, 1965

(BILLIONS OF DOLLARS)

	Legal Reserve Life Companies				Savings Banks		
	Ordinary	*Group*	*Industrial*	*Total*	*Ordinary*	*Group*	*Total*
Connecticut	9,641	5,758	504	15,903	.054	.038	.092
Massachusetts	14,973	9,226	1,220	25,419	.948	.124	1.072
New York	54,860	34,436	2,425	91,721	.785	.109	.894
Subtotal	79,474	49,420	4,149	133,043	1.787	.271	2.058
United States	497,630	306,113	39,818	843,561	1.787	.271	2.058

Current Status

The relative extent of the spread of savings bank life insurance is indicated in Table 6–2. From the table it is clear that this form of life insurance has hardly swept the field. In terms of totals, the savings banks hold only $2 billion, as against a figure approaching a trillion dollars of ordinary, group, and industrial insurance coverage in the country. However, when it is remembered that savings bank life insurance was established originally to offer a substitute for industrial insurance and that it is available in only three states, it may be more significant to note that the ordinary and group policies of the savings banks represent half the total of industrial insurance in the three savings bank life insurance states. While lives insured by savings bank life insurance comprise less than 1 per cent of the total, the significance of this form of life insurance regionally and in the market for small policies is considerably greater.

The origins of savings bank life insurance led to ceilings on the amount that could be purchased, similar to ceilings on deposits. While it would seem that these ceilings are even more difficult to justify than those on deposits, they may help explain

20. *Life Insurance Fact Book, 1966*, p. 17, and *Mutual Savings Bank Fact Book, 1966*, p. 49.

to some extent why coverage has not grown more rapidly. These ceilings have been lifted from time to time as conditions have changed. In Massachusetts an individual may obtain only $5,000 of insurance from a single savings bank, but he may obtain a total of $43,000 by combining banks. In Connecticut, however, the limit for an individual is $5,000 and in New York it was raised in early 1967 from $10,000—plus an over-all ceiling of $30,000 including a 20-year decreasing term policy—to $30,000 of regular insurance and annuity contracts yielding up to $3,000 per year.

Data for comparing buyers and policies of savings bank versus other insurance are not readily available. However, the tendency of savings banks to serve the market for smaller policies can be deduced. Of the purchases of ordinary life policies in the United States in 1965, 30 per cent were made by people with incomes between $3,000 and $4,999 and 38 per cent by those with incomes between $5,000 and $7,499. In terms of amount of insurance coverage, these groups bought half of the total.[21] However, while 37 per cent of the policies were for less than $5,000, these policies amounted to only 7 per cent of the policies sold. Fourteen per cent of the policies were purchased by those with incomes in excess of $10,000 and these policies accounted for one third of the total sold.

Somewhat earlier data, for 1960, show that 95.3 per cent of the Connecticut savings bank policies issued in that year were for $5,000 or less. Fifty-six per cent of the policies were for amounts up to $2,000. In Massachusetts 67 per cent of the policies were for $5,000 or less, and of this figure 18 per cent of the policies were for $5,000. In New York 73 per cent of the policies issued were for amounts up to $4,999, while 27 per cent were for larger amounts.

The New York Savings Banks Life Insurance Fund surveyed the occupations of applicants for insurance in 1960 and found that more than half—52.6 per cent—fell in the categories of clerical, sales, craftsmen, operatives, private household and service, and laborers, the largest group being clerical (15.9 per

21. *Life Insurance Fact Book, 1966,* p. 15.

cent). About half as many—27.4 per cent—were in the categories of professional and managerial workers.

While these data are insufficient for precise measurements, it would appear that the people for whom savings bank life insurance was designed have availed themselves of it, but not to the extent that might have been expected, and at the same time higher income groups have also taken out policies. The latter development is a rather normal one, in the sense that managerial and professional people might be expected to recognize their needs for insurance and be aware of alternatives in the market.

Brandeis and other founders of savings bank life insurance based their proposal on two expectations—that savings banks could offer insurance at lower cost than could the agency system, and that people, especially the types of people represented by savings bank depositors, would avail themselves of it. While the latter has probably developed more slowly than was anticipated at first, the former expectation has in general been true. "From a study of the net cost illustrations, it appears that the savings banks have been able to write life insurance at a net cost generally lower than most commercial companies. Particularly has this been true in the case of the Massachusetts system."[22] In the other two states, the savings banks have been able to develop less of a cost advantage.

Johnson notes another characteristic of savings bank life insurance, in that ". . . the savings bank life insurance program is without question reaching a market untapped by the company agents, inasmuch as a goodly number of all applicants for savings bank life insurance have no other insurance on their lives at time of application. In this respect the program is providing a valuable service."[23]

The basic area of disagreement between those who favor and those who object to the "self-service" type of non-agency life insurance revolves around the value of the service of the life insurance agent. Certainly, however, the services of the agent

---

22. Johnson, *op. cit.,* p. 196.
23. *Ibid.,* p. 214.

who sold industrial policies in the first decade of this century were not comparable to the services provided by the ideal agent today in the areas of estate planning, meshing policies with Social Security, minimizing taxes, and the like. There are two aspects to the question of the value of the agent. One is the view that many, perhaps most, people fail to buy insurance, at least in adequate amounts, without the efforts of the agent acting as salesman. The other view is that insurance is complicated and technical, and an agent should be consulted just as an architect should be consulted in the building of a house.

The extent to which the latter view should lead to a favorable or unfavorable view of the savings bank version of life insurance further depends on the extent to which the savings banks' insurance departments can provide advice comparable to that of company agents. In the larger banks, especially, there is no necessary reason why this advice should be inferior.

The former view—that agents are necessary to sell insurance —is true for many people and untrue for others. The original Brandeis position, however, was simply that those for whom it is untrue should have an opportunity to buy over the counter. In fact, as Lintner, Johnson, and other observers have noted, the efforts of life insurance salesmen have contributed to some degree to the success of savings bank life insurance through making much of the public aware of their needs for life insurance.

Life insurance agents will always be necessary to sell insurance to the large number of people who have not yet recognized their needs or who lack the personal initiative to buy voluntarily. But just as self-service grocery stores can offer high-quality food products at lower prices to those who are willing to come to the store, wait on themselves, and pay cash, so savings bank life insurance can offer sound insurance protection at substantial savings to those who recognize their insurance needs and have the initiative to apply for policies of their own volition.[24]

Another aspect of savings bank life insurance worthy of brief notice is its relationship to the other functions and business of savings banks. As noted in the sketches of the origins of savings bank life insurance, savings bankers generally were not enthusi-

24. Lintner, *op. cit.*, pp. 197-98.

astic about its adoption. This attitude stemmed largely from earlier views of the economic role of savings banking and from the narrow concept of the traditional savings deposit as the sole or principal "product" offered by the banks. As is discussed more fully in Chapters 5 and 9, the more recent concept is that savings banks should be centers for all the thrift needs of the "average" family.

Provision of life insurance fits naturally into the current concept of the role of savings banks, and consequently the attitude of savings bankers and savings bank organizations is now quite different from that which existed when the systems started. More specifically, rather than being an alien field of endeavor, life insurance is now more often thought of as a contribution to the over-all activity of the savings bank. The provision of life insurance can attract to the bank nondepositors who later become depositors, just as depositors can be attracted to insurance after they have entered the bank. A popular arrangement, especially in Massachusetts, is the joint deposit-insurance account, whereby a depositor both builds up a deposit by regular additions and carries a policy by having the premiums deducted from his savings account. In this manner the customer has insurance protection in case of death, but also a fund of capital in case of survival.

The marriage of life insurance with deposit banking, now approximately half a century old, also suggests other areas in which savings banks might broaden the services offered to the public. One such proposal in savings bank circles—and no more unanimously favored than was life insurance some decades ago —is that of extending the idea to a mutual fund that would be offered to depositors only. Pointing to the experience with life insurance, proponents of this extension of savings bank activity suggest that the banks could again introduce economies, improve standards, and meet some of the criticisms currently leveled at mutual funds.

CHAPTER 7

Savings Banks
in the Mortgage Markets

THE postwar resurgence and growth of the mutual savings banks are nowhere better illustrated than in their activity in mortgage lending. The growth of mortgage debt in the first 20 years after World War II was an outstanding feature of this period. Total mortgage debt increased from a mere $35.5 billion at the end of 1945 to $341.9 billion at the end of 1965.[1] All segments of the mortgage market exhibited great expansion. One- to four-family residential mortgages ballooned from $18.6 billion to $212.9 billion, showing an increase of between 11 and 12 times. Of this total, FHA and VA mortgages increased from about $4 billion to more than $70 billion, while conventional loans increased from $14 billion to more than $135 billion. Multi-family and commercial mortgages rose from $12 billion in 1945 to approximately $108 billion, also including a substantial increase in FHA mortgages, while farm mortgages increased about four-fold from less than $5 billion to more than $21 billion.

Postwar Rise of Mortgage Debt

Non-farm mortgage debt in 1965 was slightly larger than all public debts had been in 1945, and it increased in proportion to total private debt from about one fifth to nearly one third. By 1966, private debt approximated $1 trillion and total public

---

1. *Economic Report of the President, 1966*, p. 271.

and private debt reached $1.4 trillion.[2] For the first time since the war, non-farm mortgage debt exceeded federal government and agency debt in 1965.

TABLE 7-1[a]

MORTGAGE DEBT, SELECTED YEARS

(BILLIONS OF DOLLARS)

| End Of | Total | One- to Four-Family | | | | Multi-Family and Comm'l. | | Farm |
		Total	FHA	VA	Conven-tional	FHA	Conven-tional	
1945	35.5	18.6	4.1	0.2	14.3	0.2	11.9	4.8
1950	72.8	45.2	8.6	10.3	26.3	3.2	18.4	6.1
1955	129.9	88.2	14.3	24.6	49.3	4.0	28.7	9.0
1960	206.8	141.3	26.7	29.7	84.8	5.9	46.8	12.8
1965	341.9	213.5	42.0	31.1	140.4	8.0	99.0	21.2
1966[p]	366.0	225.4	44.8	31.2	149.4	8.0	109.3	23.3

p—Preliminary

Several well-known factors in the economy led to this rapid increase in real estate activity and its financing. The shortage of housing following both the depression and the war, the public's holdings of liquid assets, the increase in personal incomes, changes in total population and age composition, and policies of government and lenders all had a bearing on the situation. The number of families increased from 36.2 million in 1947 to 45.1 million in 1960, and households increased from 39.1 million to 52.6 million. Except for 1953 and 1954, new families ranged from 758,000 to 1.308 million during these years. There were relatively large increases in households with heads aged over 35.[4] Government policies tended to use stimulation of the construction industry as an anti-depression measure, and financial institutions accepted longer maturities and higher loan-to-value

2. Preliminary estimates by Council of Economic Advisers; *Economic Report of the President, 1967*, p. 278.

3. *Economic Report of the President, 1966*, p. 271, and NAMSB, *Fact Book, 1967*, p. 41.

4. U.S. Department of Commerce, Bureau of the Census, *Current Population Reports*, Series P-20, *passim*.

ratios in making loans. "Use of long-term credit is unusually large in the financing of housing, reflecting not only the extreme durability and the relatively large unit price of the structures involved, but also the substantial number of dwellings built or traded in any one year."[5]

Savings Bank Lending, 1945–65

The savings banks participated actively in and contributed significant portions of this growth of outstanding mortgages. In summary, savings bank holdings of mortgages increased more than ten-fold between 1945 and 1965, from a little over $4 billion to over $45 billion. Savings banks held less than 12 per cent of total mortgage debt in 1945 and as little as 10 per cent in 1947, but more than 13 per cent in 1965. The shift in the nature of the mortgage market during this 20-year period is suggested by the increase in the share held by savings and loan associations from about one seventh to one third of the total, while the share of holders other than these associations, savings banks, commercial banks, and insurance companies fell from about two fifths to one fifth. Commercial banks and insurance companies maintained approximately the same shares. The savings banks' growth in the mortgage markets was especially rapid in 1951–55, when the net flow of mortgage funds from savings banks averaged about 16 per cent of total flows.

The savings banks achieved a dominant position in holdings of federally underwritten mortgages. From the smallest holders of such mortgages in 1946, they went to the largest, with 31.7 per cent in 1965, or $25.5 billion out of $81.1 billion. At the same time, they maintained their position as the largest holders of mortgages on multi-family housing, with larger increases than those made by commercial banks, savings and loan associations, or life insurance companies. Closely related to the growth of mortgage holdings of savings banks was a very large increase in out-of-state lending. In the early 1950's, restrictions on out-of-state lending were generally relaxed to permit acquisition of

5. "Monetary Policy and the Residential Mortgage Market," *Federal Reserve Bulletin*, May, 1967, p. 729.

FHA and VA mortgages. By 1965, out-of-state loans were 40 per cent of total mortgage loans and were nearly all federally underwritten.

During this recent concentration on mortgage lending, the savings banks considerably surpassed the proportion of assets held in this form during the 1920's, against which there was such strong reaction in the 1930's. In this century, the proportion rose to 45 per cent between 1900 and 1915, paused and dipped during World War I, and then climbed on to 55 per cent by the end of the 1920's. The depression experience brought the ratio down to 40 per cent by the beginning of World War II, during which it fell further to 25 per cent. After a year or two of hesitation at the end of the war, the proportion started a steep climb, which persisted throughout the remaining period. Mortgages reached half of total assets in the mid-1950's and represented three fourths of total assets in 1965.

Because of differences in local real estate conditions, savings inflows, and management policies, there has naturally been some dispersion from the average ratio of mortgages to total assets. The average ratio is strongly affected by New York State, where the ratio reached 80 per cent; the six banks in Vermont had an equally high average. Other states where it exceeded 70 per cent in 1965 were Connecticut, Rhode Island, New Hampshire, New Jersey, and Washington. In Maryland and Indiana the ratio remained below 60 per cent. Out-of-state lending has been particularly affected by differences in restrictions, including tax treatment of assets. Massachusetts, for example, where out-of-state mortgages did not qualify for exemption from property taxes as did local mortgages prior to a change in the law in 1966, held less than one fifth of total mortgages as out-of-state loans, while the out-of-state loans of savings banks in Pennsylvania and Rhode Island approximated one half of total mortgages and of banks in New York State, about one third.

The widespread expansion of mortgage lending has required adoption of a variety of practices that were much less common in the past. Out-of-state lending has naturally required the services of mortgage bankers or brokers to supply the loans and to service them. Mortgage warehousing arrangements have been entered into—especially by some of the larger city banks—by means of which commercial banks provide interim financing and the savings banks acquire permanent mortgages in accordance with availability of funds. The increase in multi-family and commercial loans has brought increased use of participation loans. Construction loans do not typically bulk large in total savings bank lending, and are used primarily as sources of permanent loans; smaller banks tend to make such loans to builders and owners, while the larger banks concentrate on builders.[6]

To summarize postwar developments in mortgage lending, as described more fully in this chapter, the savings banks concentrated funds in the mortgage market in an unprecedented manner. The rise in such holdings surpassed that of any preceding housing boom. The underlying reasons for this massive shift were: (1) the persistence of demand for mortgage credit and consequent attractiveness of yields; (2) the widespread adoption of amortization of mortgage loans, increasing the liquidity and cash flow of these loans; (3) federal insurance and guarantees, which provided additional safety and liquidity; and (4) the necessary condition of state legislation authorizing out-of-state loans.

The rising ratio of mortgage loans to total assets necessarily reduced and altered the importance of securities investments. Such assets lost to a large extent their function of providing income and became all the more important as sources of liquidity and flexibility in periods of shifting yield relationships. While this development did not shift the savings banks' traditional primary reliance on internal sources of liquidity, it did at the same time bring about a re-examination of the desirability of external sources. As a result there was increased use of mortgage warehousing arrangements with commercial banks, expansion of the lending powers of the Savings Banks Trust Company, and some increase in membership in the Federal Home Loan Bank System. At the same time the need for liquidity

---

6. For a more complete discussion of mortgage lending practices, see National Association of Mutual Savings Banks, *Mutual Savings Banking,* prepared for the Commission on Money and Credit (Englewood Cliffs, N.J.: Prentice-Hall, 1962), Chap. 6.

and flexibility created pressures for broadened investment outlets in securities markets and, when increases in earnings became more difficult to achieve by shifting further to mortgages, pressures arose for relaxation of restrictions on conventional out-of-state loans.

The yield relationships that led savings banks to make out-of-state loans and loans on commercial properties created a new orientation toward mortgages in which the savings banks became active in both local and out-of-state markets and in both residential and commercial markets. Their portfolios include conventional and federally underwritten loans, loans on owner-occupied and income properties, loans on commercial and residential construction, and loans for existing as well as new housing.

The dual orientation toward local and out-of-state lending has resulted, on the one hand, in generally favorable terms for mortgage borrowers in savings bank states and, on the other hand, in flows of capital to growing and capital-deficient states with resulting development of a better mortgage market mechanism and smaller regional differentials in interest rates.[7] In a large number of states that do not have savings banks, the savings banks nevertheless provide more housing credit than do the commercial banks of those states and have more FHA and VA loans than do locally domiciled savings and loan associations. In addition, the savings banks are leading or important participants in a variety of federal housing programs and the largest lender on multi-family properties.

Over the whole period from the end of 1945 to the end of 1965, savings bank assets grew by $41.2 billion, from $17 billion to $58.2 billion. During this period mortgage holdings increased $40.2 billion, from $4.2 billion to $44.4 billion. Thus, all but a billion dollars of the increase in assets represented growth of mortgage loans. Another way of describing this development is that the increase in deposits was $37.1 billion, so that more than the increase in deposits was devoted to mortgage lending. More precisely, the sources and uses of funds for this 20-year period were:

7. See George Hanc, "Report on Out-of-State Lending," *Savings Bank Journal*, April, 1965, p. 42.

Sources	
Increase in deposits	$37.1 billion
Increase in reserve accounts	3.1
Increase in other liabilities	1.1
Reduction in governments	5.5
	$46.8

Uses	
Increase in other securities	4.5
Increase in other assets	1.3
Increase in loans	.8
Increase in mortgage loans	40.2
	$46.8

The basic factor affecting the increase in mortgage lending has been the deposit inflow, and the use of these funds has in turn been determined by the relative attractiveness of mortgages versus securities (and, within the mortgage market, by the attractions of different kinds of loans), in terms of net yields and needs for liquidity. With United States government securities and cash equaling almost three fourths of deposits at the end of World War II, the savings banks felt no pressures from the liquidity side, and in fact reduced their holdings of such securities by more than half over the next 20 years. The yield spread between mortgages and governments and other securities has, with few exceptions, favored investment in mortgages, but the relative attractiveness of government-guaranteed versus conventional and of commercial versus residential mortgages has fluctuated. The general updrift of interest rates in the postwar period, coupled with the rapid shift of assets into mortgage loans, has produced an accelerated rise in the average rate of return earned on savings bank assets, at least while both occurred.

Lending in Postwar Cycles

These interrelationships and changes in them for cyclical and other reasons are illustrated by brief reference to recent developments in the savings banks' mortgage lending. During the

1950's, the typical development was that in periods of credit restraint and relatively tight money financial institutions generally reduced their flows of funds into mortgages, as the stickiness of mortgage rates in general and the rigidity of rates on government-guaranteed loans made them less attractive relative to other capital market investments. In recessions, this same stickiness, supported by underlying requirements for residential construction, made mortgages more attractive and brought increased funds into this sector. In 1951–53, however, the savings banks swam against the tide, and while other lenders were reducing mortgage flows, savings banks considerably increased their lending. At the end of 1950, savings banks held only $8.2 billion of mortgages, a sum that represented 37 per cent of total assets. During the next three years they expanded their holdings of FHA and VA mortgages rapidly, from $3 billion to $6.5 billion, and increased their share of the total outstanding from 13.9 per cent to 20.4 per cent. VA loans alone increased from $1.5 billion to $3.1 billion, and became nearly a quarter of total mortgages held. During the three years 1951–53, mortgage holdings increased by $4.7 billion, of which $1.7 billion was financed by reductions in holdings of United States governments.

In 1954 and 1955, the total flow of mortgage funds increased rapidly, rising from $9.9 billion in 1953 to $16.2 billion in 1955. Commercial banks provided 9.9 per cent of the flow in 1953 and 15 per cent in 1955, but all principal lenders increased the amounts lent. Savings banks increased their mortgage holdings by $2.1 billion and $2.4 billion respectively, although net deposit gains were $2 billion and $1.8 billion. In 1956, while commercial banks reduced their net flow into mortgages by $700 million and savings and loan associations by $1 billion, savings banks and insurance companies maintained their annual flows at about the same level. With mortgages increasing by $2.3 billion and deposits by $1.8 billion, the savings banks again reduced holdings of governments by half a billion.

In 1957, a year of relatively tight money, mortgage flows fell off to $11.9 billion. The commercial banks reduced their lending to $600 million, only 5.2 per cent of total lending. While savings and loan associations lent about as much as in the preceding year, insurance companies and savings banks responded to higher yields in securities markets by reducing their mortgage flows. Savings banks used less than their deposit inflow of $1.7 billion to increase mortgages by $1.4 billion and also increased their corporate and other securities by $800 million—the largest such increase of the postwar period—through sale of governments and other sources. The principal reduction in net flows was in VA loans, where the statutory rate reduced the relative attractiveness of these loans. The savings banks continued conventional and FHA loans at about the same rate, but they increased VA loans, which had been increasing by over $1 billion a year, by only $640 million.

The period of credit restriction ended after the short and sharp recession beginning in mid-1957 became apparent, and Federal Reserve actions eased money supplies and market yields in 1958. Commercial banks returned to the mortgage markets, and savings institutions enjoyed large increases in deposits; the net deposit gain for savings banks was $2.3 billion. The government broadened the activities of "Fannie Mae" (The Federal National Mortgage Association, or FNMA) and the FHA, and housing starts trended upward during the year. In August, the FHA mortgage rate was raised to 5.25 per cent to encourage the flow of funds in this direction. The savings bank mortgage flow increased by 50 per cent, from $1.4 billion to $2.1 billion. The greater mortgage flow can be explained mainly by the increase in FHA loans, as conventional lending remained stable and VA loans became less attractive, with a 4.75 per cent interest rate. By the end of 1958, savings bank mortgage holdings reached $23.3 billion, more than 60 per cent of assets. Residential loans were 90 per cent of the total, and VA loans, having passed conventional loans in importance in 1955, were 35.9 per cent of total loans. FHA loans, at 23.6 per cent, brought the total of federally guaranteed residential loans to 59.5 per cent of total loans.

In spite of high interest rates in capital markets in 1959, net mortgage flows rose to an unprecedented $19 billion. The savings banks were the only principal lending category to reduce the volume of mortgage lending. In 1959 amounts deposited and

withdrawn were virtually equal, the latter being larger in the
second half of the year, and net deposit gains were only $1.2
billion. Nevertheless, the net flow of mortgage funds from savings banks declined only $400 million, remaining larger than
the net deposit gain at $1.7 billion. In this year, however, the
savings banks contributed only 9.1 per cent of the total mortgage net flow. In spite of high yields, they sold securities, both
federal and corporate, to maintain the mortgage flow. One factor maintaining the level of lending was advance commitments
made in 1958, and another was the increase in the FHA rate to
5 3/4 per cent in September, 1959. The VA rate had been raised
to 5 1/4 per cent in July, but because of the resulting differentials, FHA loans exceeded $800 million while VA loans fell
below $300 million.

Expansion of 1960's

The recession in 1960 brought conditions similar to those existing in 1953–54 and 1957–58. Federal Reserve policy was directed
toward lowering long-term interest rates while maintaining some
upward pressure on short-term rates for balance-of-payments
purposes. The FHA rate was lowered, and prices paid by FNMA
raised. FHA terms were liberalized, and further measures were
adopted to spur urban renewal and rehabilitation. As a result of
these developments, the yield spread between mortgages and
governments increased to more than 2 per cent. Net deposit
gains were not much larger than in 1959 ($1.4 billion), but the
combination of deposit inflow and yield relationships led to
slightly greater mortgage lending. Over half a billion governments again were sold or matured. FHA and conventional lending remained about the same, and VA loans increased as the
yield spread improved. By the end of the year mortgages
reached the two-thirds mark in relation to total assets. Savings
banks now held over a quarter of federally underwritten mortgages. They had become the largest holder of VA mortgages in
1957, and in 1960 they were exceeded in FHA mortgages only by
life insurance companies. In the combined categories, savings

banks were barely the largest holders, with just over $16 billion of total mortgage holdings of $26.9 billion.

The decade of the 1960's brought even more active competition for savings, and thus for earnings, than had been apparent in the 1950's. Interest in ancillary sources of earnings, such as mortgage servicing and warehousing, and in out-of-state lending was stimulated. Opportunities for lending in the fields of urban renewal, home improvement, and housing for the elderly increased with the passage of the Housing Act of 1961. At the same time, the beginning of the long recovery, in which the fears of inflation prevalent in the 1950's abated, created a situation favorable to deposit inflows and started the sharp gains made by deposit-type intermediaries. While the yield spread continued to favor mortgages, it began to narrow and to make conventional loans relatively more attractive than they had been in relation to FHA and VA loans. While the increase in mortgages exceeded the net deposit gain in 1961, the difference was not great—$2.2 billion as against $1.9 billion—as net sales of government securities fell to $100 million from $600 million the year before. By now, total holdings of governments were considerably reduced from what they had been at the start of the period, especially when viewed in relation to other assets or deposits.

The year 1961 marked the low points in terms of percentages of loans represented by multi-family and nonresidential mortgages. Nonresidential loans had represented as much as 19 per cent of total mortgages at the end of World War II, but in spite of a considerable absolute increase they fell steadily to 9.4 per cent of the total in 1961. Multi-family loans had been 35 per cent of mortgage loans in 1945, but they also declined steadily to 21.7 per cent. The counterpart of these changes was the climb of one- to four-family mortgages from 45 per cent to 68.7 per cent, representing an increase considerably greater than that of total mortgage loans. The increasing volume of funds seeking investment, the rising volume of construction of multi-family and commercial structures, and economies of scale in larger loans contributed to the upswing in this type of lending. Much of the lending on multi-family properties was in the form of FHA mortgages. On smaller properties conventional loans continued to improve in attractiveness as market rates firmed above rates on government guaranteed loans.

The new environment was dramatized in 1962, when a new record of $3.1 billion of net deposit gains was made, in contrast to the previous mark of $2.3 billion set in a climate of recession in 1958. While the competition for funds was great, the inflow of savings tended to maintain stable rates in capital markets, thus encouraging the continued shift to mortgages. Renewed activity of commercial banks in search of earnings in mortgage markets (their net flow rose from $1.6 billion to $4 billion) and continued mortgage lending by thrift institutions prevented a rise in rates although demands for mortgage funds were sufficient to cause a total net flow of $25.3 billion. The yield spread between mortgages and securities was thus beginning to be pinched, but from declining mortgage rates rather than rising bond yields, as had been the case in earlier periods of recovery.

The savings banks increased all types of mortgage loans. One- to four-family loans reached $22.1 billion, but declined slightly in over-all importance. Multi-family and commercial mortgages combined increased by almost exactly $1 billion, each increasing slightly in share of total holdings and thus more significantly as shares of annual flows. The increase in conventional residential mortgages was a record $1.1 billion and approached FHA mortgage flows, although these too showed record growth. Conventional flows were closer to FHA gains than at any time since 1957. Although the flow into VA mortgages remained below the levels of the mid-1950's, the combined flows of FHA and VA loans were large because of increasing volumes of out-of-state lending. In 1962, the savings banks were able to claim that they had loans in all 32 non-savings bank states, and loans to borrowers in these states took 37 per cent of the total flow of mortgages.

New deposit-gain records were again set in both 1963 and 1964. Net deposit gains were $3.3 billion in 1963, with mortgages rising $4 billion. The difference was financed by reductions both in government securities and in corporate and other securities and by gains in capital accounts. At this stage of the recovery bond yields began to rise slightly, while mortgage yields firmed. The result pinched the yield spread to about 1.25 per cent by the end of the year. Multi-family loans represented about one fourth of total lending, somewhat above earlier relationships. Savings banks had clearly become the predominant holder of such loans. From a slight edge over insurance companies in 1950, the savings banks held $8 billion of multi-family mortgages at the end of 1963; life insurance companies held $5.3 billion, savings and loan associations $5.2 billion, and commercial banks $1.6 billion. Government-guaranteed loans continued to increase because of the rise of out-of-state lending—from $8.4 billion to $10 billion—while at the same time savings banks continued to be the largest lender on conventional mortgages in several savings bank states.[8]

The record deposit gain in 1964 was $4.2 billion, as the economic climate remained favorable to deposit-type saving, and competition for such funds remained keen. Savings bank mortgage flows again exceeded the deposit gain, but by a small margin. The yield spread remained remarkably stable, as there was general stability in both mortgage and bond market yields. The record deposit inflow led to records in mortgage lending—$2.7 billion for one- to four-family, $1.1 billion for multi-family, and $0.5 billion for nonresidential. The total net flow of mortgage funds in the economy was a record $29.5 billion, of which the savings banks supplied 14.7 per cent. In spite of declining attractiveness of VA mortgages, the savings banks were the only principal lender to increase such loans significantly. They did so as a result of the pressures for out-of-state lending; 80 per cent of the increase in FHA and VA holdings represented such out-of-state loans. The savings banks were able to say that they were either the first or second largest holder of each of the FHA categories of loans—owner-occupied, rental, urban home redevelopment, co-operative housing, servicemen's housing, and nursing homes.

8. Connecticut, Massachusetts, Maine, New Hampshire, New York, and Rhode Island.

Lending in 1965–66

The unusually tight money conditions of the summer of 1966 and the preceding developments in 1965 are described in Chapter 4. The process of disintermediation was naturally reflected in developments generally in the mortgage market and in savings bank reaction to them. The redirection of credit flows away from savings institutions and directly into securities markets created special stringencies in mortgage credit.

While the total flow of mortgage funds was down slightly in 1965 from the record 1964 levels, one- to four-family residential mortgages expanded by a record of nearly $16 billion. In the total flow, commercial banks increased their share to the highest proportion since 1950 (19 per cent), and insurance companies to the highest level since the late 1950's (16.3 per cent). The decline in deposit growth at savings banks and savings and loan associations in 1966 accentuated the shifts in market shares. Savings and loan associations had the smallest savings growth in 13 years, and their extensions of mortgage loans fell to $3.8 billion, or less than a third of the $12.1 billion extended in 1963. Their share of the net flow of mortgage funds fell to 15.6 per cent, considerably below any other year in the postwar period. Savings banks had a net flow of $2.8 billion, or 11.4 per cent of the total. This flow was still higher than that for any year prior to 1962 and was not a precipitate drop in market shares. In contrast, commercial banks, life insurance companies, and "all other" holders increased their shares of the market significantly in 1966.

As noted in the earlier discussion of deposit behavior, savings banks stemmed the deposit outflow about mid-year, while savings and loan associations generally experienced improvement late in the year. However, the flow of funds at savings institutions available for new lending was further restricted by a slowing down of prepayments on outstanding loans. The slower turnover of real estate, because of the decline in new lending, reduced the liquidation of outstanding mortgages, and much of this effect was felt in the second half of the year.

Following the constant rise in holdings of real estate mortgages since the war, the tight money conditions of 1966 found the savings banks with 76 per cent of their assets in this form at the beginning of the year. Consequently, there was little unused liquidity with which to meet mortgage demands. The savings and loan associations, however, started the year with even less. In some areas of the country associations had found it necessary to take foreclosure or other steps and "probably owned in excess of $1 billion in real estate other than association premises."[9] Associations also lacked liquidity because they had used advances from home loan banks earlier in the expansion to increase their mortgage lending. At the beginning of 1966, advances from the home loan banks approximated $6 billion. The home loan banks generally borrow in capital markets at short term, and thus were required to roll over their debt at rising interest costs, which were in turn passed on to their members.[10] Because of conditions in capital markets, the home loan banks discontinued lending for expansion of loans and restricted their funds for cases of declining share accounts.

Virtually all of the decline in net savings bank lending in 1966 was reflected in out-of-state loans. Net mortgage acquisitions fell from $4.1 billion in 1965 to $2.8 billion in 1966, but in-state lending amounted to $1.8 billion as compared to $2 billion the year before; out-of-state lending thus fell to $1 billion. Correspondingly, the decline was also centered on federally guaranteed loans; not only was the net acquisition of FHA loans small, but VA holdings declined slightly. On balance, however, savings banks increased their mortgage holdings by 108 per cent of their net gain in savings, raising their mortgage loans to 77 per cent of total assets. Of this increase, nonresidential mortgages continued to be important and were in fact larger than the extension in 1965. Net increases in non-farm residential loans only are shown in Table 7–2. From these figures it is apparent that commercial banks maintained their lending at a relatively high

9. "Monetary Policy and the Residential Mortgage Market," *Federal Reserve Bulletin*, May, 1967, p. 733.

10. *Ibid.*

level, although at only 38 per cent of their growth in time deposits in 1966. On the other hand, while savings and loan associations put 89 per cent of their savings growth and borrowings into mortgages, their decline in lending was the most severe.

TABLE 7-2[11]

NET INCREASE IN NON-FARM RESIDENTIAL
MORTGAGE DEBT, 1964–66

(BILLIONS OF DOLLARS)

	1964	1965	1966
Commercial banks	2.5	3.5	2.7
Savings banks	3.8	3.6	2.2
Savings and loans	9.3	8.7	3.7
Life insurance companies	2.9	2.7	2.2
TOTAL	18.5	18.5	10.9
Federal agencies	−.2	.4	2.8
All others	3.2	2.7	1.4
TOTAL	21.3	21.5	15.1

In order to devote 108 per cent of savings growth to mortgage lending, the savings banks also restructured their holdings of securities. There was a net reduction of more than $700 million in holdings of governments, but at the same time the attractive yields in the corporate bond market led to a reversal of the trend toward reducing these holdings; corporates rose by $324 million. Holdings of agency securities also rose to some extent. There was a shift toward shorter maturities to protect the liquidity otherwise being reduced.

In five states, savings banks hold more mortgages than do commercial banks and savings and loan together, and in all savings bank states combined, savings banks hold slightly more mortgages than do savings and loan associations and about twice as many as are held by commercial banks.

11. *Ibid.*, p. 734.

TABLE 7-3[12]

MORTGAGE HOLDINGS OF SAVINGS BANKS,
COMMERCIAL BANKS, AND SAVINGS AND LOAN ASSOCIATIONS,
DECEMBER 31, 1965
SAVINGS BANK STATES
(MILLIONS OF DOLLARS)

	Mutual Savings Banks	Commercial Banks	Savings and Loan Associations
New York	27,432	5,974	6,935
Massachusetts	6,489	780	2,763
Connecticut	3,040	735	967
New Hampshire	691	157	220
Maine	438	197	145
Other savings bank states	6,343	14,852	30,389
TOTAL	44,433	22,695	41,419

In the 1950–65 period, the net increase in mortgage holdings of savings banks exceeded the increase for commercial banks or savings and loan associations in the savings bank states: $38.1 billion for savings banks, $35.1 billion for savings and loan associations, and $17.6 billion for commercial banks.

Out-of-State Lending

Total mortgage holdings, as shown in Table 7–4, were three fifths in-state and two fifths out-of-state, with nearly 30 per cent of total mortgages placed in non-savings bank states. Of the non-savings bank state mortgages, only a negligible portion constituted conventional mortgages, and the bulk was fairly evenly divided between FHA and VA loans.

The distribution and composition of total loans were strongly influenced by the lending of savings banks in New York State. The legislative treatment of out-of-state lending by New York is illustrative of the evolutionary nature of this type of regulation. Until the early 1950's, New York State savings banks were not

12. NAMSB data, based on FDIC, United States Savings and Loan League, F.H.L.B. Board, and NAMSB.

permitted to make out-of-state loans, but they were able to participate in loans made by the Savings Banks Trust Company, a wholly-owned central institution. Then the restrictions were lifted for direct loans if they were FHA or VA underwritten. A compromise bill broadened powers of both state-chartered commercial and savings banks in 1966, and permitted nation-wide conventional loans by savings banks up to 20 per cent of assets. Since more than 60 per cent of all savings bank mortgages were held by New York State banks in 1966, so also was the bulk of the out-of-state loans. New York State banks held $9.7 billion in non-savings-bank states in September, 1966, and these holdings constituted one third of the New York State banks' loans and 71 per cent of loans in non-savings-bank states. The next largest total of loans was held by Massachusetts banks—$6.8 billion, of which $1.1 billion, or 16.3 per cent, were in non-savings-bank states. Massachusetts and Pennsylvania held 8.1 per cent and 9.4 per cent respectively of such loans, far below the 71 per cent held by New York State banks. Pennsylvania, Rhode Island, and Minnesota, however, all had higher proportions of their own loans on such properties than did New York.

TABLE 7-4[13]

IN-STATE AND OUT-OF-STATE MORTGAGES,
SEPTEMBER 30, 1966

	Amount (Billion $)	Per Cent
Total mortgage holdings	46.6	100.0
In-state	28.1	60.4
Out-of-state	18.4	39.6
Savings bank states	4.8	10.4
Non-savings bank states	13.6	29.2
FHA	7.2	15.5
VA	6.0	12.9
Conventional	.4	.8

As might be assumed, out-of-state lending has largely represented a flow of funds from capital-surplus to capital-deficient

13. NAMSB, *National Fact Book, 1967*, p. 46.

states. The three largest recipients of loans were California, Florida, and Texas, where on September 30, 1966, outstanding loans held by savings banks were $4.3 billion, $1.4 billion, and $1.3 billion, respectively. Other leading sources of loan demand were Virginia, Georgia, and Alabama.

Loan Terms

The rapid growth of savings banks' mortgages and their dominant position in some areas suggest that their lending practices are sufficiently liberal to be effectively competitive. Allowing for the inaccuracies of the data, average interest rates and other terms offered by savings banks tend to be on the liberal side. These are summarized for 1966 in Table 7–5.

TABLE 7-5[14]

AVERAGE INTEREST RATE AND OTHER TERMS,
CONVENTIONAL FIRST MORTGAGE LOANS,
SINGLE FAMILY HOMES, 1966

	Interest rate (%)	Fees and charges (%)	Maturity (years)	Loan to price ratio	Purchase price* ($000)
New home purchase					
All institutions	6.11	.69	24.4	72.8	23.7
Mutual savings banks	5.89	.07	24.1	68.7	23.3
Commercial banks	6.03	.20	19.6	64.5	26.1
Savings and loan associations	6.20	.90	24.5	75.5	22.2
Life insurance companies	6.11	.14	26.7	69.9	28.4
Mortgage companies	6.00	.95	27.0	73.5	25.4
Existing home purchase					
All institutions	6.24	.59	20.0	70.9	18.9
Mutual savings banks	5.94	.20	21.6	68.4	20.5
Commercial banks	6.11	.22	16.8	65.3	19.4
Savings and loan associations	6.37	.87	21.1	74.2	17.9
Life insurance companies	6.07	.13	24.7	69.0	28.9
Mortgage companies	6.22	.31	23.4	71.5	30.9

*1964

14. FHLB Board and NAMSB. Unweighted averages of monthly loan terms approved during the year, confined to loans originated by lender. Fees and charges are discounts and payments resulting in income, expressed as percentages of principal.

Despite reduced out-of-state mortgage acquisitions in 1966, savings banks continued to hold larger portfolios of residential mortgage loans than locally-based commercial banks in many of the 32 non-savings bank states. And they remained larger holders of federally underwritten mortgages than local savings and loan associations in a majority of these states, as well as the leading investors in FHA and VA loans in the nation as a whole.[15]

Savings banks tend to charge low interest rates on both new and existing homes. Commercial banks and savings and loan associations tend to get higher rates. Savings banks are near the bottom with respect to fees and other charges. The maturity of their loans is roughly average for all lenders, commercial banks tending toward quicker maturities and the other lenders tending toward maturities that are as long or longer. Savings and loan associations tend to lend higher proportions of the purchase price; this practice is consistent with their higher average interest rate. The average purchase price is roughly the same for savings banks as the average for all lenders, but savings and loan associations are somewhat below the average, and insurance companies are a bit above the average.

Mortgage Loans And Earnings

The rise in the ratio of mortgage loans to total assets from roughly one fourth to three fourths in the postwar period has strongly influenced the rates earned on total assets, as has the upward drift of interest rates during most of the period. Since 1950, the savings banks have altered their statement of condition from one closely resembling that of life insurance companies to one similar to that of savings and loan associations. With the latter already holding mortgages in the range of 80 per cent to 85 per cent of total assets, the proportion of deposit growth going into mortgages has been even higher for savings banks. Total earnings—and thus dividends—have become more and more closely identified with yields on mortgages.

The situation is pictured in Chart 7–1, which is based on

---

15. NAMSB, *Annual Report, 1967*, p. 12.

Table 7–6. Although the scale of the chart perhaps exaggerates the steepness of the rise in yields, it also brings out the manner

TABLE 7-6[16]

MORTGAGE AND SECURITY YIELDS,
1949–65

	FHA Mortgages	*Savings Bank Mortgages*	*Treasury Bonds*	*Savings Bank Securities*	*Savings Bank Total Assets*
1949	4.34%	4.39%	2.31%	2.46%	2.95%
1950	4.16	4.24	2.32	2.47	3.01
1951	4.26	4.17	2.57	2.49	3.11
1952	4.29	4.11	2.68	2.59	3.20
1953	4.63	4.14	2.94	2.68	3.30
1954	4.60	4.21	2.55	2.73	3.40
1955	4.64	4.25	2.84	2.79	3.53
1956	4.85	4.33	3.08	2.88	3.65
1957	5.44	4.39	3.47	3.01	3.80
1958	5.49	4.50	3.43	3.17	3.92
1959	5.81	4.63	4.08	3.31	4.08
1960	6.16	4.75	4.02	3.49	4.25
1961	5.76	4.89	3.90	3.62	4.41
1962	5.60	5.02	3.95	3.76	4.56
1963	5.46	5.13	4.00	3.83	4.68
1964	5.45	5.18	4.15	3.96	4.79
1965	5.47	5.22	4.21	4.07	4.89

16. Sources: FHA yields, *Business Cycle Developments,* July, 1964, December, 1964, January, 1966; savings bank earnings on mortgages, bonds, and total assets, NAMSB; Treasury bonds, *Economic Report of the President, 1966* and *Federal Reserve Bulletin.* The data should be taken as indications rather than precise measures of mortgage yields. The secondary market FHA yield is based on prices of FHA-insured mortgages on new homes, estimated on the basis of opinion reports from FHA field offices. Before July, 1961, prices are for an assumed original maturity of 25 years on mortgages assumed to be prepaid in 12 years; after that date, an assumed original maturity of 30 years, and prepaid in 15 years. The yield earned on savings bank mortgages is equally imprecise, as it is based on the yields reported by individual savings banks and includes banks that do as well as those that do not service their own mortgages, those that buy and those that originate, and so on. Treatment of fees, charges, and discounts may vary.

in which rising mortgage yields have raised the average yield on mortgages held by savings banks and, combined with the rising proportion of mortgage loans, the average yield on savings bank assets. The yield on savings bank securities—below 2.5 per cent in 1949—has been pulled up by the sharp upward trend in bond yields, but, as might be expected for such a long period, the average portfolio yield has lagged behind prevailing market yields. The same is true of mortgage yields, represented by the yield on FHA mortgages in the secondary market.[17] The virtually constant and steep rise in market yields during the 1950's permitted the continuing addition of higher-yielding loans to the portfolio, thus raising the average yield. Older mortgages paid off were in general loans made at lower rates of interest. Thus, not only the net flow but the gross flow of funds into mortgage loans contributed to the rise in earnings. As in a standard textbook explanation of marginal and average costs, so long as market yields have been above portfolio yields, additions to the portfolio have raised the average portfolio yield. This situation is particularly noticeable during the period of softer rates after 1960. Although mortgage yields eased, they remained well above the yield on existing portfolios and, of course, further above the yield on Treasury securities, even though the latter rose.

Chart 7–1 illustrates the fact that the average yield on savings bank mortgages approached much more closely the market yields in 1963 and thereafter than had been the case previously. This relationship tended to imply that the steepness of the rise in earnings could not be maintained, because there was little margin remaining to be exploited and because mortgages already constituted a large fraction of total assets. Even with the higher level of rates established in 1966—which in mid-1967 appeared to be unexpectedly sticky—there is less room to increase the percentage of assets held in this form than there was in the decade of the 1950's. An offsetting factor, however, is the larger gross flow of new lending based on repayments of the larger holdings.

17. For sources of data and comment on the reliability of these figures, see note to Table 7-6.

Chart 7–1

Earnings Rates, Savings Bank Assets

1949—66

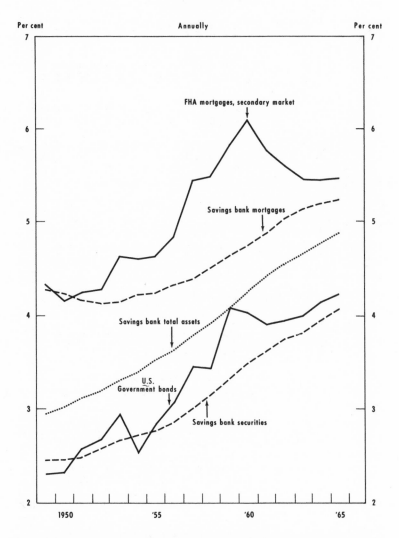

Sources of data: National Association of Mutual Savings Banks, Federal Housing Administration, and Board of Governors of the Federal Reserve System

TABLE 7-7[18]

RATIOS OF MORTGAGE LOAN PORTFOLIO ACTIVITY, SAVINGS BANKS, 1949–66

| | Ratio to loans outstanding at beginning of year | | | | | | | | Ratio of net gains to new loans acquired | | | |
| | New loans acquired | | | | Repayments | | | | | | | |
	Total	FHA	VA	Conv.	Total	FHA	VA	Conv.	Total	FHA	VA	Conv.
1949	28.0	67.0	42.2	20.5	12.6	17.2	.7	14.1	54.9	74.3	98.4	31.3
1950	37.1	89.6	47.4	25.1	14.0	11.6	12.5	14.8	62.3	87.1	73.6	41.1
1951	34.6	69.3	38.2	23.2	14.6	2.7	23.4	15.7	57.8	96.1	38.8	32.3
1952	28.3	27.7	39.9	25.1	13.6	6.2	8.5	18.5	52.0	77.7	78.7	26.2
1953	26.6	17.4	46.2	24.2	12.7	6.4	9.4	17.3	52.0	63.2	79.7	28.5
1954	28.8	16.9	48.1	26.3	12.8	8.5	6.3	18.2	55.5	49.7	86.8	30.8
1955	30.3	18.3	44.8	28.0	14.0	9.8	8.7	19.5	53.9	46.5	80.5	30.4
1956	25.3	15.0	31.0	26.6	12.3	8.4	7.4	18.2	51.6	43.9	76.3	31.8
1957	17.5	12.0	14.6	23.1	10.3	7.1	5.8	16.0	41.1	40.7	60.1	30.7
1958	20.7	26.2	13.9	23.8	10.7	7.2	6.8	16.1	48.0	72.7	51.1	32.1
1959	19.0	22.2	9.8	25.3	11.1	7.4	6.8	17.2	41.5	66.5	31.0	32.3
1960	17.8	18.9	10.6	23.1	10.0	6.0	6.0	15.8	43.7	68.0	43.3	31.5
1961	18.2	21.2	9.5	23.5	10.0	7.7	7.0	14.1	44.9	63.7	26.4	40.1
1962	21.4	23.4	13.6	26.2	10.6	8.4	8.3	13.9	50.5	64.0	38.8	47.1
1963	23.9	25.8	16.4	28.0	11.6	10.3	9.1	14.4	51.3	60.0	44.8	48.5
1964	23.5	26.3	15.1	27.3	11.5	10.9	9.0	13.7	50.8	58.4	39.9	49.7
1965	21.3	22.1	12.3	26.7	11.2	9.8	9.4	13.4	47.4	55.6	23.4	49.7
1966	15.8	13.8	8.4	21.6	9.8	8.9	7.9	11.5	38.2	35.4	6.5	46.8

18. NAMSB *Fact Books.*

Another offsetting factor would occur if savings banks obtained extended permission generally to make conventional loans on a nationwide basis. This development might take place through state legislation or through federal chartering. If the flow of out-of-state lending should shift to conventional loans, an additional increment would be added annually to average portfolio mortgage yields.

A clearer view of the effects of large annual additions to the mortgage portfolio is provided by the data in Table 7–7, showing the gross flow of new mortgage loans made in relation to repayments and the resulting net addition to portfolios. In the earlier years covered by the table, new loans made were in excess of one quarter or even one third of loans already held. The increases in FHA and VA loans were even larger, partly because of the relatively small base from which they were measured. For the mortgage portfolio as a whole, repayments after the first few years have approximated half of the new loans made, resulting in net acquisitions of roughly half the new loans. Repayments have had a downward trend as a proportion of new loans made. The decline has been influenced by the growing importance of federally underwritten loans and longer maturities. It is apparent, however, that since 1960, repayments of federally underwritten loans have moved upward, at least through 1964 and seemingly stopped the decline in the over-all portfolio. Concentration of new loans in this category in the early years—FHA loans nearly doubled in 1951, and VA loans often increased by more than three fourths in the early 1950's—coupled with low repayment ratios resulted in high proportions of new loans of this type remaining as net gains in the portfolio. Since 1960, however, the increased emphasis on conventional loans has been apparent in the rising proportion of new loans kept as net gains, from less than one third to approximately one half.

The average size of loan held has been pulled up throughout the postwar period by rising valuations, higher loan-to-value ratios, and, in recent years, by larger amounts of multi-family and commercial mortgages. The average mortgage loan held in 1950 was $7,727, while the average loan made in that year was $8,949. This relationship has existed throughout the period, pulling up the size of the average loan held, as illustrated in Table 7–8.

TABLE 7-8[19]

AVERAGE SIZE OF MORTGAGE LOANS,
SELECTED YEARS

	Loans held at end of year (in dollars)				New loans during year (in dollars)			
	Total	FHA	VA	Conv. & other	Total	FHA	VA	Conv. & other
1950	7,727	9,982	6,564	7,571	8,949	13,823	7,040	8,016
1955	9,607	11,399	8,783	9,474	11,710	10,852	11,219	12,608
1960*	10,850	11,705	9,346	11,882	14,244	13,714	10,635	16,790

Decline of Other Assets

The dominant position achieved by mortgage loans has been accompanied by a corresponding decline in relative holdings of other assets. The shifts taking place during the postwar period are pictured in Chart 3–1. Along with the increasing emphasis on liquidity and flexibility in the portfolio of government bonds, there has also been a small but significant increase in holdings of equity investments. State legislation varies considerably in allowing limited investments in common and preferred stocks, some of which go back many decades for historical roots and some of which originated in the inflationary environment after World War II. In New England holdings of bank shares are prevalent, while they are not permitted in New York State. In Maine and Massachusetts holdings of insurance company shares are also significant.

While equity investments are not large on a national basis, in a few states they are significant fractions of total security holdings and of total assets. These are summarized in Table 7–9. Total holdings of equities approximated $1.5 billion at the end of 1965, and more than two thirds of this amount were common

19. NAMSB.

stocks. In New York State the proportion between common and preferred shares is nearly 50–50. Typically, savings banks have channeled more funds into equities in periods of relatively low prices and reduced the flows when prices were higher. Some of the older savings banks have substantial unrealized capital gains, and welcome sources of income, from holdings of common stock. There were net liquidations in the uncertain markets of 1966, matched by additions of preferred stocks. The accelerated deposit inflow and recovery of prices in 1967 led to purchases of equities to bring total holdings to $1.65 billion at mid-year.[21]

TABLE 7-9[20]

CORPORATE STOCKS HELD BY SAVINGS BANKS
DECEMBER 31, 1965

| | | Per Cent of | |
| | *Amount* | *Security* | *Total* |
State	*(Million Dollars)*	*Holdings*	*Assets*
New York	656	13.4	1.9
Massachusetts	328	12.6	3.4
Connecticut	217	24.4	5.1
Rhode Island	61	30.9	6.2
New Hampshire	51	25.3	5.1
Pennsylvania	51	4.7	1.4
New Jersey	37	6.6	1.7
Maine	31	14.7	4.5
Vermont	2	7.8	.8
Other	38	6.2	1.5
TOTAL	1,471	13.0	2.4

20. George Hanc, "Equity Investments of Mutual Savings Banks in 1965," *Savings Bank Journal,* June, 1966, p. 115.

21. George Hanc, "First-half Equity Investments by Savings Banks at Record Level," *Ibid.,* December, 1967, p. 23.

III | Savings Banks in the Economy

CHAPTER 8

Savings Banking Abroad

SAVINGS banks in their modern form arose in a surprising number of countries at approximately the same time. At roughly the beginning of the nineteenth century the growth of city populations dependent on wages, a result of the Industrial Revolution, led philanthropic and wealthy citizens and associations, as well as different levels of government, to consider ways and means of alleviating some of the problems of poverty and dependency that accompanied changing economic conditions. The idea of encouraging self-reliance and personal thrift spread rapidly from country to country, and nonprofit savings banks were established across Western Europe and Scandinavia.

As a result of the more or less simultaneous beginnings and common purposes, there are many similarities between the savings bank systems of different countries. As the American savings banks were copied from those in Scotland and England, so the European systems borrowed from each other. In fact, there grew up what became known as the savings bank movement, a term that is rather difficult to define precisely, because it carries different meanings for different individuals and in different places. Even today it is apparent that leaders of savings banking consider these banks something more than business institutions in mutual form. They feel that thrift is something to be encouraged for social as well as economic reasons and that savings banks have a missionary and welfare function. This attitude unquestionably lends a zeal and an enthusiasm to savings bank leadership, but at the same time it creates paradoxes and managerial problems in which expenses of expansion and promotion of the system must be weighed against earnings for depositors in the competition for funds.

While there are many international similarities, there are also many contrasts. In some countries savings banks were started under or have come under government sponsorship of some sort, ranging from municipal management to guarantee of deposits to encouragement of saving through tax treatment or premiums of various kinds. In some countries the savings banks have virtually unlimited powers of lending and investing and of accepting deposits; in others investments are limited to government securities, and no loans are made at all.[1] In Germany, for example, demand deposits are an important source of funds, the giro system of transferring funds is highly developed, and short term business loans are common. In some areas there may be a single savings bank with numerous branches; in others the system resembles unit banking. In some countries savings banks dominate the mortgage market, while in others they make no mortgage loans at all. As in the United States, what might be called the accidents of history have brought about the present national situations; either the savings banks acquired additional powers and freedoms, or competing institutions dominated various segments of the savings and capital markets.

Germany

The German system of savings banking would probably be considered the most highly developed and most free in obtaining and using funds. A few banks were started by private philanthropy before 1800, but the period of rapid development came around the turn of the century when Berlin, followed by other cities, established savings banks. Municipal savings banks were

---

1. Some of the material for this chapter was gathered in Europe in 1966. At the time of publication it was possible to up-date some of this material but not all; hence, for comparability many of the data are left as of the end of 1964.

soon operating in all the Laender (states) of the country. In 1932, the savings banks became legally independent, but municipalities guarantee the banks, and up to one half or two thirds of the board of trustees, depending on the district, represent the sponsoring governments. There are 863 savings banks in West Germany; 13 of these, including some of the largest and oldest, are private banks. The other 850 are public institutions sponsored by municipalities or other government bodies. Besides municipal banks there are district, rural, and town banks, as well as some operated by associations of local governments. Branches are widespread; there are in all some 12,300 branches of different types.

Management of the banks is selected by boards of trustees, who are in turn elected by government representatives. The number of trustees that may be chosen from among government representatives is limited, and no one connected with another type of banking institution may be elected.[2]

It is the policy of the German savings banks to invest deposited funds in the same district that provided the funds. An important use of funds is local residential mortgages. From 1950 to 1964, the savings banks supplied roughly half of the housing financing in West Germany. In addition, demand deposits provide funds from which loans are made to local businesses. The savings banks take pride in this financing of local housing and business and have resisted any system, such as exists in some other countries, whereby funds would be centralized and invested in government securities. "The savings banks have at all times stressed the independence of their investment policy and have jealously defended it against any attempts at imposing compulsory investment regulations upon them."[3]

The importance of the savings banks in the savings market is shown by the figures in Table 8-1; 60 per cent of all savings accounts were held by the savings bank system at the end of 1964.

In addition to savings deposits of 60 billion marks, the savings

2. *Die Deutsche Sparkassenorganisation,* (Stuttgart: 1965), Deutscher Sparkassenverlag, and *World Thrift, Congress Issue,* (Amsterdam: International Savings Bank Institute, March-April, 1966).

3. *Die Deutsche Sparkassenorganisation,* p. 9.

banks held 18 billion marks of clearing deposits. Assets amounted to approximately 93 billion marks, nearly one third of which was mortgage loans. Other long-term loans were 6.3 per cent, short- and medium-term loans to businesses and individuals 11.9 per cent, loans to local authorities 9 per cent, securities 13.5 per cent, and the remainder about 17 per cent liquid assets and 12 per cent other assets.

TABLE 8-1[4]

SAVINGS DEPOSITS, GERMANY, 1964

Depository	Amount (Million DM)	Per Cent
Savings banks and savings bank central banks	60,018.0	60.0
Post office, state or central	5,195.9	5.2
Joint stock banks	14,680.9	14.7
Co-operative banks and their central banks	20,050.4	20.1
Other banks	15.3	- -
TOTAL	99,960.6	100.0

A significant feature of the German savings banks, as also of the banks in some other countries, is that after payment of dividends to depositors and allocations to security reserves, surplus earnings are paid over to the municipalities or similar bodies for social purposes. This feature helps to support the idea of the social welfare aspect of savings banking.

The existence of clearing accounts at the savings banks provides them with short-term funds for working capital loans to business and has also led to the development of an efficient clearing system. This system is composed of the regional Savings Banks Central Banks *(Girozentralen)* and a central clearing center, the German Clearing Center-German Municipal Bank *(Deutsche Girozentrale-Deutsche Kommunalbank)*. There are 13 regional central banks, whose main function is operation of the "giro" or clearing system of transferring credits between customers of savings banks both intra- and inter-regionally. In

4. *World Thrift,* p. 237.

addition, they serve as central banks for the savings banks and for municipal and other public bodies and make long-term loans on real estate and to municipalities. All but one operate related building societies. They manage the liquid assets of member savings banks and lend to those banks requiring temporary funds, or they participate in loans originated by the banks. The Girozentralen also carry out security transactions for the banks and provide safekeeping facilities for them.

The 13 regional central banks in turn use the Deutsche Girozentrale-Deutsche Kommunalbank as their central bank. While maintaining their liquidity requirements at the central bank, the regional banks make loans to local governments and public services, purchase long-term securities from the smaller government units, and sell debentures to raise funds for mortgage loans to housing developments.

The Deutsche Girozentrale-Deutsche Kommunalbank originated in 1918, and since 1947 has operated principally in Duesseldorf. As the central bank for the regional central banks, it holds their liquid reserves and handles clearings between them. Thus, it has funds that it uses in both short- and long-term markets, although for the latter it also raises funds through the sale of debentures. Funds raised in this manner are usually lent to municipalities through the regional banks.[5]

The principal difference between the giro transfer system and the check-clearing system familiar to Americans is that the process starts at the bank of the transmitter of funds, rather than with receipt of a check at the recipient's bank. Funds may be transferred to the account of a recipient, whether he has a savings transfer account, a regular savings account, or an account at the post office or at a commercial bank. In the latter cases, clearing is accomplished through the central bank's account there or through the bank of issue. If the payee happens to have no account, either at a savings bank or elsewhere, he is paid cash by his local savings bank. The savings bank giro system is by far the largest clearing system in Germany, handling well over nine million accounts. Nearly all businessmen have giro accounts,

---

5. *Millionen zahlen duerch Spargiro, Millionen erhalten Kredit duerch Spargiro* (Stuttgart: Deutscher Sparkassenverlag, 1964).

and there are individual and salary accounts into which wages are paid. Statements are available daily and are placed in boxes outside the savings banks, where depositors may pick them up.

Another striking characteristic of the German system is the *Bausparkassen,* or building societies affiliated with savings banks. Typically, these are operated by the regional Girozentralen, although of the total of 14 (each operating in a defined region or state of the Republic), two are divisions of local savings banks and three are legally independent corporations. The Bausparkassen were set up after the inflation following World War I because of the destruction of savings capital and the housing shortage. In some respects they resembled savings and loan associations in their early days. That is, groups of people formed mutual organizations in which they committed themselves to save and from which they were entitled, in order of priority, to borrow approximately the amount of their individual savings for the purpose of acquiring housing. As capital markets improved and mortgage funds became more available, the purpose was changed in 1929 to that of making second mortgages junior to first mortgages made by the savings banks, under "saving-for-building" plans.

The Bausparkassen now range in size from about 100 million marks to more than one billion. Their principal activity is still saving-for-building contracts. Once the contract sum is agreed upon, the saver pays monthly into a savings account four marks per 1,000 marks of the contract sum, or more at any time if he prefers. After 18 months, and when his savings account reaches 40 per cent of the contract sum, he becomes eligible to receive that sum, although in order of priority determined by the amount saved and the length of time over which it has been accumulated. When the sum is disbursed, he receives the part that he saved, plus interest at 3.5 per cent. Repayment of the remaining part, plus interest at 5 per cent, is scheduled at the rate of 6 marks per 1,000 monthly. In addition to lending to savers, the Bausparkassen have in recent years made similar loans to nonsavers at somewhat higher rates of interest, raising the funds partly by sale of securities and partly from local savings banks. The difficulties of finding houses or land have led the Bausparkassen to extend their activities into subsidiaries, which prepare building sites and construct housing developments, as well as to affiliate with several other construction companies. In 1964, about 10,000 properties were acquired by savers through this system.

The saving-for-building scheme is also one of several plans encouraged by the government through the payment of premiums or through tax relief. After six years, the amount saved, whether used for housing or not, can be withdrawn with an additional premium from the state of from 25 per cent to 35 per cent up to a maximum premium of 400 marks per year. If used for housing, the expenditure may instead be treated as a deduction from taxable income. Similar arrangements may be made with savings banks or other banks accepting savings for periods of three years or longer. A more general plan is the premium-saving scheme, under which a saver may make lump-sum or installment deposits or purchase securities and receive premiums after five years of from 20 per cent to 30 per cent of the savings, depending upon the size of his family. As in some other countries, there are also savings plans linked to lotteries. Lottery tickets are sold for nine marks, eight going into a savings account and one into a drawing. There is a drawing every 30 days and a variety of winnings. The top prize is usually 1,000 marks, but special prizes go as high as 10,000.

Besides the building plans, there are also others in which saving is connected to subsequent loans. Saving-for-marriage plans provide for regular savings for two years or more before marriage. At the time of marriage loans equal to or larger than the savings are available at low interest rates. Similar plans are available to young businessmen and craftsmen, allowing them to borrow up to five times the amount saved regularly over three years, to set themselves up in business.

The wide extension of savings bank services in Germany is evidenced in many other ways. Deposits and withdrawals may be made at any savings bank, not only the depositor's own bank or branch of it. When in Austria, a depositor may make a withdrawal from any Austrian savings bank at the standard rate of exchange. Many depositors with giro accounts leave standing orders with their savings banks to pay a variety of bills for them. The banks offer a variety of savings deposits, about a third of the total comprising either those with a legal period of notice or an agreed-upon period. Besides the plans already mentioned, there are savings schemes for school children, for clubs, and for factory workers, and savings-plus-insurance plans, whereby a contractual sum is to be saved regularly and is covered by insurance in case of death. Savings banks buy and sell securities for their depositors, provide them with foreign currency or travelers' checks, collect domestic and foreign items, and administer property.

The German banks are the envy of savings bankers elsewhere, perhaps most for their powers of dealing with transfer accounts and for their freedom in lending and investing. With some restrictions, the savings banks may in general make virtually any kind of loan, secured or unsecured, for any purpose to any borrower. Mortgage loans are restricted to 50 per cent of assets, but individual loans have no upper limit, nor do long-term loans to corporations. Real estate may be owned up to the amount of guarantee capital.

The banks are not completely without regulation. Federal officials are empowered to require liquid holdings, and state laws may add further requirements. Reserve requirements (unpopular with the savings banks) provide for deposits at the German Federal Bank of up to 30 per cent of demand deposits, 20 per cent of time deposits, and 10 per cent of savings deposits.

The Netherlands

In terms of freedom of action, the savings banks of the Netherlands are in some respects similar to those in Germany. Tradition, conservatism, and ties to other institutions are more restrictive, however, than are government regulations. There is, in fact, no legislation directly regulating the savings banks, but the central bank possesses some rather undefined powers of regulation. It controls maturities of assets and certain asset proportions but has little enforcement power other than publicity and indirection. The savings banks, however, are governed by consensus, and the national association both audits the banks and checks on their compliance with regulations.

The private and mutual type of savings bank received a setback with numerous failures around 1830, after which newly established banks tended to avoid the word "mutual" in their titles. There are now five municipal savings banks and 248 private banks sponsored by associations or foundations. Since there is no savings bank legislation, new banks may be formed virtually at will; an individual may set up a savings bank so far as legal restrictions are concerned, and this occasionally happens. Consequently, failures of small banks are not unknown. Those banks that are organized as mutuals, however, all belong to the national association and are thus operated under its rules and surveillance. The five municipal banks are, of course, guaranteed by their respective cities. In these banks trustees are elected by the municipal governments following recommendations of the banks. The private mutuals elect trustees by various methods, often by the American plan of co-option.

The early banks were often formed in connection with other public services, such as mutual libraries or swimming pools, and these organizations (called "departments") still in some cases have the right to be represented on the boards of savings banks. Before World War II, where these connections still existed, part of the net earnings of the savings bank was paid to these related operations. The trustees are barred from receiving compensation. They typically elect the officers, set rates of compensation, and decide on premises, and an executive or investment committee approves investments. The chairman of the board usually chairs this committee. Ties with other institutions are common; in one case, for example, the chairman is a commercial banker and another trustee is chairman of an insurance company.

As in Germany, the banks operate a giro system, but the post office and city systems (as in Amsterdam) are much more important. The latter systems are operated as public services, comparable to the postal system, and as a result demand deposits are relatively unnecessary for payments. People generally use the postal and city systems for all sorts of payments typically made in the United States by check. Standing orders can be left for payment of utility and other regular bills. The system can also be used to pay people who do not have accounts, as they can cash orders at post offices.

An unusual feature of the accounts in the Netherlands is the prevalence of anonymous accounts. These accounts may be in some irrelevant name, such as "coffee," "trousers," or "spectacles," but they are also identified by number. The holder of the passbook can make withdrawals without signature. If the book is lost payments can be stopped, but with no liability to the bank for payments already made. The principal advantages seem to be that they provide privacy. There are no difficulties of inheritance, and they would sometimes be used for income tax purposes, although it is claimed that most depositors would owe little or no tax. Bank records are confidential and cannot be shown to income tax authorities without a court order; in the memory of one executive, who had been with a large bank for 18 years, there never was such an order, only a special law after World War II to help trace black marketing.

Most of the deposits are held by individuals, and most of these are "regular" accounts or accounts with notice periods not exceeding a year. Wages and salaries are often paid into these accounts. Depositors may withdraw limited amounts from any other savings bank. In fact, the European banks are attempting to work out arrangements whereby withdrawals may be made in any country. Although giro operations are carried out through the savings deposits, demand deposits subject to check are not carried. In 1966, the savings banks adopted a saving-for-marriage plan similar to the German plan, and they also offer school, factory, and life insurance plans.

Government encouragement of private saving is based not so much on a fluctuating policy of combating inflation as on one of encouraging the formation of private property. Under one plan, young people aged 15 through 20 (23 for soldiers) may contract to save regularly for six years, at the end of which period the state pays a tax-free premium of 10 per cent. In case of marriage, the premium may be paid after three years of regular saving. Another plan benefits state employees; after four years of regular saving, a tax-free premium of 15 per cent or 25 per cent, depending on salary, is paid. The plan is continuous in the sense that after the fifth or sixth year, for example, additional funds become eligible for the premium, since they have been on deposit for four years. The premium can also be paid for amounts withdrawn for housing, life insurance, marriage, education, securities, or transfer to a building society. Under comparable arrangements, private employers may pay similar tax-free premiums to employees' accounts. A similar plan open to all has been under consideration for some years.

Central bank rulings prevent business and agricultural loans, especially short-term loans. Savings banks lend frequently to mortgage banks, which also raise mortgage capital by bond sales. Other short-term loans are made to public bodies. A limited amount of personal loans may be made under regulations. Long-term loans are also made to public bodies and to organizations guaranteed by a public body or whose shares are listed on the Amsterdam Stock Exchange. Except in the case of public corporations, these loans are usually secured by mortgages up to two thirds of the valuation. Under specific limitations, other assets include liquid assets, securities, and real estate. Cash reserves are required on a sliding scale geared to the rate of turnover of deposits; these reserves are kept at the central bank. The banks also have a Cooperative Liquidity Fund, which manages the liquid resources of the savings banks for them.

As compared with 1,867 savings bank branches and 253 main offices, there were 2,197 postal savings offices at the end of 1964. The savings banks held 4.6 billion guilders of savings deposits, as against 3.9 billion in postal savings, but ranked second to the cooperative or "farmers'" banks, which held 7.1 billion.[6] The joint stock banks, while becoming more interested in savings accounts than they had been in the past, held 2 billion. The Farmers Banks were originally what their name implies, in co-operative form, but they have acquired wide powers and are the equivalent of commercial banks, although still the largest holder of savings. These banks usually hold 40 per cent to 50 per cent of assets in public bonds, make large loans to public bodies, and have only 10 per cent to 20 per cent in mortgages. The

6. *World Thrift,* p. 238.

specialists in mortgage lending in the Netherlands are the mortgage companies, which, as noted earlier, obtain some of their funds from the savings banks.

A rather unusual type of savings institution, known as the Spaarkas, exists in the Netherlands. There is a limited-liability corporation in form, and it operates according to a tontine system, under which subscribers agree to save certain amounts monthly for 14 years. Some of the subscribers die and some drop out during this period, and at the end the capital is divided among the survivors. The scheme may be called a "year bank," "fund," or "club." The plan is re-opened each year, and funds paid in for that particular maturity are kept separate from the others. The plan may be linked to insurance to protect the amount actually paid in by a subscriber. The assets of these enterprises resemble those of commercial banks.

Belgium

Belgium provides an example of a highly nationalized system. The *Caisse Générale d'Épargne et de Retraite de Belgique* (General Savings Bank and Pension Fund of Belgium) is the parent organization. It includes the savings department, which in turn has more than 30 branches. Deposits and withdrawals for the account of the savings bank may also be made at post offices and offices of the Bank of Belgium. The king appoints the members of the General Council (equivalent to trustees), a body of from 15 to 25 members, not more than two of whom may be connected with other financial institutions. This body elects a Board of Administration consisting of eight members, including the chairman. This board appoints the management, except for the top two officials, who are appointed by the king.

The bank holds regular and notice savings accounts and time deposits that receive higher interest than do the former. Above a ceiling of 350,000 francs, savings deposits receive a lower interest rate than do smaller deposits. Individuals may not have demand deposits, although certain government and social organizations may, but individuals may arrange for the bank to pay recurrent bills such as public utilities. The only premium type of saving is that for newborn babies; for them a voucher for 100 francs is available, which, if matched by at least an equal amount, may be used to open an account. School savings plans are common.

The bank's loans are principally for housing, and preference is given low-income borrowers and depositors of the bank. Loans may be up to ceilings of from 50 per cent to 90 per cent of valuation, depending on a variety of circumstances. "Social" housing is favored. The only permitted investments, other than liquid assets, are government securities at different levels and industrial bonds under various restrictions.

France

In contrast to the Belgian system, the French system has 570 local savings banks, which operate about 4,000 branches, but the system is highly concentrated because of the existence of a governmental Deposit Bank, the *Caisse des Dépôts et Consignations* in Paris. The banks are guaranteed by the state as private institutions "of public utility." Trustees are selected in a manner similar to that used in the United States; they must be people of local standing, and they select the management.[7]

The Deposit Bank is a semi-public institution that accepts deposits from the public and from postal savings. The savings banks deposit all of their funds at this bank and may direct the Deposit Bank, within the rules, how it wishes half of the total to be invested. The Deposit Bank may invest the remaining half as the local bank wishes or it may exercise government priorities, as for example for housing.

Individuals may have up to 15,000 francs in regular savings deposits on which the interest (3 per cent in 1966) is tax free. They may have a second account up to the same maximum and choose between declaring the interest as income or having 25 per cent deducted at the source. Saving for home ownership is encouraged by a plan of *Epargne-logement,* under which a saver makes regular deposits for a period of time up to a total of 40,000 francs and thus becomes eligible for a loan of up to

7. Bernard Guémas, *Les Caisses d'Épargne* (2nd ed.; Paris: Les Éditions de L'Épargne, 1963).

100,000 francs, a premium of up to 4,000 francs, and tax exemption of the interest and premium. In this scheme the interest is 2 per cent for both the deposits and the loan. The loan is repayable in from two to ten years. Demand deposits are not held by the savings banks, except in Alsace and Lorraine, where "grandfather clauses" apply.

The savings banks pass on their funds—except limited holdings of cash—to the Deposit Bank. Their recommendations for uses of these funds may include local public works of several kinds. Thus, the principal investments made by the Deposit Bank are in local governments and corporations, government-issued or guaranteed bonds, other bonds on an approved list, and bonds issued by the Mortgage Bank (Crédit Foncier), the source of mortgage lending. In Alsace and Lorraine the savings banks retain the power to make residential mortgages with part of their resources.

Although the banks' deposits are guaranteed, they take pride in the safety provided by the reserves held by both the Deposit Bank for their benefit and the banks themselves. The savings banks' income consists of interest received from the Deposit Bank. The funds represented by the banks' surplus accounts may be used other than through the Deposit Bank.

Italy

In Italy the savings banks are local or regional and have in general been founded by individuals or associations without government guarantee. The largest savings bank in the world, the Cassa di Risparmio delle Provincie Lombarde, is in Milan. Its size stems from its issuance of bonds as well as from its holdings of deposits; the total of both is over $3.5 billion. It has about three and one-half million depositors, out of a regional population of eight million, and the average deposit is the equivalent of about $500.[8]

Although the banks are private organizations—with trustees selected by members in the case of banks founded by individuals

---

8. From Quill Pen to Transistor (Milan: Cassa di Risparmio delle Provincie Lombarde, 1962), and annual reports.

and by the founding organization in other cases—the chairman and the deputy chairman are appointed by the Minister of Finance after receiving recommendations from the Governor of the Bank of Italy. These bank officials are not necessarily full-time officers of their banks, and they may be compensated in proportion to the time they devote to this work.

There are 81 savings banks in the various cities and regions and an additional ten "pawn banks of the first category," which are very similar to the savings banks. The widespread facilities of the savings banks are suggested by the fact that they have nearly 3,000 branches. The Italian banks have wide loan and investment powers and hold demand, time, and savings deposits. Interest rates paid on deposits are subject to cartel agreements covering all types of banks and are relatively low compared to those in other countries.

The social movement aspect of savings banking is strong in Italy. The banks may donate as much as half of net earnings to charities or welfare projects, the other half being added to surplus. For example, the annual report of the Cassa di Risparmio delle Provincie Lombarde for 1965 remarks:

> Undeterred by the year's difficult economic conditions, the Cassa di Risparmio in no way cut down on its customary gifts for social, relief and charity purposes, which it has regarded since its foundation as part of its fundamental aims. As in 1964, the Institute again spent more than $4,000,000 on such contributions, which, though often only small in individual amount, helped to provide the life-blood of some 5,500 institutions. More than $1,056,000 of the total went to education and training, $448,000 to relief, more than $800,000 to purposes of general public usefulness, and $1,136,000 to social projects under the ambitious programmes of the Cassa's own Social Welfare Foundation.
>
> The share of education bears witness to the Cassa's conviction that any nation's social and economic problems can be solved only if its new generations are given a sound moral and cultural background.

This use of earnings appears to be an important factor in attracting small depositors to the savings banks as well. In addition, the social needs of a community carry weight with the banks in their selection of loans and investments. The same annual report notes that "As before, it remained the Cassa's policy to encourage medium-sized and small firms in industry and crafts, in trade and services—witness the large number of separate credits outstanding and their rather low average amount of around $10,800."

Up to 10 per cent of the total deposits may be classified as those of small savers and are paid favorable rates of interest. These deposits may also be opened for educational institutions and other welfare groups and be administered by other banks, although the savings banks hold much the greatest part.

The savings banks are required by the Savings Bank Act to belong to their respective regional association, which accumulates a joint reserve fund out of contributions of 20 per cent of net earnings from each member. There is also a central bank, which administers the savings banks' liquid funds.

The restrictions on savings bank activity are largely in their own by-laws. They make a variety of secured and unsecured short-term loans and in some cases assume the function of collecting local taxes and managing the localities' finances. The only legal restriction on mortgage loans is that they have "sufficient" security. The model by-laws of the Italian savings banks, however, suggest limiting mortgage loans to 15 per cent of assets. Unsecured loans to individuals may be made, but in restricted amounts.

Austria

Many similarities may be found between the savings banks of Austria and Germany. Although many rules and regulations exist in Austria, the banks nevertheless have considerable freedom in their uses of funds. There are 173 local savings banks with slightly more than 300 branches. The majority are public banks—seven district and 133 municipal—and 33 are private associations. The local councils of the communities guaranteeing the public banks elect trustees of these banks; an annual General Meeting elects those of the private banks. In the case of the municipal banks, management is selected from among the trustees. The League of Austrian Savings Banks is charged with auditing the banks and has certain enforcement powers. The banks have giro accounts, subject to either transfer order or check, time deposits that must exceed 50,000 schillings, and savings deposits with either the legal notice period of 30 days or longer contractual periods. Wages and salaries are commonly paid into giro accounts.

The banks have a central bank, *Girozentrale der österreichischen Sparkassen, A.G.,* which administers their central reserves and acts as a central clearing house. With few exceptions the banks are required to deposit their liquid funds with this central bank. There is also a central investment company, *Sparinvest-Kapitalanlagegesellschaft m.b.H,* the majority of whose capital stock is owned by the savings banks' central bank. Savings bank depositors may invest in the certificates issued by this company.

Under ceilings on individual and aggregate loans, a wide variety of secured and unsecured short- and medium-term loans is made. Long-term loans are either mortgage loans, which may reach 50 per cent of deposits, or loans to provincial and local governments. Real estate may be owned up to the amount of the bank's reserves, and investments made in securities. Some of the savings banks are active in foreign exchange markets.

Liquidity regulations require that the banks maintain liquid assets, as defined, of 30 per cent of savings deposits and 50 per cent of other deposits. In addition there are required reserves ranging to a maximum of 15 per cent of deposits.

Spain

In Spain there are 83 savings banks with approximately 3,000 branches. These banks range from small local institutions to large banks operating over a large region. They have been established by churches, associations, individuals, and governments, and all have the same legal status, except that provincial banks are guaranteed by the provinces. Trustees are likely to be chosen as representatives of founding or sponsoring groups. The banks are subject to supervision by the *Instituto de Crédito de las Cajas de Ahorro,* in turn a branch of the Ministry of Finance, which has veto power over selection of trustees and management. The Institute exercises some of the functions of a central bank, in that it is the clearing center for giro and other inter-savings-bank transactions, and it audits and supervises the savings banks.

Ordinary savings deposits are withdrawable on demand, and about one fourth of savings deposits have a six-month's notice period. Withdrawals may be made at any savings bank. Demand and time deposits are also carried; the demand deposits are giro and checking accounts. There are savings schemes similar to those found in other countries, for marriage, youths, workers, and those tied to insurance. A recent ordinance establishes uniform rates of interest.

The banks are required to invest half of their deposits in government or industrial bonds on an approved list. In addition, they may use up to 30 per cent of their funds for purposes "of social importance." These include specific maximum percentages for "social house building;" "middle-class credits" for farmers, handicraftsmen, small industries and fisheries, agricultural and trading cooperatives, and the like; and "middle-class credit" for small traders and small savers for acquiring agricultural or housing property or securities or for becoming self-employed. Secured and unsecured loans are made for different maturities to individuals, businesses, and governmental units.[9]

Portugal

Portugal has both a State Savings Bank, with over 300 branches, and 22 local savings banks, one of which (Lisbon) has six branches. The government guarantees the former, while the latter are in the form of mutual societies. Trustees of the State Savings Bank are appointed by the Minister of Finance, and the members elect the trustees of the mutuals. Special legislation covers the State Savings Bank; the mutuals are governed by general legislation relative to mutual societies.

Legally, deposits are demand, with agreed period of notice, or

9. *World Thrift,* p. 206.

with specific maturity; hence, savings deposits as such are not recognized, and, unless of the other types, they are considered to be demand deposits. Interest is paid on them, however. These deposits are transferable either by check or through the giro system.

Both the State and the mutual savings banks have broad powers. "Except for foreign exchange business, the Savings Banks in continental Portugal are authorized to transact all normal banking business."[10] An exception is that savings banks in general are not allowed to discount bills. There are no limits to individual or total secured loans, including mortgage loans. Only the State Bank grants unsecured loans, which it may make to large enterprises. Other assets naturally include a variety of securities.

Scandinavia

The savings banks of Denmark, Norway, Sweden, and Finland may be described together because of both their general similarities and the degree of co-operation among them. "Scandinavia" will be used here to include all four countries.[11] Although the Scandinavian countries did not become industrialized as early as some others, savings banks originated at roughly the same time in much the same way—in 1810 in Denmark and within about a decade in the other countries. Their numbers grew rapidly after the middle of the century and, in general, until World War II. Since then mergers have reduced the number of banks but not of bank offices. The savings banks were often the first type of bank to be established, and they consequently acquired fairly widespread powers. The trend, furthermore, is toward widening of powers for all types of financial institutions, rather than toward specialization.

Table 8–2 shows the distribution of deposits among various types of banks at the beginning of 1965 (1964 in the case of Denmark). In addition to these amounts, life insurance savings amounted to about $780 million in Denmark, $256 million in

10. *World Thrift,* p. 202.
11. Nordens Centrala Sparbanksforeningars Delegation, *Savings Banks in the Nordic Countries* (Stockholm, 1966).

Finland, $1,077 million in Norway, and $2,907 million in Sweden. While Denmark does not have a postal savings system, a significant portion of savings is placed through the bond market. In Finland and Sweden, farmers' co-operative banks are important links in the financial structure.

TABLE 8-2[12]

DEPOSITS IN SCANDINAVIAN FINANCIAL INSTITUTIONS

(MILLIONS OF U.S. DOLLARS)

	Denmark	Finland	Norway	Sweden
Savings banks	1,475	840	1,386	3,803
Post Office Savings	- - -	221	156	1,178
Commercial banks	2,506	1,085	1,108	5,145
Agricultural banks	15	538	- - -	417
Others	- - -	112	- - -	655

In all four countries the banks are subject to government supervision, although in Finland it is carried out by the savings banks' association for the Ministry of Finance. Typically, the banks have reserves in the form of an original "founders' fund," which has been augmented from earnings. Besides annual additions to reserves or surplus, there are small donations to community or welfare purposes. Normal income is not taxed to the banks in Denmark. In Sweden a combination of state and municipal taxes amounts to about 50 per cent of profits. The system is similar in Finland, except that income from interest on loans for housing gets preferential treatment. In Norway, there is a progressive tax on net profits, a proportional municipal tax of up to 19 per cent, and taxes on capital.

All of the banks are of the trustee type. Denmark has two varieties, one with guarantors who elect trustees, the other with self-perpetuating boards. In Finland the depositors elect all trustees, and in Norway they elect three fourths of the trustees, the other fourth being appointed by municipal officials. Since legislation in 1955, half of the Swedish trustees are selected by gov-

12. *Ibid.*, p. 10.

ernment and half by the trustees themselves. At the Stockholm bank, the city council elects 16, the county elects eight, and the other 24 are co-opted. Trustees elected by the councils may not be connected with other banks, but those selected by the trustees may be. The trustees usually elect a smaller body of directors who are more closely identified with the banks.

In each country the savings banks have established a central or commercial bank, which accepts deposits from the public as well as from savings banks, holds liquid assets, makes loans to the savings banks as well as to others, and serves as a clearing house. In each country the savings banks have checking accounts as well as savings deposits, although the latter are far greater. That holdings of accounts is extremely widespread is shown by the fact that there are 72 accounts per 100 inhabitants in Finland and 95 or 96 in each of the other countries.

Sweden is the only one of the four countries that has a ceiling on savings deposits—the equivalent of $38,600, with some exceptions. Finland has two kinds of "index" accounts, whereby the savings banks undertake to provide against depreciation of the currency. On "A accounts" the banks promise to compensate for 100 per cent of the decline in purchasing power, while paying 2.5 per cent interest; on "B accounts" the compensation is 50 per cent, but the interest is 4 per cent. Both school savings and savings club plans are in wide use. All have savings schemes in which periodic and regular saving qualifies the saver for premiums or loans or both. Tax exemptions for the saver include a general deduction from income of interest used for certain purposes and other deductions based on age and, in Denmark, on price-level changes. Employees up to 40 years of age may deposit as much as 20 per cent of salary annually tax free if the proceeds are used to start their own businesses. Interest on ordinary accounts is completely free of tax in Finland. In Norway a limited amount of interest is free of tax, and the deposits are free of capital tax. Similar arrangements exist in Sweden.

The scarcity and expense of housing in the Scandinavian countries, has led to the development of saving schemes. In Sweden a leading savings bank has established a housing affiliate, which constructs housing developments. When a development is opened, savers are eligible to purchase a house and obtain a loan on the basis of priority determined by the number of months they have saved regularly.

Mortgage loans run for very long periods by American standards, often from 30 to 50 or even 60 years. The interest rate is variable, tied to some index such as the central bank rate, but the government pays the interest in excess of 4.5 per cent. There is usually a second mortgage, often maturing in 15 years. The savings banks now prefer to make the second mortgage rather than the first. Mortgage institutes make many of the first mortgage loans. These institutes raise funds by selling bonds, largely to savings banks, insurance companies, and government pension funds. They are likely to be affiliated with other financial institutions; the savings banks, in fact, have such an institute.

TABLE 8-3[13]

PRINCIPAL SAVINGS BANK ASSETS

(MILLIONS OF U.S. DOLLARS)

	Denmark	Finland	Norway	Sweden
Cash and bank deposits	96	125	193	134
Bonds	259	15	312	391
Municipal loans	175	38	- - -	251
Mortgage loans	664	415	545	2,780
Personal security loans	101	115	271	137
Other loans	237	151	178	347
Real estate and other	76	92	32	101

Thus, the Scandinavian savings banks are important lenders for construction, both multiple and single, but the relative importance of mortgage loans is greatest in Sweden. In Norway government issues of bonds for housing purposes replace to some extent direct mortgage loans. Generally speaking, however, securities are purchased largely for purposes of liquidity. The principal categories of assets at the beginning of 1965 (again, 1964 in the case of Denmark) are shown in Table 8–3. In all four

13. *Ibid.,* p. 40.

countries, significant fractions of total loans are employed in agriculture, as well as in trade and industry. In Finland the savings banks provide a third or more of total housing and agricultural credit. They are the principal lenders to farmers in Norway. Directly and indirectly, the savings banks in Sweden are the principal source of housing credit.

Switzerland

The savings banks of Switzerland, although important institutions, are somewhat difficult to classify, because there is one general banking law under which all banks are founded and operate, and savings banks may be founded in different forms and utilize different powers. They may have shareholders, be mutual, or like the *Caisse d'Épargne de la République et Canton de Genève,* take the form of a trust. The largest savings bank, in Lausanne, is owned by a mortgage bank. The cantonal and commercial banks hold in the aggregate considerably more savings deposits than do the savings banks. The relative figures are shown in Table 8–4.

TABLE 8-4[14]

SAVINGS DEPOSITS WITH SWISS BANKS,
END OF 1964

(MILLIONS OF SWISS FRANCS)

	Amount	Per Cent
Local savings banks	2,821.8	11.7
Cantonal banks	14,988.4	40.3
Joint stock banks	15,246.5	41.0
Co-operative banks	2,446.1	6.6
Other banks	610.5	1.6
TOTAL	37,176.1	100.0

The Swiss savings banks typically offer savings deposits subject to immediate withdrawal (ordinary deposit) and deposits sub-

14. *World Thrift,* p. 237.

ject to notice at a half per cent higher interest, and certificates of deposit ranging from three to six months up to five years. Except for requirements of cash and liquidity, the savings banks are relatively free in selection of assets. As the commercial banks are invading traditional savings bank areas, the savings banks are taking on more commercial bank functions; this is one stimulus to the use of certificates. Typically, they hold about two thirds of assets in mortgages and one third in cash and public bonds.

In the case of the Geneva bank, which was established as a philanthropic trust for the benefit of the poor, the trustees are appointed by the canton of Geneva. The political parties propose candidates, who are selected proportionately. The role of the bank is to suggest proper qualifications. The trustees often hold political office or are otherwise interested in cantonal government. They select a bank committee of a manager and four directors.

The cantonal banks may be totally government owned or partly private. Banking generally is subject to a cartel arrangement, including the five largest commercial banks, the union of 28 state banks, the union of 150 local and regional banks, and more than 1,000 small local banks in the villages.

While the Swiss are conscious of the philanthropic origins of the savings banks, they tend to shy away from the idea of encouraging "thrift" at a loss. They are more inclined to view the benefits of thrift as economic, in combating inflation, than as social. They think more in terms of serving the depositor than of serving the abstract idea of thrift. The political selection of trustees, however, colors some management decisions, such as placing funds in low-rent housing projects (80 per cent loans guaranteed by the state) rather than in first mortgage loans. As in Scandinavia, mortgage loans have exceedingly long maturities, and none at all in some cases. The Swiss, who are not reluctant to carry permanent debt for their housing, have probably the highest per capita mortgage debt of any country. Loans are made technically for three years, and the lender has the privilege of changing the rate on six months' notice.

Australia

Outside of Europe, the principal savings banking countries are Australia, New Zealand, and Canada. In Australia there are three categories of savings banks: (1) the Commonwealth Savings Bank of Australia, established and guaranteed by the Commonwealth Government; (2) three state savings banks, in Melbourne, Adelaide, and Perth, with 658 branches and more than 1,700 sub-offices; and (3) two trustee savings banks in Hobart and Launceston, Tasmania, with more than a hundred branches and sub-offices. The Commonwealth Savings Bank has 910 branches and more than 8,200 agencies for accepting deposits.

The trustees of the Commonwealth Bank consist of the managing director and deputy managing director, the Secretary to the Commonwealth Department of the Treasury, and eight others; they are appointed by the Governor General. The state governments appoint the trustees of the state banks; only persons connected with other banking institutions are ineligible. Trustees of the trustee savings banks are elected by the district justices of the peace. In both state and trustee banks the trustees select the general manager.

All of the savings banks, of course, maintain savings deposits, but only one of the state banks permits corporations to hold them. The two trustee savings banks have deposits with a variety of notice periods. Savings schemes are similar to those found generally in Europe. The federal government pays a premium of one third of the amount saved toward home acquisition costs by married couples under 36 years of age, up to A$500.[15] Generally speaking, depositors may make withdrawals from other savings banks. Checking accounts are held, generally at the state banks of Victoria and South Australia, only by non-profit institutions at the Commonwealth Savings Bank. These two state banks also hold time deposits.

The savings banks may invest in or lend on securities issued or guaranteed by the Commonwealth or state governments, or

---

15. The Australian dollar is the equivalent of U.S. $1.12.

lend on the security of land. The Commonwealth Bank and the Victoria Bank also make limited amounts of personal loans. All the banks make long-term loans to individuals, non-profit institutions, building societies, and governments. The state savings banks also lend to business enterprises. Long-term loans are generally secured by mortgage. Other assets are generally liquid assets. The Commonwealth Bank and the trustee banks are required to maintain 10 per cent of deposits in specified liquid assets.

New Zealand

In form and function the savings banks in New Zealand resemble more closely the savings bank system in England and Scotland. There are 13 trustee savings banks with about 150 branch offices. The banks are guaranteed by the state and must hold at least 50 per cent of their assets in government bonds. The Governor General appoints the trustees, who select the management. Up to 2,000 New Zealand pounds may be held in both regular savings accounts and "investment accounts," which have a maturity of 12 months and receive a higher interest. In addition, 500 pounds may be kept in each of five other accounts for specific purposes. The New Zealand scheme for encouraging saving for a home provides an extra 5 per cent of the sum saved, up to a maximum premium of 50 pounds. Virtually the only loans made are those to local authorities and mortgage loans that are limited to two thirds of the property value.

Canada

In Canada, the Popular Savings Banks *(Caisses populaires Desjardins)* operate only in the Province of Quebec and are in fact similar in many respects to savings and loan associations, as they are co-operative societies and are governed by the Savings and Loan Bank Law. Those who have subscribed for shares (each share at $5.00) are members and participate in the election of trustees. Only members may have deposits and obtain loans. No distinction is made between demand and savings deposits, the same deposit being paid interest and subject to check. The shares are considered to be in the nature of time deposits, because they can be redeemed. Proceeds of loans are credited to the savings deposits. Of the short-term loans, about half are on signature, the other half provide co-signers or collateral. Long-term loans are primarily first mortgage loans. The banks are supervised by a central association, whose approval must be obtained for all loans of more than $40,000 and for specific investments in national, provincial, or local bonds or bonds of church organizations or co-operative societies. Rules of the central association require that 50 per cent of the deposits and shares be invested in cash or balances (15 per cent) or bonds (35 per cent), although large banks are granted exemptions. Altogether, there are nearly 1,300 banks, many rather small.

United Kingdom

The trustee savings banks of the United Kingdom are described last and in somewhat greater detail because of their close historical relationship to the development of savings banking in the United States. The British system is also of interest because of its close ties to the government, its ability to progress with limited investment powers, and the unity with which the banks in England and Scotland operate.[16] A continuing merger movement has brought the number of banks to less than 80 (in 1966), but they have nearly 1,300 branches. The trustee savings banks have been integrated into a National Savings system, which also provides government savings certificates and a postal system.

In the United Kingdom the various segments of the capital market are fairly well staked off and dominated by specialized

16. The basic source of historical material for the trustee savings banks is H. Oliver Horne, *A History of Savings Banks* (London and New York: Oxford University Press, 1947). There are also useful briefer histories, such as A. R. B. Haldane, *One Hundred and Fifty Years of Trustee Savings Banks* (London: Trustee Savings Banks Association, 1960), and numerous volumes on individual banks. The *Radcliffe Report* describes the role of the savings banks in the financial structure, and current data are provided by the association and National Savings Committee.

institutions. The savings banks make no mortgage loans at all, while the building societies dominate this market. Until the pressures of recent years, commercial banks exhibited little interest in having savings accounts or in making mortgage loans.

Early Development. Following the establishment of the Rev. Henry Duncan's savings bank in Ruthwell, Scotland, the idea was picked up by philanthropists elsewhere, and banks were ·established in Aberdeen, Perth, Edinburgh, and other towns. It was not possible to enforce the paternalistic rules of Duncan's parish in the cities, and a considerable amount of pamphleteering took place in the early days to debate the merits of the "Edinburgh" plan versus the Ruthwell model and to determine who should have the credit for founding the first "modern" savings bank.[17] In both cases, the trustees solved the original problem of the use of funds by depositing them with the Scottish commercial banks, which paid interest for them. There were already some 80 savings banks in England when the first banks were being founded in the United States, but the English commercial banks did not pay interest on deposits. Thus, investments had to be made, and the two problems of potential depreciation and inadequate management arose. The solution, as early as 1817, was that the savings banks were to pay to the Bank of England, for the account of the National Debt Commissioners, the funds deposited with them. By this act of Parliament the government provided an umbrella for the savings banks, which were hurt by the high interest rates that followed the Napoleonic War. The government agreed to pay to the banks £4 11s. 3d per 100, which permitted the banks to pass on 4 per cent to the depositors. A similar act covered Ireland.

Three questions later developed out of this protection from the government, in some respects similar to those raised in American state legislatures. When interest rates later fell, the government was unwilling to continue paying rates above the market; how far should the government go in supporting the savings bank

17. The dispute is reviewed in John Herries McCulloch and Kenneth J. Stirling, *The Edinburgh Savings Bank, 1836-1936* (Edinburgh: H. & J. Pillans & Wilson, 1936).

movement? (By the end of 1818, there were already 465 banks, including 182 in Scotland.)[18] Another question was how to restrict the benefits granted to the banks to those segments of the population for whom they were intended. The third question was that of who was responsible, trustees or government, for the safety of the funds deposited, since they had in turn to be invested with the government. By a process of evolution these questions now seem to be resolved, although the first one will probably always be a basis for disagreement. As in many states, there are limits to the size of deposits. As to responsibility, the government guarantees those deposits now invested in governments, but does not guarantee the Special Investment Department (described below), which may invest funds in limited other ways.

Early Difficulties. Even with the high rate paid in the early days, the savings bank movement fell into difficulties, no doubt partly because of its rapid growth. Although the savings banks' account with the National Debt Commissioners created a deficit, amounting to a subsidy, management weaknesses led to failures and a general disenchantment with the banks on the part of the public and in Parliament. As Chancellor of the Exchequer, Gladstone attempted in the 1850's to reach agreement with the banks whereby they would accept government supervision in exchange for government guarantee of deposits. Failure of this effort lent strength to the proposal for establishment of Post Office Savings Banks, which were authorized in 1861. This development led to the immediate failure or voluntary closing of some 30 savings banks, to efforts on the part of leading savings bankers to salvage what was possible, and to a savings bank law in 1863. The law identified the powers and responsibilities of trustees, making them primarily responsible for complying with regulations of auditing and bonding officers, and provided that all deposits would be paid over to the National Debt Commissioners.

The government was willing to pay at this time £3 5s and to allow the banks to pay depositors 3 per cent, or slightly more, while the government itself paid £2 10s per 100 at the Post

18. Haldane, *op. cit.,* pp. 14-15.

Office. There followed a period in which several savings banks failed, most of them small, but including one large bank in Birmingham, while the Post Office System expanded.[19]

In 1870, a few of the Scottish savings banks, led by the Savings Bank of Glasgow, took advantage of the proposition that what was not prohibited was permissible and, relying on an unrepealed obscure provision of an earlier law, set up what they called Special Investment Departments. In these departments they would accept deposits that they would invest otherwise than directly with the government. Subsequent reductions in the rate paid by the government squeezed some of the smaller banks even further, leading to still more failures, while the Glasgow bank and others with Special Investment Departments grew in spite of Post Office competition.

The situation led to a Parliamentary investigation and new legislation in 1891. Efforts by critics of the banks to make Special Investment Departments illegal were defeated. Lax administration at many small banks was attacked by establishment of an Inspection Committee. While the larger savings banks were well run and more than able to cover their expenses, many smaller ones were inefficient and creating deficits. The number of savings banks was down to 281 by 1892. At this time it was ruled that Special Investment Departments were not legally able to invest in local government securities, as they had been doing, but only in national government securities through the market. Thus, another roadblock was thrown in the path of the English banks, but, with their usual adroitness, some of the Scottish banks found a solution by forming investment trusts.

At a time when it looked as if the savings banks had about reached the end of their existence, a turning point was reached in 1904, when an act of Parliament again opened up the opportunity to establish Special Investment Departments with the power to invest in local "mortgages"—actually local government securities based on tax revenues. Some growth of the banks took place until World War I, when all ceilings on deposits were

19. The failure in Birmingham led to establishment of a municipal bank, the only one in England. It was later, from time to time, considered a model for changing the system.

removed but the government refused to pay higher rates in line with market levels to the Ordinary Department. Consequently, most individual saving took the form of government securities paying 5 per cent. These high rates in turn brought about depreciation of the portfolios of the Special Investment Departments and eventually brought them also under the supervision of the National Debt Commissioners. Investments, rates paid to depositors, and expenditures have since been subject to supervision. Provisions making easier the merging of savings banks were also made.

National Savings System. An important step in establishing the future nature of trustee savings banks was taken during the decade of the 1920's. One part of this step was to bring together the National Savings Committees, which had been formed during the war, and the two types of savings banks, postal and trustee, into a unified system of national savings. This integration in turn led the government to approve extension of the trustee savings bank system through establishment of additional branches, but such expansion naturally raised the problem of financing. The solution fortunately lay at hand, as the surplus funds of those solvent banks that had closed in the face of competition from the Post Office Savings after 1861 had lain unused and accumulating interest at the Bank of England. These funds were freed by an act passed in 1929 to be used for the establishment of savings bank branches, on the recommendation of the Inspection Committee and the savings banks' association. In particular, this made possible expansion in the south of England, where there were few banks large enough to finance construction of branches.

The government pegged interest rates during World War II, and, while selling certificates and other types of "savings bonds" to the public, also encouraged saving through the trustee savings banks and postal savings, as these funds were also channeled to the Exchequer. Consequently, the two types of savings banks experienced greatly increased deposits, as well as numbers of accounts, during the war. After the war, however, the old question of the appropriate rate to be paid by the government to the banks was again raised, and it appeared possible that the government might adopt different rates to be paid to different banks on the basis of their needs for funds. Partly to forestall this development a plan was devised, called Mutual Assistance, whereby the earnings of the larger and more prosperous banks were partly to be paid into a common fund from which interest-free loans would be made to smaller and less prosperous banks. The plan has been altered several times since 1947, and a fifth scheme began in 1966. The plan was altered not only to support the smaller banks with undeveloped territories, but also to finance expansion of branches. Part of the funds become available as outright grants, part as loans.

The most striking characteristic of the system in the United Kingdom is the existence of the Ordinary Department and Special Investment Department side by side. In the Ordinary Department the depositors' funds are channeled directly to the Exchequer at the current rate paid by the Exchequer. In the Special Investment Department funds are invested through the market, roughly half in national government securities and half in local government obligations. The latter represent borrowings for a variety of public works—public housing (county council houses), hospitals, and the like—and are similar to general obligation municipal securities in the United States. In periods of high interest rates, funds tend to flow into the Special Investment Departments. The success of these departments led the Post Office to adopt a similar arrangement beginning in 1966. There seem to be three reasons why depositors continue to use the Ordinary Department in the face of a decided difference in rates paid. First, it is necessary to have a minimum balance in the Ordinary Department before an account may be opened in the Special Investment Department. Second, there are some depositors who probably feel that the higher rate in the Special Investment Department reflects higher risk.[20] Third, deposits in the Ordinary Department are withdrawable on demand, while a notice period is normally enforced in the Special Investment De-

20. Government guarantee of deposits is confined to the Ordinary Department.

partment. To some extent the differential in rates paid is reduced by the tax exemption allowed interest in the Ordinary Department. In the summer of 1966, the Ordinary Departments were paying 2.5 per cent, tax free, after receiving 3.125 per cent from the government, while the Special Investment Departments were generally paying 5.25 per cent, taxable.

The savings banks are also authorized to purchase and hold government securities for their depositors' accounts and to credit the interest to their savings accounts. In addition, the banks were successful in obtaining legislation in 1964 permitting them to operate checking accounts in order to move the deposits with more active turnover from the Ordinary Department. These accounts are cleared through the commercial banking system and a clearing center.

The building societies are roughly three times the aggregate size of the trustee savings banks and are the principal mortgage lenders. They pay an average rate of tax for their members, so that in effect the interest received by the latter is tax free. Thus, the 4 per cent to 4.5 per cent paid by these societies generally in 1966 was the equivalent of about 6.75 per cent before tax. The societies do not encourage sporadic deposits, but prefer larger and more stable subscriptions; thus, the savings banks tend to lose the larger accounts subject to higher tax rates to the building societies.

Social Aspects. The concept of savings banking as a social movement and a considerable feeling of unity among the savings banks are strong in the United Kingdom. The latter is encouraged by common regulation, by the small number of strong and active banks in the association, and by the continuing operation of Mutual Assistance. Applications for approval of expenditures for buildings, branches, and the like go to the National Debt Commission, which confers with the association, especially in the cases of banks receiving Mutual Assistance. For banks paying into Mutual Assistance, approval of these matters and of investments and rates paid is more *pro forma*.

The limited investments that may be selected and the extent

of regulation raise questions as to the value and importance of the role of the trustees. This problem is one that interests leaders of the savings banks. In fact, the trustees approve the selection of specific investments (in the Special Investment Department) and make decisions on branching, management, and other personnel. Legally, four of the trustees hold title to the bank's assets. Trustees are forbidden to profit from their position; the General Manager (president) of a bank may not be a trustee for this reason. The larger and better known banks are able to recruit able trustees because of the prestige attaching to the position and because there is still an atmosphere of public service attached to the boards. Where the prestige is of value in the trustee's principal occupation, this factor tends to be important. Many of the smaller local banks, however, find it difficult to fill their boards with competent people. In fact, some of these banks have no management of their own; the trustees pay a fee to an individual, usually a solicitor, who provides the necessary staff.

The social-movement aspect of savings banking is apparent in the attitude toward branching and in the operation of Mutual Assistance. The larger banks apparently expect to have at any one time several new or otherwise unprofitable branches. The necessity of covering interest in the Ordinary Department and of being competitive in the Special Investment Department raises constant problems of how many and how unprofitable these branches may be. For this reason, the management of the banks is constantly seeking efficiency and low-cost operation. Savings bank leaders are of course interested in obtaining expanded lending powers, but they naturally face opposition from both building societies and commercial banks. Perhaps because of this opposition, many savings bankers appear to be more interested in efforts to obtain powers to offer unit trusts (mutual funds) than to win mortgage lending powers.

The different parts of National Savings and the relative position of the trustee savings banks in it are shown in Table 8–5. It is clear that savings certificates, postal savings, and the Ordinary and Special Investment Departments combined are roughly equal.

TABLE 8-5[21]

AMOUNTS IN NATIONAL SAVINGS,
FEBRUARY, 1966

(MILLIONS OF POUNDS)

	Amount	Per Cent
Savings Certificates		
Principal	1,939.4	23.3
Accrued interest	625.00	7.5
Defense bonds	799.7	9.6
Post Office Savings Bank	1,838.9	21.9
Trustee Savings Banks		
Ordinary Department	1,063.8	12.7
Special Investment Department	1,017.9	12.2
Other "stock" on Post Office Register	177.6	2.1
Premium savings bonds*	542.8	6.5
National Development bonds	356.2	4.3
TOTAL	8,361.3	100.0

*Premium bonds are sold under an arrangement whereby the interest, instead of being paid to the investor, is placed in a lottery. They are sold in multiples of one pound and the maximum individual holding is 1,000 bonds. After being held three months a bond is eligible for monthly drawings. The interest at 4.5% becomes the prize fund, of which each £100,000 is divided into 2,751 prizes ranging from £25 to one prize of £5,000.

The relative position of the savings banks and National Savings generally in the savings market is shown in Table 8–6. This table also shows the rapid rate of growth of the savings banks between 1954 and 1964. That rate, however, was exceeded by insurance companies and building societies.

Summary

Students of savings banking can find in savings banks in Europe and elsewhere examples of virtually any change they might like to install in the system of a given country. The banks vary in

21. National Savings Committee, *Monthly Bulletin of Statistics and Economic Information*, April 1966.

TABLE 8-6[22]

Savings Media, 1954 and 1964

(Millions of Pounds)

	1954	1964	Per Cent Change
National savings certificates	2,342.0	2,711.1	16
Post Office Savings Bank	1,727.3	1,814.0	5
Trustee savings banks	1,003.1	1,893.7	89
Other stock on Post Office Register	186.6	177.3	– 5
Defense bonds	793.3	1,081.6	36
Premium savings bonds	- - -	477.5	- -
National Development bonds	- - -	134.6	- -
TOTAL	6,052.3	8,298.8	37
Life assurance	2,405.0	6,411.0	167
Building societies	1,847.3	4,719.1	155
Industrial assurance companies	840.1	1,458.5	74
Friendly societies	224.5	280.4	25
Other societies	16.1	23.7	47
Industrial and provident societies	559.3	852.8	52
Trade unions	74.8	112.5	50
Railway savings banks	42.9	43.4	1
Authorized unit trusts	(n.a.)	429.0	- -
Superannuation and other trust funds	290.6	595.3	105
London clearing bank deposits	2,456.0	3,079.0	25
GRAND TOTAL	15,041.0	26,673.1	77

their ability to compete for funds in being able to offer a limited or varied array of deposit arrangements and in being able to employ the funds gained either in a limited list of "safe" securities, with no discretion at all in the case of the Ordinary Departments in the United Kingdom or in virtually any suitable asset in the opinion of management in some other countries. The banks vary from making no mortgage loans in some countries to dominating the mortgage markets of others, and the same is true with respect to agricultural, personal, and some types of business loans. In Germany and elsewhere the savings

22. *Ibid.*

banks operate immense giro systems and operate freely in foreign exchange.

The original philanthropic origins of the banks, so similar in nearly all countries, have colored the activities and the thinking of management through the years. In some countries, notably Italy, the savings banks think of themselves at least as much as social institutions as businesses, and in Great Britain the uniformity of operations and of goals intensifies the unity among the banks and strengthens the feeling that they represent a "movement." The question of whether the banks in the different countries are businesses that happen to operate as mutual institutions or social institutions bears heavily on the extent to which the various national governments restrict, protect, or encourage the banks with investment and other regulations and tax treatment. By the same token, the attitude toward this basic question of the nature of savings banking determines the legal and social attitudes toward trustees. All these considerations can throw light on the questions raised in the United States by the savings banks' efforts to expand their areas of operation both geographically and functionally.

Regardless of variations along these lines, however, a general recognition of the savings banks as desirable institutions is apparent in the European countries. The necessities of reconstruction after the war and the desirability of economic growth thereafter have undoubtedly led to an appreciation of the importance of investment in real assets and in the potential role of personal saving in the investment process. Consequently, the official reaction has been one of encouraging personal saving. Usually this policy is reflected in some form of liberalization of savings bank powers. Exemptions of interest from income tax and of deposits from capital taxes, authorization whereby the savings banks may purchase securities for their depositors or sell them shares of investment funds managed by the banks, subsidization of housing schemes, and encouragement of contractual savings plans are all examples of these measures.

CHAPTER 9

Mutual Savings Banks
and the Future

Expansion of the savings bank system naturally presupposes a need for such institutions. This presupposition may be examined in two stages: first, the desirability of having additional thrift facilities; and second, the appropriateness of providing them through the trustee and mutual principles. Clearly, the social need for thrift facilities is completely different from what it was when the mutual savings banks were originated. The very great increase in the general level of incomes in the United States and the restructuring of income, whereby employee income represents a larger fraction of the total and a considerably greater degree of uniformity, have brought new dimensions to the concept of thrift for the bulk of the population. While it is still true that the disadvantaged and lowest-income groups can benefit from encouragement to save for the proverbial rainy day and to make a start on accumulating property, for millions of the population the emphasis has changed to that of "saving for the sunny day." Social security plans have taken the edge off the most severe economic dangers of a few generations ago, and for many people the accumulation of liquid savings is not designed to prevent disaster so much as to make possible future expenditures or acquisitions and to provide additional income.

New Forms of Thrift

As the general level of income has risen and economic sophistication has kept pace, at least to some extent, the traditional savings deposit has been found to be an inadequate answer to all the new desires to save. On the one hand, a considerable volume of saving now takes place through the process of consumer credit, whereby the desired asset is purchased first and saved for later through retirement of the liability incurred. On the other hand, a broader spectrum of assets becomes desirable once the needs for holdings of liquid funds are met. The original growth of life insurance reflected this broadening, and in recent decades the climbing percentage of home ownership has also reflected it. Another reflection has been the expanding ownership of corporate securities. Thus, if the savings banks are to continue to be important institutions in the savings market, it appears necessary for them to be able to offer services more closely related to these new needs in addition to the traditional savings deposit.

The new services require changes on both sides of the balance sheet. New types of deposits—such as notice and bonus accounts —have, of course, already been devised. But a logical extension of savings bank traditional services would be the ability to purchase securities directly for savings bank depositors, and a further extension of this concept would be for the banks to manage investment funds for interested depositors. Such an extension, indeed, would not be a revolutionary change from the service of offering a variety of insurance policies that now exists in three of the principal savings bank states. A basic difference between the American savings bank system and the more broadly developed system in some European countries is the complete divorce (with a few minor exceptions) of demand deposit business from American savings banks. An extension of savings bank powers to receive and make payments for depositors through correspondent commercial banks would be one step toward offering more complete services to depositors.

Also, on the asset side of the balance sheet, if savings banks are to participate in the acquisition of durable assets by depositors through the use of consumer credit, it will be necessary for them to have the power to make this type of loan. While the savings banks in some states may do so, in some important savings bank states (notably New York) they may not. Since consumer credit is admittedly an expensive form of credit, there are two advantages from a social point of view in having these loans made by the savings banks. One lies in the increased supply of funds in this market, tending toward lower costs, and the other is in the mutual form of organization, in which higher earnings flow back to the borrowing depositors.

Public Policies Toward Thrift

As became evident in Europe after World War II, the growth of the economy is partly dependent on the degree to which the public voluntarily saves. While the overall rate of gross saving in the United States is considerably less, in terms of gross national product, than it has been in several European and other countries, national policies here were exceptionally successful in promoting growth and higher employment with stability of prices, especially from 1960 to 1965. Eventually, this long period of expansion naturally reached levels of full utilization of resources, after which growth could not be maintained at the same annual rates. Under these circumstances, a reduction of aggregate expenditure to an equivalent level with real output once again became desirable, and in the household sector of the economy this has meant an economic desirability of more saving and less consumption. But in a sense there is never enough saving, only a deficiency of investment. In this sense, thrift is never a vice, and when it tends to outrun investment it is the latter that needs adjusting. Thus, with rising levels of real investment necessary in the economy for the foreseeable future to provide employment opportunities for the growing population and also to provide much-needed construction of public works, the channeling of private income into capital remains a desirable objective.

Assuming that financial institutions will respond to economic needs, as tends to happen in a market economy, there remains the question of the extent to which mutual savings banks should be encouraged to participate. As described at some length in Chapter 8 (dealing with savings banking systems in Europe and elsewhere), governments encourage savings bank activities with a variety of means—income tax exemptions of interest on deposits, cash premiums as rewards for completing contractual savings schemes, several kinds of saving-for-housing plans, and even lottery arrangements. It is not certain, however, that these arrangements, at least in the long run, actually raise the level of personal saving above what it would be in any event, although they probably affect the relative flows of saving. "In fact, one may well wonder—at least as far as the continent of Europe is concerned—whether the municipality and complexity of the measures adopted do not result in exactly the opposite to what was intended."[1]

If it is determined that savings banks should be permitted a larger role in the development of thrift institutions, an adequate measure would be equalization of lending powers among different types of institutions, as recommended by the Commission on Money and Credit, and relaxation of the restrictions on chartering and branching now embedded in state legislation. Political debate accompanying efforts in this direction tends to involve the appropriateness of the trustee and mutual principles. The appropriateness of these principles in a market- and profit-oriented economy deserves some consideration.

Mutuality

Trusteeship and mutuality characterized the early savings banks because of their philanthropic origins. Since the savings banks were not designed to earn a profit for their founders, but to divide earnings among the depositors, the mutual form was appropriate, and since the property had to be established in some form, the trustee arrangement was employed, as it was in the cases of hospitals, orphanages, or other philanthropic institutions. The ability of the mutual organization to survive was demonstrated not only by the longevity of the savings banks, but by the development of leading life insurance companies based on the same principle. One view of the mutual organiza-

1. Nicholas G. Krul, "Some Aspects of Saving and the Development of the Savings Banks," *World Thrift*, (Amsterdam: International Savings Banks Institute, 1966), p. 63.

tion can be that, in the modern world of business units, the impersonal relationship that exists between owners, managers, and employees is much the same, whether the owners are a separate group of stockholders or are the customers. As ownership of a corporation can be transferred by sale and purchase of stock, ownership of a mutual savings bank changes as people open or close accounts. While legal ownership resides with the trustees, beneficial ownership is basically with the depositors. In this view, management is as unaffected by the composition of the ownership group in the one case as in the other.

Actually, however, both types of ownership tend to develop industry loyalties. Commercial bankers are aware of being members of a group, and this feeling is naturally encouraged by industry leadership and associations. At the same time, mutual savings bankers enjoy a distinctive existence, and they take pride in the history and traditions of savings banking. While a mutual savings banker is as interested as his commercial banking competitor in maximizing earnings through adroit loan and investment policies and efficient operations, his motivation is partly similar and partly different. Both are partly motivated by self-interest and by the "instinct of workmanship"—the pleasure of doing a good job. The savings banker, however, has an added motivation to some degree, and that is the recognition of the mutual principle itself.

Full evaluation of this difference would require an extensive study in the field of industrial psychology, but the fact that it exists is rather apparent. It is illustrated in the persistent feeling among savings bank circles that thrift in itself is "a good thing" and that the basic function of savings banks is to encourage thrift. The fact that this encouragement may require the banks to operate in much the same fashion as any profit-seeking financial institution, in order to be able to attract funds, only partly obscures the basic objective. As is also noted in the discussion of European savings banks (Chapter 8), this view of thrift provides a solidarity among savings bank interests, and today it is only partly a result of the philanthropic origins. While there is general recognition of the fact that savings banks, in order to serve their customers, must be competitive in markets for both assets and funds, the end in view—at least in the minds of the vocal leaders of the industry—is the provision of thrift services to an ever larger market.

The influence of the mutual principle on savings bank executives works partly through the conviction that thrift is good for the individual saver, but also through the conviction that it is good social policy. "The task of savings banks is to promote thrift in the broadest sense in order to increase the general level of personal property and welfare. . . . As laid down in the declaration of Milan in 1924, savings banks should not only collect savings but should also provide educational information. The work of savings banks is not a business, but a mission."[2] "Savings banks are not financial institutions. This is not their main purpose. The main purpose of savings banks is a social mission. . . ."[3] While these are European views, they are not far removed from the view of one American savings banker: "A mutual savings bank has as its basic mission the continuous promotion of true thrift at the community level, affording its depositors stability, safety, ready availability of funds, sound investment and liquidity. . . ."[4]

Thus, savings bankers are constantly faced with a trade-off between using funds for expanding facilities and for promotional activities, on the one hand, and for improving rates paid to depositors on the other. One view, perhaps the "hard-headed" one, would be that every possible penny should be used to pay maximum returns to savers with some earnings set aside as surplus to improve future earnings; while at the other extreme it could be held that only the minimum return necessary to maintain deposits should be paid, while earnings could be diverted

2. Walter Sadleder (General Secretary, League of Austrian Savings Banks), at International Savings Bank Conference, New York, May 2-4, 1966.

3. Manuel de Aranegui (President, Provincial Savings Bank of Alava, Spain), at same conference.

4. Jason W. Stockbridge (President, Central Savings Bank, Baltimore), at same conference. For a defense of the mutual form of organization in the thrift field, see the testimony of Adolf A. Berle at the 1963 Hearings on the federal charter bill (pp. 299-308).

to promotion and to unprofitable branches and small accounts for those who "need" them.

A recent attempt by the International Savings Bank Institute to draw up a statement of basic principles illustrates, in the careful way in which the statement is framed, the difficulty. It states: "Savings Banks are financial institutions which provide for the general public financial services and education in saving. Their main object is therefore to promote thrift—and not primarily to earn a profit—and to supply the maximum usefulness to the public and their community."

Profit and Surplus

The question of profit is in any event somewhat a problem of semantics for a mutual institution. Since earnings after expenses can only be paid to depositors, transferred to surplus, or in some countries donated to charities and welfare organizations, the "profit" is essentially the return paid to the depositors plus that kept for their protection and future earning power. The essential difference between a joint stock savings bank and a mutual bank is that in the joint stock bank the net worth is supplied by stockholders (original or subsequent), who thus assume the risk of loss of this net worth in return for the annual earnings made possible by the whole of the assets, while in a mutual bank the depositor assumes this position. By becoming a depositor, he automatically benefits from the existence of any surplus, but, in the absence of deposit insurance, his risk extends to his deposit.

Thus, if a mutual bank had (for the sake of simplicity) deposits of $900,000 and surplus accounts of $100,000 for each $1 million of assets, and if operating earnings were 5 per cent of assets, it would have $50,000 to divide among expenses and taxes, dividends, and retention of earnings, per million of deposits. Taking an approximation of actual ratios, operating expenses and taxes would require about $7,500; $40,000 would be credited to depositors' accounts; and $2,500 would be retained or would represent write-offs. If a privately owned bank had the same capital structure, the $2,500 would represent profit on the investment, assuming that income taxes are included in the first item.

It is this characteristic of mutuality that complicates, both philosophically and legalistically, the problem of ownership of the surplus and what should be done with it should a solvent savings bank cease operations. On the one hand, the current generation of savings depositors may have had nothing to do with the accumulation of the present surplus; and on the other hand, when a depositor closes an account, he has no claim to any part of the surplus that may have been earned with "his" funds. Thus, there exists in savings bank circles the opinion that a savings bank represents a kind of community trust in which the surplus accumulated over the years becomes a trust fund for the benefit of those who wish to use the services of the bank. Earlier versions of the federal charter bill recognized the situation by providing that the net assets of any federal savings bank that liquidates voluntarily would be distributed to the Federal Savings Insurance Corporation, after all claims were satisfied.

The eleemosynary aspects of savings banking have been stressed in various early court decisions. In New York State, the courts have found a savings bank to be "a charitable institution, the sole corporate purpose of which is to securely protect money deposited up to a certain fixed amount by individuals, and by investing it in such limited and prudent ways as the legislature has prescribed, to secure safe and moderate return by way of interest upon moneys held."[5]

Savings banks are not organized as business enterprises. They have no stockholders, and are not to engage in speculation, or money-making in a business sense. They are simply to take the deposits, usually small, which are offered, aggregate them and keep and invest them safely, paying such interest to the depositors as is thus made, after deducting expenses and paying the principal on demand.[6]

The Supreme Court has stated that while a savings bank is "not strictly eleemosynary," its purpose is "to furnish a safe depository

5. *People v. Binghamton Trust Co.,* 139 N.Y. 185, 34 N.E. 898 (1893).
6. *Hun v. Cary,* 82 N.Y. 65 (1880).

for the money of those members of the community disposed to trust their property to its keeping."[7]

Trustee System

The nature of mutual banks in turn relates to the existence of trustees. Since the relationship between a savings bank and its depositors is considered to be that of debtor and creditor, there is a basic difference between savings banks and other types of co-operative institutions, such as savings and loan associations, where the customers are owners rather than creditors. Since there are no stockholders in the mutual organization, it must be owned by someone, and some form of trusteeship is thus necessary. How the trustees are to be selected, however, may be determined in many ways. Historically in the United States it was natural for the trustees to be a self-perpetuating body, although there have been a few examples of other arrangements, because of their original similarities to other philanthropic organizations. A variety of methods of selecting trustees has been developed in Europe, partly because of the varied origins of the banks. At first glance, it appears anomalous that the ultimate responsibility for the management of savings banks, especially of the large city savings banks, should reside in the same form of organization as guides the libraries, hospitals, and orphanages. It is paradoxical that these large, essentially business enterprises should have the equivalent of boards of directors who differ so radically from their counterparts in two respects—their election of their own membership and the ban on their profiting from their position.

In this respect, European experience may be useful. In some jurisdictions, local governments appoint or elect trustees. While this arrangement cannot be said to work badly, it admittedly tends to turn the savings banks into loan and investment channels that they might not choose on purely market consideratons. In other jurisdictions, depositors or "members" elect trustees. In

7. Wm. H. Kniffin, *The Savings Bank and Its Practical Work* (New York: The Bankers Publishing Co., 1928), p. 21.

these cases, the system appears to have the same disadvantages as occur when it is used in the United States, and in this sense it has the same artificiality usually apparent when stockholders elect directors of corporations. They "elect," but usually do not "select." Relatively few members of European banks are actually interested or informed in the matter, and trustees come close to being self-selecting in the process of determining candidates. The democracy sought in this method seldom actually exists. In other jurisdictions, two or three methods are used jointly.

The best defense for the traditional American system is that it has worked well for a century and a half; on the basis of pragmatism it would be difficult to improve upon. For their own protection and that of the bank, and because of their legal responsibilities, the natural interest of trustees is to select capable people to fill vacancies. Two differences between European and American practice may be applicable, however. One is that in some countries the rule against trustees benefiting from their position is even more restrictive than in the United States, in that the principal officer of the bank cannot be a trustee, since he is paid a salary. This rule appears to be unnecessarily stringent in that it prevents the manager from serving, at least formally, as a trustee. If the rule is designed to prevent the trustees from rewarding one of their own with the presidency, it could be revised to prevent a trustee from becoming a paid officer, but allow the officer to become a trustee.

The other difference is the more widespread prohibition or limitation of trustees who have affiliations with other financial institutions. It was a natural development in the United States that in their search for capable people trustees sometimes found them in other banks. In the early days savings banks were not thought of as competitive with commercial banks. In some cases, savings banks were formed to keep such deposits out of commercial banks, and in these instances the commercial bankers who started the savings banks naturally served on their boards. Regardless of the integrity of the individuals involved, a complete absence of conflict of interest sometimes became difficult. As Keyes noted years ago, the savings bank sometimes came off second best in cases of these affiliations. Also, development of savings bank life insurance was retarded by similar ones. As noted elsewhere, in some European countries where this rule does not exist, the savings banks feel that their efforts to expand operations and legal powers are discouraged by trustees who maintain that other institutions are handling the matters adequately. The difficulty is that many capable and devoted trustees would be excluded if they could have no affiliation with other financial businesses.

The nature of mutual savings banking is further illustrated by comparison with savings and loan associations, especially the mutual type, which comprises some 85 per cent of the total assets in associations. The essential differences revolve around the fact that the associations are owned by shareholders, who may now legally be called depositors in some states. Thus, the shareholders elect directors at annual meetings. This arrangement stems partly from the origins of the building and loan associations, in which acquiring housing was the primary motivation rather than providing a place for savings. It also explains to a considerable extent why savings and loan associations were widely established after the extension of savings banking slowed down. In contrast to the usual reasons for establishing savings banks, self-interest could play a role even in the establishment of mutual savings and loans. "The organizing groups often were comprised of people who stood to gain in one way or another through a more advantageous flow of credit to the community and through the economic activity the associations were designed to make possible."[8] In other words, founding groups were often engaged in construction, building supplies, or other branches of business related to housing. In addition, the concept of "corporate opportunity" permitted the legitimate profiting from association activities through a director engaging in related insurance, development, or legal services stimulated by association lending.

The original concept of savings banking has led to continuing

8. Norman Strunk, "A Federal System of Mutual Savings Banks?", *Savings and Loan News,* May, 1963, p. 37.

legislation that prohibits even indirect profiting from the position of trustee. While a person who is a trustee may also hold a salaried position, his compensation must be solely for his service in the latter position, except for "reasonable" compensation for attendance at meetings of the board of trustees or its committees. Indirect gain from the bank's lending or other activities would be considered a breach of trust. Thus, there is a certain logic to the historic practice of self-perpetuating boards, since a board oriented in this fashion might be relied upon to protect its own nature better than might a system in which candidates may present themselves to the depositors for election.

A bare recital of the fact that shareholders of savings and loan associations elect the directors of their institutions might create an impression of a large annual gathering of shareholders for the purpose, but this image would, of course, be inaccurate. In practice the system widely used is that shareholders give proxies of indefinite duration (that is, good until revoked) with which directors normally determine the composition of the board. While there have been instances—especially in the 1930's and a few isolated cases at other times—in which shareholders found reason to exercise their voting rights, the proxy system is the normal procedure.

Because of the normal compromises in the legislative process, the appeal of the appearance of greater democracy in the savings and loan arrangement was eventually adopted in the bill providing for federal charters for savings banks. The name is changed from trustee to director, and depositor voting is provided. However, continuation of trustees is provided for those existing savings banks that might convert to federal charters. Either the self-perpetuating type or election by incorporators may be approved for the successor institution by the Federal Home Loan Bank Board. Newly chartered federal savings banks or converting savings and loan institutions would normally have depositor voting, under the general supervision of the Federal Home Loan Bank Board, which could authorize proxies of limited duration, regulate proxy material and solicitation, and issue general regulations covering the mechanics of elections.

Comparison with Savings and Loans

In their day-to-day operations mutual savings banks and savings and loan associations have come to resemble each other to a high degree. The reformation of savings and loan charters in the 1930's frankly copied the deposit side of savings banking, that is, the usual passbook, deposit and withdrawal privileges, and the like, while it outmoded the earlier paid-up and serial shares. While the investment powers of savings and loan associations are much narrower, in the 20 years after World War II the advantages of mortgage lending over security investments made the asset side of the two institutions' balance sheets similar also. In certain specifics, however, differences remain or have arisen, owing largely to the structure of the two businesses. The savings and loan associations are much more numerous and smaller in average size; they have therefore specialized in originating local conventional mortgages, especially in comparison to the large city savings banks, which have not only acquired larger multi-family mortgages but also made guaranteed loans out of state. The advantages of the more flexible investment powers of the savings banks were demonstrated in late 1966 and in 1967. When the deposit inflow reversed its direction and brought in record amounts of funds, the savings banks were able to invest in corporate securities at unusually high yields in the absence of mortgage loan demand, and the funds can presumably be shifted to mortgages when demand for such funds warrants.

Another difference generally characteristic of the two institutions is that the savings and loan associations have welcomed their ability to borrow from the Federal Home Loan banks and often have more than their actual share of capital invested in mortgage loans, while savings banks have typically invested only deposited funds, out of which they also provide their own liquidity. In recent years, however, some banks have exhibited a greater willingness to borrow from their own institutions set up for the purpose or have joined the Home Loan Bank System.

The natural trend toward similarity brought about by postwar yield relationships was accelerated by the controversy in the late 1950's over the taxation of mutual financial institutions. While mutual institutions were exempt from income tax before 1951, the Revenue Act of that year provided that both savings banks and associations would thereafter pay tax on net income in excess of retentions sufficient to create surplus accounts of 12 per cent of liabilities. The subsequent efforts of commercial banks to accomplish enactment of more severe taxation of the mutuals resulted eventually in the Revenue Act of 1962, which limited retentions more strictly and related them to bad debt reserves more closely. While a savings and loan association has to show that it qualifies under the Act and a savings bank does not, they compute taxes in the same manner.

The similarities and differences between mutual savings banks and mutual savings and loan associations have been noted at some length, partly because discussion of the suitability of extending the savings bank system rests on the advantages or disadvantages of the mutual and trustee principles. Since both institutions are mutual, an attack on one represents an attack on the other, while the savings banks would like to maintain the trustee system as far as possible in obtaining authority to expand. Whether the mutual arrangement is appropriate for financial institutions does not appear to be an exceedingly fruitful field of debate. The success since the turn of the century of the mutual life insurance companies attests to their adaptability to modern economic conditions, and the rapid development of the savings and loan institutions to a level of assets in excess of $100 billion points to the appropriateness of these institutions. An important factor in their growth, of course, was the general disinclination of commercial banks to expand in the mortgage market until recent years, while another was the restrictions on savings bank growth in the states where they were not chartered.

Savings Bank Functions

Whether the savings banks' efforts to expand their system will succeed will eventually depend, given the requisite efforts, on the answers to several simple and basic questions. First, do they perform an economically useful function? When the savings banks were virtually the sole institution to offer the small saver a safe and liquid earning asset, their growth was rapid. When they continued to offer this "product" in competition with newer competitors in the form of life insurance policies and other financial assets their relative importance declined rapidly. Consequently, the current interest of the savings bank leaders is to acquire generally some of the powers that are permitted in individual states and to expand their powers eventually along the lines of European savings banks in order to become centers of family finance, providing—ideally—all the financial assets and all the loans and financing required by the family of modest means. Dr. Grover W. Ensley, Executive Vice President of the savings banks' national association, has listed the functions of such a family finance center as

> . . . a broad range of thrift and lending services—packaging regular and special-purpose savings accounts, savings bank life insurance, and perhaps depositors' mutual funds on the savings side with education, consumer, and mortgage loans on the lending side. But the package must also contain a very important third group of services, which would include financial counseling, greater speed and convenience, and imaginative use of automation to revolutionize customer services.[9]

The Executive Vice President's annual report for May, 1967, defines the "one ultimate goal" of the association's activities as that of making "savings banks, both the large and the small, the nation's foremost family financial service centers," and the means as "broadening and improving the package of thrift, credit, and other financial services offered by all members of the industry; strengthening the industry internally; expanding the industry geographically."[10]

A second question would be, do they perform this service economically? The term is, of course, relative, and requires com-

---

9. "Creating a Financial Service Package for a Young America," address before Savings Banks Public Relations Forum, Lake George, N.Y., May 27, 1965.

10. *Annual Report*, May, 1967, pp. 17-18. These statements need to be interpreted in the light of the subsequent introduction of the Federal Savings Institutions Act as a replacement for the federal charter bill.

parison with other financial institutions. Savings bank cost ratios compare favorably with those of competing institutions. Being in general fewer and larger than savings and loan associations, savings banks have relatively low ratios of operating expenses to deposits and to operating income. Savings and loan associations have also spent more for promotion and for borrowing costs. While the nature of commercial bank operations is different, in view of roughly half of total deposits being demand deposits, these same ratios are also lower for savings banks than for commercial banks. In comparison with savings and loans, preliminary figures for 1965 indicate that the savings banks' operating expenses were 14 per cent of operating income and .65 per cent of assets, while associations' ratios were 19 per cent and 1.23 per cent.

A question related to the two foregoing questions is, do they earn a profit? In the case of mutuals, of course, the question implies a rephrasing of whether they are advantageous to their depositors. Savings banks paid average dividends of 4.13 per cent in 1965. Insured savings and loan associations paid average dividends of 4.33 per cent; in the Boston and New York Federal Home Loan Bank Districts, covering the bulk of the savings banks, the figures were 4.18 per cent and 4.19 per cent.[11] The differential between rates paid by these two institutions has been narrowing in recent years. While on a national basis the differential was approximately half of one per cent in 1960, it declined each year thereafter to less than one quarter of one per cent in 1965 and disappeared in 1966. As the savings banks rapidly increased their holdings of mortgage loans, their earnings rose at a more rapid rate than did the earnings of associations, which already had the bulk of their assets in this form. In those states that have savings banks, moreover, average rates paid by the banks caught up with and surpassed the savings and loan average in 1964.

A final question relates to the general conformity of mutual institutions to social criteria of business operations. It is conceivable that affirmative answers could be supplied for the fore-

11. *Savings and Loan Fact Book, 1966,* p. 77; NAMSB, *National Fact Book, 1966,* p. 29.

going questions, and yet on grounds of anti-social behavior, monopoly, social costs, or the like an economical, efficient, and profitable business might be considered undesirable. The safety record, advances in operating methods, financing of urban renewal, respect for the trustee system, and other aspects of savings bank history suggest creditable marks on this score. The point of attack for competing institutions is limited almost completely to the contention that tax treatment of mutuals creates an unfair competitive advantage.

The Tax Problem

The nub of the tax problem is simply that for mutual savings institutions net income, after expenses, interest payments to depositors, and appropriate allocations to reserves, does not flow to stockholders as profits but further increases the reserves or surplus of the institution. In the case of a stock institution, the interest payment is clearly a cost of doing business; the smaller the interest payment and any tax-free allocations to reserves, the larger the taxable corporate income. While the short-run self-interest of a stock bank is to minimize interest payments to maximize income, the short-run advantage for a mutual institution may be to maximize interest payments to attract funds. In the long run, however, both institutions benefit from accumulating surplus, assuming that profitable assets are available. The problem then becomes one of tax treatment of retained earnings and whether some of these should be considered as held for future losses or as true net profits.

When recognition is given to earnings allocated to loss reserves, it becomes necessary to adopt some criterion for judging their adequacy. The solution reached in the Revenue Act of 1962 is that mutual lenders may allocate 60 per cent of income after dividends to reserves free of income tax, subject to a ceiling of 6 per cent of eligible loans. As an alternative, institutions with low reserves may elect to deduct 3 per cent of the year's increase in eligible loans. An overriding ceiling of 12 per cent of surplus and reserve accounts to deposits also applies. Commercial banks may, in general, allocate income to reserves tax free up to 2.4 per cent of qualifying loans, which include consumer, business, and uninsured mortgage loans. Thus, for both mutual and stock lenders, an increase in amounts paid as interest results in a net cost to the institution of roughly half of the increase, after considering taxes. The fact that the members in a mutual institution benefit in either one way or the other—that is, through higher dividends or larger allocations to surplus—tends to provide a long-run advantage for the mutual depositor under any given tax formula.

While it would appear that the arguments over "tax equality" and over extension of the savings bank system are logically separate issues, the former tend to be injected into consideration of the latter. The savings bank position is essentially that there is no tax advantage for mutual institutions in the current law, and some individual savings bankers take the position that the income, however defined, of mutual institutions should not be taxed in any event until it reaches the individual recipient.

Any difference in tax treatment between savings and commercial banks is attributed by the former to differences in the business being carried on. "If these basic differences did not exist—that is, if commercial banks operated in the same manner as savings banks, their tax payments would be essentially similar."[12] It is pointed out that interest paid on savings deposits is equally deductible for each type of institution, and that each has provision for loss reserves adapted to its own operations. The fact that commercial banks' income tax payments have dropped while their proportion of deposits in time and savings form has risen, and the ability of savings banks to minimize tax liabilities over the recent period of rising loans subject to the 3 per cent reserve allocation are each cited in support of one position or its opposite.

Potential Role of Mutuals

While the advantage of the mutual depositor in being both creditor and recipient of retained earnings has led to considera-

---

12. Dr. Grover W. Ensley, "Federal Charters for Mutual Savings Banks in the Public Interest," address before the National Savings Conference of the American Bankers Association, March 14, 1967.

ble political debate over the tax treatment of mutuals, little thought appears to have been given to an alternative approach. Different forms of legal organization offer advantages in different circumstances and in different lines of business. Otherwise it would be a matter of indifference whether a given business were a sole proprietorship, partnership, corporation, or mutual. Tailors and barbers are usually sole proprietorships, legal firms are normally partnerships, and manufacturing enterprises are generally incorporated. Co-operative forms of organization have often succeeded in distribution and finance. Further, a presumption of the desirability of maximum consumer choice suggests a tolerance for specialty stores, discount houses, chain stores, department stores, and other types of enterprise in a given line of commerce. All, or at least many, of these are considered unfair competition by many of those engaged in the other forms.

European experience suggests that there is nothing inherently inconsistent in mutual banks operating in a wide area of financial services. In some countries the evolution of the banking structure was such that mutual savings banks, being the only banking institutions in many localities, assumed the functions required by an expanding economy. While remaining oriented toward personal thrift, they implemented this orientation with many other banking services, including a payments mechanism. Later, commercial banks and other, sometimes specialized, types of financial institutions responded to market demands for specific services. Thus, in Germany, for example, the savings banks offer what would be called in the United States full-service banking, while the commercial banks not only offer the usual range of services but act as investment bankers and are more closely identified with individual commercial enterprises than is allowed in the United States.

In the United States the evolution of the banking structure has been, broadly speaking, for different types of banks to begin in specialized markets. Commercial banks specialized in short-term commercial lending and financing commerce, savings banks in the accumulation of small savings for investment largely in securities, and savings and loan associations in financing home purchases. As the country spread westward, commercial banks were established in new territories to finance longer-term needs, and they found it desirable to accept savings deposits. Savings and loan associations were established to stimulate construction, and in some state jurisdictions they gained other loan powers. But the trend has been for commercial banks to broaden their scope of operations, especially in recent decades, so that the end result is a banking structure with a non-specialized full-service institution and two relatively similar specialized institutions, all three competing in the mortgage and savings markets.

The natural political result of this competition is that the specialized institutions have attempted to obtain changes in regulations that would enable them to operate in fields not previously open to them as commercial banks had already done. This attempt has been accentuated in recent years by the increased competition for funds, higher market rates of interest, and the consequent need for corresponding assets. The process tends to be a piecemeal one: The savings and loan associations obtain permission to make improvement loans; the savings banks obtain permission to make out-of-state mortgage loans; and the commercial banks obtain rulings permitting leasing and other new functions. As a reflection of competition, this gradual piecemeal expansion of powers to offer attractive wares is probably desirable. As a long-run solution to the basic problems of establishing a rational financial structure it has little to recommend it.

The danger inherent in specialized institutions is that when the special need for which they were designed loses its urgency, they lose their market powers. As a specialized institution, the mutual savings bank reached a position of dominance in the savings market and then lost this position to others. As a specialized institution, the savings and loan association grew spectacularly in the postwar environment, but by 1965 was being squeezed between commercial bank competition for time deposits and the earnings from its portfolio of long-term assets. One conceivable solution for this danger, of course, would simply allow specialized institutions to die out when their special competency is no longer in demand. If there are other functions to which they are adaptable, however, adaptation is obviously the more economical course. Thus, the problem of how to adjust then becomes one of choosing between piecemeal changes in laws and regulations or a broader approach.

One clear-cut approach to the problem, and one that has received little attention in spite of the comprehensive studies of the Commission on Money and Credit and the President's Committee on Financial Institutions, would be to consider a broad equalization of powers for all types of banks. If all types of banks had legal authority to operate in virtually any field of banking—as is true, for example, in Switzerland—each bank could decide in terms of its own particular market whether to specialize or to offer services over a wide spectrum. Shifts in demands for funds would presumably be more quickly and adequately met, initiative would not be restricted to traditional and restricted areas, and competition would presumably be more free. Consumer choice would be maximized, and local conditions would be reflected in variations of services available, while a free flow of capital would be encouraged between both uses and geographical areas.

> It is insufficient merely to grant to mutual thrift institutions broader lending powers. Desirable as this may be, it would seem to leave us about where we are now—with a number of different types of depositories known as commercial banks, savings banks, savings and loan associations, et cetera, operating under an almost bewildering maze of federal and state laws and regulations, competing under ground rules that differ, if not conflict, for each type of institution—rules that differ even among members of the same type of institution, depending on the source of their charters. . . . To meet the problem of the mutual thrift institutions, I suggest that we need a major change in our philosophy about them. We must not regard them as permanently tied to a specialized function, but as potential candidates for full service financial status.[13]

To follow the suggestion of Governor Robertson just quoted implies a full acceptance of mutual institutions as members of the financial structure, not only as remnants of a situation that

---

13. J. L. Robertson, "An Alternative to Fossilization," remarks at the 75th Diamond Jubilee Anniversary Convention, Illinois Bankers Association, May 17, 1966.

historically led to their establishment, but as banks capable of meeting today's demands of the public. These demands will presumably be met; how fully and at what market price depends on the adaptability of existing organizations. A continuance of traditional legislative restrictions slows down adaptability and forces it into the only paths left open, principally the conversion of mutual savings banks and savings and loan associations into commercial banks with state or federal charters. The consequence will be a decline in the number and importance of mutual institutions, as well as cumbersome adaptation to market forces. On the other hand, in Governor Robertson's words again, ". . . I see no theoretical or supervisory reason why commercial bank operations could not be handled entirely on a mutual basis."[14]

Prospects

Whether all mutual institutions would want to expand broadly into other areas of operation is questionable. The commercial banking industry is itself an extremely heterogeneous one, with thousands of small banks doing an essentially savings banking business and a few very large banks operating in many markets. As there is room for the chain clothing store, the thrift shop, and the specialty fashion shop, all operating as clothing stores, there presumably would remain opportunities for local thrift institutions specializing in mortgage loans. Furthermore, new functions bring new responsibilities, and a savings bank operating departments now closed to it would become subject to reserve requirements, additional supervision, and, no doubt, requirements relating to capital adequacy and other matters. Many mutuals would, of course, find it desirable to expand.

An important aspect of the question of legislating for specialized or for all-purpose financial institutions is that of the effectiveness of monetary policies given one or the other type of financial structure. While there is considerable literature based mainly on the efforts of the Federal Reserve to restrain inflation in the 1950's, little attention has been paid to the restrictions

14. *Loc. cit.*

that may be imposed on monetary actions by repercussions on nonbank intermediaries. For example, the manipulations of Regulation Q and the complexities of commercial bank competition for funds more recently have raised questions as to the costs of Federal Reserve actions in terms of their effects on savings institutions with portfolios of long-term assets, which yield considerably less than current market rates. The imposition of "temporary" ceilings on interest rates paid by savings institutions in 1966 was an example of the need to expand regulatory powers in the absence of more equal competitive abilities in a period of unusually tight money.

The limitations on the development of savings banking imposed by lack of charter legislation in two thirds of the states and by the impediments to amending legislation in the other third emphasize the key role of the federal charter bill in deciding the future of the industry. The existence of opposition to the bill illustrates recognition of this fact by competitors of the savings banks. Unless and until savings banks can be established in areas of the country now without them and existing savings banks can obtain broader competitive powers, growth must be restricted to the annual increments of net new money and amounts of dividends credited to accounts.

The future of mutual savings banking depends largely, therefore, not only on the success of the industry in expanding the geographical area in which these banks may operate, but also on its ability to expand the functions it may offer to the public. By its nature as a mutual organization, a savings bank is not normally able to grow spectacularly at any time, because of its inability to attract investor capital. The growth of a mutual bank is dependent almost solely on its ability to attract net new money from depositors. If the banks were to attract relatively large new deposits because of new types of deposits and loan services, they would probably still be retarded by capital requirements, although here, perhaps, new devices such as capital debentures might be useful. In any event, a sudden spectacular resurgence of savings banking to the dominant position it once enjoyed nationally is hardly to be expected, in the absence of conversion of other institutions. At the same time, the enthusiasm of the industry's leaders, its progress in developing future leaders, its ties with progressive savings banking systems abroad, and its steady success in promoting federal charter legislation suggest that the relative decline in importance of these banks has been checked and that the route to broader participation in the economy has been opened.

Selected Bibliography

Books

American Bankers Association, The. *The Commercial Banking Industry*. Englewood Cliffs, N. J.: Prentice-Hall, 1962. (A monograph prepared for the Commission on Money and Credit.)

Berger, Meyer. *Growth of an Ideal, 1850-1950: The Story of the Manhattan Savings Bank*. New York: Manhattan Savings Bank, 1950.

Berle, Adolf A., Jr. *The Bank That Banks Built: The Story of the Savings Banks Trust Company, 1933-1958*. New York: Harper & Bros., 1959.

Brabrook, E. W. *Provident Societies and Industrial Welfare*. London: Blackie & Son, 1898.

Buley, R. Carlyle. *The American Life Convention, 1906-1952*. New York: Appleton-Century-Crofts, 1953.

Clough, S. B. *A Century of American Life Insurance: A History of the Mutual Life Insurance Company of New York, 1843-1943*. New York: Columbia University Press, 1946.

Commission on Money and Credit. *Report: Money and Credit*. Englewood Cliffs, N.J.: Prentice-Hall, 1961.

Ewalt, Josephine Hedges. *A Business Reborn: The Savings and Loan Story, 1930-1960*. Chicago: American Savings and Loan Institute Press, 1962.

Friedman, Milton, and Schwartz, Anna Jacobson. *A Monetary History of the United States, 1867-1960*. Princeton, N.J.: Princeton University Press, 1963.

Goldsmith, Raymond W. *Financial Intermediaries in the American Economy Since 1900*. Princeton, N.J.: Princeton University Press, 1958.

————. *A Study of Saving in the United States.* Princeton, N.J.: Princeton University Press, 1955.

Grebler, Leo; Blank, David M.; and Winnick, Louis. *Capital Formation in Residential Real Estate.* Princeton, N.J.: Princeton University Press, 1956.

Grebler, Leo, and Brigham, Eugene F. *Savings and Mortgage Markets in California.* Pasadena: California Savings and Loan League, 1963.

Gurley, John G., and Shaw, Edward S. *Money in a Theory of Finance.* Washington, D.C.: The Brookings Institution, 1960.

Haldane, A. R. B. *One Hundred and Fifty Years of Trustee Savings Banks.* London: Trustee Savings Banks Association, 1960.

Hall, Sally. *Dr. Duncan of Ruthwell.* Edinburgh: Oliphant, Anderson and Ferrier, 1910.

Hamilton, James Henry. *Savings and Savings Institutions.* New York: Macmillan Company, 1902.

Hammond, Bray. *Banks and Politics in America.* Princeton, N.J.: Princeton University Press, 1957.

Horne, H. Oliver. *A History of Savings Banks.* London: Oxford University Press, 1947.

Kendall, Leon T. *The Savings and Loan Business.* Englewood Cliffs, N.J.: Prentice-Hall, 1962. (A monograph prepared for the Commission on Money and Credit.)

Keyes, Emerson W. *A History of Savings Banks in the United States.* New York: Bradford Rhodes, 1876.

Klaman, Saul B. *The Postwar Residential Mortgage Market.* Princeton, N.J.: Princeton University Press, 1961.

Kniffin, William H. *The Savings Bank and Its Practical Work.* New York: The Bankers Publishing Company, 1928.

Kreps, Clifton H., Jr., and Tapkin, David T. *Improving the Competition for Funds Between Commercial Banks and Thrift Institutions.* Chapel Hill, N.C.: School of Business Administration, University of North Carolina, 1963.

Kuznets, Simon. *Capital in the American Economy: Its Formation and Financing.* Princeton, N.J.: Princeton University Press, 1961.

————. *National Income and Capital Formation, 1919-1935.* New York: National Bureau of Economic Research, 1937.

Lewins, William. *A History of Banks for Savings in Great Britain and Ireland*. London: Sampson Low, Son & Marston, 1866.

Life Insurance Association of America. *Life Insurance Companies as Financial Institutions*. Englewood Cliffs, N.J.: Prentice-Hall, 1962. (A monograph prepared for the Commission on Money and Credit.)

Lintner, John. *Mutual Savings Banks in the Savings and Mortgage Markets*. Cambridge, Mass.: Graduate School of Business Administration, Harvard University, 1948.

McCulloch, John Herries, and Stirling, Kenneth J. *The Edinburgh Savings Bank: A Review of Its Century of Service, 1836-1936*. Edinburgh: H. & J. Pillans & Wilson, 1936.

Mason, Alpheus T. *The Brandeis Way*. Princeton, N.J.: Princeton University Press, 1938 (o.p.).

Miller, Harry E. *Banking Theories in the United States Before 1860*. Cambridge, Mass.: Harvard University Press, 1927.

National Association of Mutual Savings Banks. *Annual Reports of the Executive Vice President*. New York.

————. *Mutual Savings Banking*. Englewood Cliffs, N.J.: Prentice-Hall, 1962. (A monograph prepared for the Commission on Money and Credit.)

————. *National Fact Books*. New York.

Orcutt, William Dana. *The Miracle of Mutual Savings: As Illustrated by One Hundred Years of The Bowery Savings Bank*. New York: The Bowery Savings Bank, 1934.

Savings Division, The American Bankers Association. *Response to Change: A Century of Commercial Bank Activity in the Savings Field*. New York: The American Bankers Association, 1965.

Schweiger, Irving, and McGee, John S. *Chicago Banking*. Chicago: Graduate School of Business, University of Chicago, 1961.

Sherman, Franklin J. *The Modern Story of Mutual Savings Banks*. New York: J. J. Little and Ives, 1934.

Thon, Robert W., Jr. *Mutual Savings Banks in Baltimore*. Baltimore: The Johns Hopkins Press, 1935.

Trustee Savings Banks Association. *Trustee Savings Banks Year Book, 1966*. London: Cox & Wyman, 1966.

Welfling, Weldon. *Savings Banking in New York State*. Durham, N.C.: Duke University Press, 1939.

Whitehill, Walter Muir. *The Provident Institution for Savings in the Town of Boston, 1816-1966*. Boston: The Provident Institution for Savings, 1966.

Willcox, James W. *A History of the Philadelphia Saving Fund Society, 1816-1916*. Philadelphia: J. P. Lippincott, 1916.

Articles

Ascheim, Joseph. "Commercial Banks and Financial Intermediaries: Fallacies and Policy Implications." *Journal of Political Economy,* Vol. 67, No. 1 (February, 1959).

Birnbaum, Eugene A. "The Growth of Financial Intermediaries as a Factor in the Effectiveness of Monetary Policies." International Monetary Fund *Staff Papers,* November, 1958.

Carson, Deane. "Bank Earnings and the Competition for Savings Deposits." *Journal of Political Economy,* Vol. LXVII, No. 6 (December, 1959).

Gurley, John G., and Shaw, E. S. "Financial Intermediaries and the Savings-Investment Process." *Journal of Finance,* Vol. 11, No. 2 (May, 1956).

Friend, Irwin, "Determinants of the Volume and Composition of Saving with Special Reference to the Influence of Monetary Policy." Research Study Six in *Impacts of Monetary Policy*. Commission on Money and Credit, 1963.

Guttentag, Jack M., and Herman, Edward S. "Banking Structure and Performance." *The Bulletin,* Graduate School of Business Administration, New York University, No. 41/43 (February, 1967).

Institute of Life Insurance. *Life Insurance Fact Book*. New York, annual.

International Savings Bank Institute (Amsterdam). *World Thrift,. Congress Issue,* March–April, 1966.

Kaufman, George G., and Latta, Cynthia. "Near Banks and Local Savings." *National Banking Review,* Vol. 3, No. 4 (June, 1966), p. 539.

Keith, E. Gordon. "The Impact of Federal Taxation on the Flow of Personal Savings Through Investment Intermediaries." Research Study Six in *Private Financial Institutions*. Commission on Money and Credit, 1963.

Klaman, Saul B., and Lawson, Donald E. "For Savings Banks and S&L's: Change, or Else." *Challenge,* July–August, 1967, p. 16.

Linke, Charles M. "The Evolution of Interest Rate Regulation on Commercial Bank Deposits in the United States." *National Banking Review,* Vol. 3, No. 4 (June, 1966), p. 449.

National Association of Mutual Savings Banks. *Savings Bank Journal.* New York.

Schwind, Robert L. "Conversion and Acquisition of Savings Institutions." *The Banking Law Journal,* Vol. 82, Number 10 (October, 1965), p. 847.

Smith, Warren L. "Financial Intermediaries and Monetary Controls." *Quarterly Journal of Economics,* Vol. 23, No. 4 (November, 1959).

Strunk, Norman. "A Federal System of Mutual Savings Banks?" *Savings and Loan News* (May, 1963), p. 36.

Thorn, Richard S. "Nonbank Financial Intermediaries, Credit Expansion, and Monetary Policy." International Monetary Fund *Staff Papers* (November, 1958).

United States Savings and Loan League. *Conference on Savings and Residential Financing.* Chicago, annual.

————. *Savings and Loan Fact Book.* Chicago, annual.

————. *Savings and Loan News.* Chicago.

Werboff, Lawrence L., and Rozen, Marvin E. "Market Shares and Competition Among Financial Institutions," Research Study Four in *Private Financial Institutions*. Commission on Money and Credit, 1963.

Government Publications

Board of Governors of the Federal Reserve System. *All-Bank Statistics, U.S., 1896-1955.* Washington, D.C., 1959.

————. *Annual Reports.* Washington, D.C.

————. *Banking and Monetary Statistics.* Washington, D.C., 1943.

————. *Flow of Funds in the United States, 1939-1953*. Washington, D.C., 1955.

————. *Flow of Funds: Supplements*. Washington, D.C.

————. *Federal Reserve Bulletin*. Washington, D.C.

Commissioner of Banks, Massachusetts. *Annual Reports*. Boston.

Committee on Banking and Currency. *The Federal Savings Bank Bill: A Staff Analysis of H.R. 11433, and Identical Bills*. Washington, D.C., 1966.

Committee on Banking and Currency, Subcommittee on Bank Supervision and Insurance, 88th Congress, First Session. *Hearings on H.R. 258 (and Identical Bills)*, Washington, D.C. 1963.

Committee on Banking and Currency, Subcommittee on Bank Supervision and Insurance, 89th Congress, Second Session. *Hearings on H.R. 11508, a Bill to Authorize the Establishment of Federal Mutual Savings Banks*. Washington, D.C., 1966.

Committee on Banking and Currency, Subcommittee on Domestic Finance, 88th Congress. *Comparative Regulations of Financial Institutions*. Washington, D.C., 1963.

Committee on Banking and Currency, 90th Congress, First Session. *Federal Savings Institutions*. Washington, D.C., 1967.

Comptroller of the Currency. *Annual Reports*. Washington, D.C. (Various years.)

Economic Report of the President, Together with the Annual Report of the Council of Economic Advisers. Washington, D.C. (Various years.)

Federal Deposit Insurance Corporation. *Annual Reports*. Washington, D.C.

————. *Summary of Accounts and Deposits in All Mutual Savings Banks*. Washington, D.C. (Various years.)

Federal Home Loan Bank Board. *Annual Reports*. Washington, D.C.

Superintendent of Banks, New York State. *Annual Reports*. Albany.

U.S. Department of Commerce. *U.S. Income and Output*. Washington, D.C., 1958.

Index